Playing
Partners

Playing Partners

A Father, a Son, and Their Shared Addiction to Golf

GEORGE PEPER
EPILOGUE BY SCOTT PEPER

WARNER BOOKS

An AOL Time Warner Company

Warner Books, Inc., 1271 Avenue of the Americas, New York, NY 10020

Visit our Web site at www.twbookmark.com.

 An AOL Time Warner Company

Printed in the United States of America

First Printing: May 2003

10   9   8   7   6   5   4   3   2   1

The Library of Congress Control Number: 2002096285

ISBN: 0-446-52707-6

To Libby, my one true partner,
with love on our twenty-fifth

Contents

Playing Partners

1

Blessed
Onlyness

My father's name was Gerhard.

Now, imagine growing up in a middle-class New York suburb, just after World War II, with a father named Gerhard. I still shudder over that day in second grade when, in a primitive stab at ethnic profiling, Mrs. Sanford strolled the room asking each of us to recite the names of our parents.

"Shirley and Bill," "Mary and Bob," "Eileen and Lester," chirped my homogeneous classmates at the William Street Elementary School. Then she reached my desk.

"Doris and Gerhard," I mumbled quickly.

"Doris and what?"

"Gerhard."

"Ah, Gerhard . . . that's a *good German* name," she said, serving two dozen eight-year-olds their first oxymoron.

At recess later that day my direst fears were realized when Dicky Smyers planted an accusative finger in my chest and said, "Your dad's a Nazi."

Well, my father was emphatically not a heel-clicker. That said, he was about as American as apple strudel. Born in a small town in Schleswig-Holstein in 1903, he left home at age nineteen, hopping a steamship from Bremerhaven to New York in search of his fortune. At Ellis Island, when he reached the front of the line, they asked him his name.

"Gerhard Peper," he said, pronouncing it as if it were a producer of pulp products.

"No way, pal," said the immigration clerk. "Over here, with a name spelled like that, no one's gonna call you 'Paper.' It's either 'Gerry Peeper' or 'Gerry Pepper,' take your pick."

Dad opted for the marginally more euphonious "Pepper." However, he declined sprightly "Gerry," gutting it out in the New World with darkly thudding "Gerhard." In one way this turned out to be a canny move. By 1940 Americans would be vilifying every soldier in Hitler's army as a "Gerry."

By that time my father was a card-carrying American. Had he fought in that war, he would have fought for the United States—against his own brother—but he was too old to serve. Ten years later, when I arrived, he was, again, too old to serve—as my father. At age forty-six he could have been my grandfather.

Old and old school he was, a man who worked ten hours a day, six days a week his entire adult life. Fresh off the boat, he'd signed on as a carpenter's assistant, hoping to raise enough money to put himself through medical school. But economic reality forced him to abandon that plan in favor of a more affordable alternative—chiropractic college—moonlighting as a busboy during four years of schooling in Iowa.

A week before graduation he threw a dart at the U.S. map

and speared Pearl River, New York, "The Town of Friendly People," a tiny hamlet twenty miles north of Manhattan. In 1933 it was there that he set up a two-room office.

One of his first patients was my mother. She was eleven years younger than he, a sophomore at Mount Holyoke College. Her major was German, and she had plenty in common with Dad, beginning with Teutonic blood on both sides of her family. In fact, during the nineteenth century her maternal grandparents had emigrated to the United States with the most astonishing of surnames: Peper. Yes, one-*p*-in-the-middle Pepers dangle from virtually every branch of my family tree. I'm not sure whether that makes me a hybrid or a mutation. I do know I'm the product of a union that somehow lasted forty-three years before my mother's death in 1977.

Although stern and humorless on the surface, my father had a sort of oompah-band schmaltz that endeared him to just about everyone, beginning with Mom. He called her Toots (the truth is, he called all women Toots, but Mom was Toots #1); he hugged and kissed her openly and often and constantly proclaimed her "the star of my sleepless nights."

In a similar way he schmoozed his female patients, who unfailingly fell for his little-old-winemaker charm. Although Dad claimed to hate socializing—and people in general—he was invariably the life of the party. He had a fine, strong singing voice, could waltz like Astaire, and spoke five languages fluently, albeit with a heavy German accent.

A classic family story involves the lady of a certain age whose chiropractic treatment required spinal and cranial X rays.

"Okay, Toots," said Dad as he fired up his machine, "are you wearing any bridges?" (False teeth apparently inhibit a clear view of the medulla and environs.)

"Yes, of course," she said.

"Then I'm afraid you'll have to remove them," he said, directing her to the lavatory.

Moments later the woman reappeared, stark naked from the waist down. "Bridges," as pronounced by Dad, had registered as "britches."

Language barrier aside, he was a terrific chiropractor. Although most of his patients came in search of relief from lower-back pain, he had success helping people with everything from epilepsy to multiple sclerosis. But he also knew his limits, frequently recommending patients to local physicians who in turn referred their sacroiliac sufferers his way. In a profession that has provoked unending skepticism Dad was legit: honest, caring, dedicated, and thorough.

Personally, I never understood the whole chiropractic shtick. How manipulating a section of the neck or spine could possibly repair any internal malady was beyond me. My father once told me it was like turning on a light. "You flip a switch on the wall," he said, "and up on the ceiling a bulb goes on. That's what I do with the spinal cord." Kind of scary, if you ask me. I can attest, however, that throughout my twelve years of public school, I missed only a handful of days, largely due to Dad's knack of squelching colds and related ailments by means of a quick "adjustment."

Since his office was attached to our house, members of the immediate family could be whisked in for checkups and routine servicing. Every examination was a two-part process. He'd begin by gliding a strange two-pronged instrument—sort of a pregnant magnet—up the back of one's neck. This produced a red-ink readout resembling a six-month chart of the Nasdaq. After a perusal of its peaks and valleys he moved to part two, which involved one of two ominous machines, known privately by me as Godzilla and the Rack.

Godzilla was comprised of four or five spring-loaded

leather cushions. It was powered by a groaning electric engine and angled up and down like a construction crane when my father stepped on a pedal at its base. In its at-rest position Godzilla inclined about twenty degrees below vertical. The patient boarded it, facedown in the firm cleavage of its paper-covered pillows. Then Dad hit the gas and down it steamed until parallel to the floor—adjustment mode.

The Rack was more low-tech—a rigid Naugahyde chaise lounge on which the patient assumed a more or less fetal position. The Rack's only distinctive feature was a raised headrest with a small cavity into which one inserted the ear of Dad's choice.

Once I was in position on either apparatus, Dad would cradle my head in his huge hands, sliding soft, puffy fingers ominously across my neck, temples, cheeks, and jaw as he searched for the perfect time and place to make his move. This unsettling foreplay could last anywhere from five to thirty seconds, depending on how quickly he found his inspiration. Then, with the suddenness of a lightning bolt, he'd snap his hands, usually causing an audible click inside my neck. Adjustment completed.

"Now lie still for a couple of minutes," he'd say as my eyeballs returned to their sockets. Invariably, I'd fall fast asleep. By the next morning my earache, runny nose, sore throat, and/or cough was miraculously gone. These days, as I address my computer—three Aleves in my stomach and a back pillow at the base of my chair—I'm aching for one of those adjustments.

On the flip side my father could inflict almost as much pain as he relieved. He was old-country strict, brooked no disobedience, and believed strongly in corporal punishment. Major misbehavior brought a few swift lashes from "the belt" or "the switch." The belt was not a major threat, since my father mostly wore suspenders, but the stick—a pliant, well-aged branch from one of our oak trees—was always within easy reach in the center of the kitchen resting ironically atop a kitschy "Home Sweet Home" sign.

Dad's stubbornness was probably his worst quality. He never backed off, even when he was patently out of line and knew it, and he never took blame. The only time I ever heard him apologize to my mother was when he said, "I'm sorry, Toots, you're wrong."

He and Mom had frequent and loud arguments on everything from politics to patio furniture. They were both highly intelligent, but Mom had more verbal finesse and she wasn't above using it in their debates. "It must be absolutely wonderful to be so sure of yourself all the time," she'd say. "I so envy you your state of perpetual self-confidence." He never had a response for that one.

She was particularly fond of taunting him about his overeating. (At age twenty he'd had a swimmer's body—by forty he'd become a whale.) Remember that television show from the sixties, *The Alfred Hitchcock Hour,* which began with the famed director striding into his own ovoid silhouette? Dad could have filled in for Hitch, and he worked at that role, three squares a day.

"My God, Gerhard," Mom would say as he tucked into pork chop number seven, "you're digging your grave with your teeth!" This invariably triggered a spirited exchange on the pros and cons of gluttony. It was Dad, however, who usually got the last if not best word, stomping from the room while delivering his bread-and-butter closer: "Toots, you can go shit in your hat!"

Like most kids, I couldn't imagine my parents having sex, and in the case of our family the irrefutable evidence was meager. Married in 1934, Mom and Dad took eight years to produce my brother, Eric, and another eight to come up with me.

One consequence was that Eric and I had separate and unequal childhoods when it came to paternal participation. Middle-aged Gerhard was an outdoorsman. He loved to hunt and fish, and he taught Eric to love those things, too. Together they disappeared for weekends to bag bass, birds, and bucks. When Eric came home with his first 14-point whitetail, it was one of the proudest days of my father's life.

By the time I reached the *Field & Stream* years Dad was a senior citizen with arthritic joints, varicose veins, poor hearing, and a self-described "bum ticker." A year or so before my birth he'd suffered a heart attack that had brought an abrupt end to his wilderness trekking. There would be no hunting and fishing with George.

Truth be told, that was fine with me. I hated summer camp, found the Boy Scouts vaguely homosexual, and never quite saw the delight in rising at 4:00 A.M. in order to bring about the demise of a duck. Unlike Thoreau, I am at *two* with Nature.

Guns attracted me briefly, as they do so many boys, and one year I got an air rifle for my birthday. It was fun plugging tin cans and toy soldiers with those copper BBs. Then one day I drew a bead on a robin that had perched on a telephone wire near our house. Now, at a distance of fifty paces I had never hit anything, but this time I did: a thunderbolt to the bird's little skull. It was as if I'd shot myself. At eleven years old I'd become a cold and demented murderer. My hunting career ended right there.

As for fishing I lack the requisite patience. As a hopelessly type A personality I don't stop to smell the flowers, let alone the fish. Results are what I crave, preferably immediate results. At a bare minimum I need the assurance of action.

Sitting in a rowboat and staring at the surface of a lake is my idea of water torture. Ocean fishing can be pleasurable, of course, especially when I have a companion to hold the waist of my shorts as I lurch seaward and projectile-vomit my three most recent meals.

Without question my most gratifying day as an outdoorsman came at about age ten, when from the end of a dock at Greenwood Lake, New Jersey, I caught precisely one hundred sunfish. I'd set myself a goal early that morning and had gone at it with disturbing zeal, molding a loaf's worth of Wonder bread into pea-sized pellets that slid easily onto the hook. (The most effective bait, I've found, is the kind that's equally palatable to both fish and fisherman.) All day long I horsed in those pathetic perch—tossing them back as fast as they arrived—until somewhere around Miller Time the centenary sucker hit the planks.

Although I made a hundred conquests that day, in actuality I caught only about a dozen fish—the same dozen over and over again. After a while I came to recognize each glazed gaze and mutilated maw. They didn't seem to be having as much fun as I was.

In any case, there was no outdoor life between George and Gerhard Peper, no bonding in the boondocks. In fact, not much in the way of shared recreation.

Dad was, to coin a word, asportual. Having been raised in another culture, he had little affinity for American games. During my formative years his idea of leisure-time fun was a few hours of weeding the pachysandra, followed by some light hauling to the compost heap.

I didn't miss his presence, except when it came to one activity: baseball. I loved baseball. In fact, between the ages of eight and twelve, I lived baseball.

Whatever money I could scrounge went into the purchase

of Topps baseball cards. They came in packs of six or seven, accompanied somewhat gratuitously by a brittle rectangle of bubble gum. No serious collector will ever forget those brightly colored wrappers, the sweet smell of the gum, the slick film of sugar that coated the top card, or those two-and-a-half-by-three-and-a-half-inch treasures themselves.

Each pack was a new adventure, to be embraced with the pathetic fervor of a Super Lotto player. Praying for Hank Aaron or Al Kaline or Nellie Foxx, I'd invariably draw Don Blasingame or Tom Sturdivant or Felix Mantilla. But the big names popped up just often enough to sustain the addiction. I've often wondered what sort of marketing Machiavelli in the Topps offices decided how many Mays and Koufax cards to sprinkle into the flow, and just where and when to seed them.

If you collected baseball cards, you didn't go halfway—at least I didn't. Each summer my consuming goal was to complete the collection. Judicious card management was thus important. I housed my collection in an old Dutch Masters cigar box that never left my room, and kept with it a checklist that showed cards procured and cards needed. The cards were rubber-banded by teams, with separate packs for rookies, all-stars, and other specials. The duplicate Blasingames never saw the box; they joined my traveling squad for flipping and swapping with friends.

I fancied myself a better-than-average flipper, with a deft wrist flick that served me well in the game where a single card was propped against a wall and players took turns skimming cards at it, Frisbee style, until someone toppled the leaner and raked in the pile.

One golden summer, probably 1961 or '62, through a combination of prudent collecting, artful flipping, and good fortune, I was able to amass the entire year's collection. The cards came out in several series, and that year I completed all seven or eight series—several hundred cards in all. I have no idea what I did with that cigar box, but if I had it today, it would probably be worth more than my house.

By the fifth grade my obsession had reached the point where all I wanted was to own a copy of *The Complete Baseball Encyclopedia*. That spring my mother told me that if I could finish the school year with a 90 average, she'd buy it for me. I can still remember the Saturday in June when I walked into Lord & Taylor in Westchester and plucked it from the shelf—a big, blue volume, boundlessly packed with statistics and information. I spent hours and hours with that book, and for a while I knew just about everything in it, or thought I did.

Most of all, I knew the Yankees. In the early 1960s no red-blooded American boy within a hundred miles of New York City could know otherwise. McDougald, Kubek, Richardson, and Skowron in the infield; Berra and Howard splitting the chores behind the plate; the Chairman of the Board, Whitey Ford, leading a pitching staff that also included Bob Turley, Ryne Duren, and Eli Grba. And, of course, that outfield: unsung Hector Lopez playing left foil to "the M Boys," Mantle and Maris.

In the summer of 1961, when Mickey and Roger made their fabled joint run at Babe Ruth's single-season home run record of sixty, I was with them every step of the way, watching weekend games on channel 11 and listening to night games on WPIX, as Mel Allen, Red Barber, and Phil Rizzuto relayed every "Ballantine Blast" and "White Owl Wallop."

Rarely was I able to stay awake through the end of a night game, but on one special evening the entire baseball world remained wide-eyed and rapt until the final out. It was game number 154—not the last game of the season, but the last chance for Maris, who had made the stronger bid, to tie or beat the record in the same number of games in which Babe had set it.

He came into the game with fifty-eight, two short of the record, and he gave it everything he had. He hit number fifty-nine, and in his second-to-last at-bat he hit a long foul ball into the seats. But the Yankees' opponents that night, the Baltimore Orioles, did not want to go into the record books as the team that let the record fall, and so they brought in their legendary stopper, knuckleballing Hoyt Wilhelm. Roger's last at-bat was a check-swing ground ball. Ultimately, however, he would finish the season with sixty-one home runs, albeit a season of 162 games.

I was happy for Roger—all Yankee fans were. But we were also sorry it wasn't Mickey who'd done the deed. It was Mickey, after all, who had thrilled and frustrated and enchanted us more than any other Yankee. He was our hero, maybe our last hero, a guy who played with an innocent love of the game, who played through pain and never gave less than 100 percent.

In the fourth grade, when we were assigned to do a book report on a biography, I chose Mickey Mantle's. I learned about his childhood in Texas, how his dad encouraged him to hit the ball both left- and right-handed. I also learned how to pronounce the word "osteomyelitis," the disease that ended his career.

I even tried switch-hitting in Little League. Well, sort of. The truth is, I didn't make Little League. I tried and failed—in mortifying style. I'm not sure whether it's a measure of my otherwise charmed life or the singular devastation of the event, but to this day I have never experienced a worse moment.

The epicenter of my hometown was the high school football field. Set on Central Avenue and walled on its four sides by the school, the library, the firehouse, and a dozen downtown stores, it was Pearl River's answer to the Roman Forum. One Saturday each spring—traditionally the coldest, dampest day in March—most of the town's male population assembled on that field at dawn for the solemn rite of Little League try-outs. It was one big Elks Club/Knights of Columbus/Boosters/Jaycees/Kiwanis spermfest.

For some kids this was a terrific day, a chance to showcase their considerable skills. For me it was the most traumatic event of the year, an annual persecution that loomed ominously for weeks, even more harrowing than the moment in the annual school physical when the doctor said, "Now turn your head and cough."

In 1961—the same year Roger Maris earned eternal fame—I won undying infamy in my first Little League tryouts.

My number was 164. In black Magic Marker it had been printed on a white four-by-six-inch card, and handed to me, along with a safety pin, by one of the myriad Baseball Moms stationed behind folding tables at the firehouse end of the field. "Pin this on your chest, son," she said, "and when the eleven-year-olds are called, run out to the position you want to try out for."

Baseball Moms and Dads were all over the field that day, taking names and giving numbers, selling doughnuts and raffle tickets, and generally choreographing the chaos. The Moms came in a variety of shapes and sizes, but the Baseball Dads were a definite breed: broad-shouldered, big-bellied, chain-smoking guys—foremen and firemen with nicknames like Chick and Mooney. The biggest bulls in the B.D. herd carried clipboards, identifying them as team managers and coaches. On each clipboard was a list of our names and numbers, and next to each name were two small boxes. A check mark in box one meant we'd made Little League; in box two we were toast, relegated to the ignominy of the minors.

My parents weren't part of this scene. Mom had been my den mother in Cub Scouts, but she was always more interested in mind-nurturing than athletics. The closest she got to the football field was her monthly Wednesday night meeting as president of the Pearl River Library Board. As for Dad the only time he ever hefted a bat, glove, or ball was when he cleaned out the garage. He did take the family to Yankee Stadium once, but I suspect the highlight for him that day was the appearance of the "Beer here!" guy.

Generally, I was comfortable being a baseball orphan—even a little proud that my parents were a notch above dugout demographics. In the days leading up to the 1961 tryouts, however, I was needful. At school, baseball hadn't started up yet, so no one was throwing the ball around. My closest friends were too wimpy to play catch with me, and the other guys were too good. My brother was in college. So for backyard practice all I had was the garage door, which I pelted furiously with a sponge-rubber ball.

My father's main contribution was to board up the garage door windows so I could wing high hard ones with impunity. I knew it wasn't his thing to toss a ball back and forth, and I never resented him for it, but I nonetheless yearned for some advice, some guidance, some encouragement—something to give me confidence as the tryouts approached.

"Eleven-year-olds, take the field," blared the loudspeaker, and out I trotted with a dozen or so classmates into center field. I'd chosen the outfield because it seemed relatively uncomplicated. Catch the ball and throw it to second base. No hot liners, no handcuffing bounces. It was away from the action, and that suited me fine.

The outfield also gave me a chance to show off my only athletic asset: a strong throwing arm. My biceps and triceps hadn't developed (truth is, at age fifty-three I'm still waiting), but for some reason I could throw things hard and long. Back then the Kennedy administration had started something called the President's Council on Youth Fitness, which involved a battery of tests measuring strength, speed, and agility. In events such as the shuttle run and standing broad jump my performance put me in the gelatinous middle of schoolboy vigor, but on the softball throw I was presidential timber. I could chuck that puppy a country mile.

Besides, center field was where the Mick played.

So there I was that cold, damp March morning, standing in a line of similarly terrified eleven-year-olds, awaiting our moments in the spotlight. The assignment was straightforward. Field three or four fly balls and two or three grounders. The exact number varied because the fungo-swatting Baseball Dad usually failed to apply bat to ball with sufficient precision to produce three uncontestably catchable fly balls in a row. Invariably, he'd either pop one up to the catcher (a shot that B.D.'s like to field themselves, usually one-handed and sometimes backhanded), push or pull one beyond reasonable chase-down range, or catch one on the screws and nail it into the cheap seats. Such shots complicated things for the clipboard carriers.

On the question of my candidacy, however, there would be no discussion. I had hoped to be one of the first kids called—less time to get nervous—but I turned out to be one of the last. With only two of us left to go, the mike finally blared, "Number 164."

Stiff-legged and dry of throat, I stepped forward, delivering a couple of pseudoconfident fist pounds to the neat's-foot-oiled pocket of my Tony Kubek Autograph Trap-o-Matic glove. Back at home plate the B.D. tossed up a ball, reared back, and served me a picture-perfect pop fly—the kind baseball announcers used to call "a can o' corn"—arcing gracefully into the gray sky and straight at me. With two or three steps I was positioned perfectly under it, poised to make the catch and fire a strike to the kid standing on second.

And then I choked. I'm not sure how or why, but that baseball never struck my glove; instead, it hit me—smack on the prow of my forehead—and knocked me flat on my pathetic ass.

The next thing I knew, I was staring skyward at the faces of a half dozen B.D.'s, circling above me like an E.R. team. Their expressions ranged from shock to concern to stifled mirth. "Don't move, kid," said one of them, "we've got an ice pack coming."

Like an injured football hero, I was assisted from the field, but with no cheers from the stands—just silent stares. My head throbbed, and a Grade AAA Large egg had begun to form. By Monday I would look like a prepubescent unicorn.

What hurt most, of course, was my pride. I'd just suffered a moment of utter mortification, in front of my friends, my classmates, and the entire baseball fraternity of my hometown.

All that afternoon I lay on my bed and cried. There was no denying or deflecting my failure, but at age eleven I was unable to accept that. So the tears of shame turned eventually to tears of self-pity and then anger—anger at the tryout system, at the weather, and at my nonathletic friends, but above all, anger at my father, for being too busy, too old, too flabby, and too German. Maybe he *was* a Nazi. All I knew was, I was the only eleven-year-old in town whose father was a fifty-seven-year-old, potbellied, foreign-born, nonathletic chiropractor. And *that's* why I'd flubbed the fly ball.

I felt very alone on that day, but I wasn't. My mother had sensed my pain acutely, as she had on countless occasions throughout my childhood. Nearly a decade later, almost as an offhand remark, she made a confession that shocked me. She said that if she'd had her life to live over again, she would never have married my father. Not because she was unhappy with her marriage, but because of what it had done to me. "It was just too much for you to handle," she said.

She may have been right. Still, my childhood was scarcely a saga of hardship and neurosis. I never doubted that both my parents loved me, and they gave me just about every material thing I ever wanted, despite the fact that we weren't remotely wealthy. (One Christmas, I remember my mother reporting that my father had just had his best year, earning $18,000.)

It was the nonmaterial giving, however, the time and attention from father to son, that was lacking. We were never estranged or hostile; we just had little in common. There wasn't enough intersecting DNA to make us inherently close, and neither Dad nor I was very good about making the kind of move that busts down barriers.

But as I headed into my teens and developed the myriad psychoses that come with that phase, our relationship worsened. My father, I decided, was a huge embarrassment to me. At age thirteen, remember, being cool is everything, and Gerhard Wilhelm Peper was the living antithesis of cool. Beyond his triple-A liabilities—age, ancestry, and avoirdupois—he had the absolutely fatal flaw for any parent of a teenager: an absence of fashion sense.

In his office he was harmless: dark slacks, short-sleeved white shirt, and tie every day. His only major faux pas was the suspenders, which I forgave him because of the exigencies of his build. (Once the waistband of his slacks slipped below the equator of his pot, the slacks dropped due south. Suspenders were his sole defense against gravity.) Like many doctors, he wore a white lab coat, but Dad's was made of a strange filmy plastic—evocative of a shower curtain—with twin breast pockets that screamed "barbershop surplus."

The real killer, however, was his leisurewear. On some days the overall look was one notch from circus clown. Around the house on summer weekends he favored Bermuda shorts and sleeveless wife-beater T-shirts, completing the ensemble with over-the-calf black socks and a pair of bulbous orthotic space-man shoes. The socks were actually a blessing, as Dad's legs were not suitable for public display—untanned, and remark-ably birdlike for a man of his size. Moreover, along with a tor-tuous network of varicose veins, they were marked by dozens of dark subcutaneous spots, like baby blueberries.

One summer at the beach, when I asked about the spots, he said, "Those are buckshot."

"Buckshot? What's that?"

"Pellets from a shotgun. I was in a hunting accident," he said a bit sheepishly.

That was Mom's cue. "Fifteen years ago one of your father's pals, Johnny Herman, cleverly mistook him for a par-tridge." Years later I saw the X rays showing the pellets still there. It's a small wonder my father died of old age instead of lead poisoning.

Mom tried to give Dad some sartorial savoir faire, but she had an uphill battle. To begin with, he was color-blind—greens and blues all looked gray to him. So she sectored his tie rack with labels that read "navy blue suit," "brown suit," etc. But color coordination was only part of the challenge. Since Dad had no interest in fashion, he donned items of apparel pretty much in the order he found them, with little attention to whether they harmonized. One Saturday morning, after run-ning a series of errands, he came in the back door with a smile from ear to ear.

"Everyone in town was so friendly today," he said.

My mother, peeling carrots over the sink, glanced at him, chuckled, and summarily burst his bubble. "It's no wonder," she said. "You're wearing a shirt of one plaid and shorts of another. They were laughing at you."

Suffice it to say, I wasn't disappointed when Dad no-showed at school concerts, bake sales, and parent-teacher conferences.

By the time I entered puberty my brother had entered college. He'd also fallen in love with a terrific girl, had slimmed his theretofore corpulent six feet three inches down to a rippling two hundred pounds, and had begun to find his way in the world. By contrast, I was battling near-terminal acne, morphing my childhood crew cut hilariously into a Beatles mop, and precariously straddling two mutually exclusive cliques—the cool set (comprised of natural athletes and future super-models) and the socially leprous, slide-rule-toting smart kids—all the while wondering whether I'd ever kiss a girl. As I careened within this vortex, Dad offered no help at all.

On one summer morning in 1962, however, he did reach out to me, with an invitation that changed the course of my life.

"I'm going over to Blue Hill this afternoon," he said. "Why don't you come with me and pull the cart. You might enjoy it."

Blue Hill was our local golf course, a place that had recently gone public after nearly forty years as a very private club. The confluence of Arnold Palmer, television, and golf nut President Dwight Eisenhower had ignited nationwide curiosity, and even in little Pearl River, people were beginning to catch the golf bug.

I can't recall why I tagged along on that day—maybe it was the two-dollar cart-pulling fee Dad offered me. Certainly, I had no interest in golf. No one my age played. In fact, almost no one I knew played golf—I don't think even the Baseball Dads were into it. Back then the prototypical golfer was my father: fat, fifty-something, and dressed like a pimp on holiday.

Still, I went along. Somewhere in the recesses of my brain there must have been a need, a curiosity. Both of my parents had played the game for years; and at roughly my age Eric had taken it up, developing enough skill to make his high school and college teams. I suppose it was unavoidable that I would give the game a look. Or maybe the need was more basic—maybe, subconsciously, I needed to spend a few hours with my father.

I remember well his dusty old leather bag, with its odd collection of implements, Kroydons and Wilsons mostly, including one iron with a maroon shaft and a big, round, dot-punched face that was stamped with the word "niblick." In the zippered bottom pocket of the bag lived a half dozen or so balls—Spalding Dots—along with a crusty brown left-hand glove that had, mysteriously, no fingers.

My father's golf shoes were enormous: size 13EEEs with shiny steel cleats that added nearly two inches to his six-foot frame. I wasn't ready for the sound the cleats made that first day when he walked from the parking lot to the pro shop, but I remember liking it. It gave Dad a military, almost gladiatorial quality, like a professional football player clomping through the tunnel to the stadium.

That aura evaporated at the first tee. Although I knew almost nothing about the game, it was clear to me from swing number one that Dad had less than textbook form. I never asked him, but my guess is that he was purely self-taught. He didn't make the kind of money that allowed for golf lessons, and surely, no instructor would have equipped him with the fundamentals he had.

His interlocking grip—the pinkie of the right hand interlaced between the second and third fingers of the left—was a particularly curious choice, since each of Dad's fingers was roughly the size of a bratwurst. His preshot routine was a series of semiviolent waggles, accomplished with the spasmodic hinging and unhinging of not his wrists, but his elbows. He'd snatch the clubhead straight up from the ball and set it back in place, snatch it up and set it back, snatch it and set it. On a given shot the precise number of snatch-ups was unpredictable, but the count occasionally hit double digits. It was a bit like the cheek-slathering foreplay he favored in his chiropractic adjustments—not until he felt the inspiration would he make his move.

Because of his advanced age and generous torso, a full, flowing swing was pretty much out of the question, so what Dad featured instead was a convulsive three-part move comprised of a yank, a lurch, and a snatch. He began by whipping the club back into an abbreviated backswing, then punched through the ball with his powerful arms and hands before finishing with his signature move, a paroxysmal pullback of the club shaft to his chest, as if snatching it from a white-hot fire. This was all accomplished from a flat-footed stance and at atom-splitting speed.

By contrast, his pace of play was pitifully slow. Club selection could take decades, and each of his shots was preceded by a painstakingly executed practice swing—sometimes two. Putting was the worst of all. He went through the same nutty up-and-down waggles as in the long game, but then, just prior to the stroke, he observed a puzzling ritual. He'd place the putter carefully behind the ball, then lift it up and set it directly *in front of the ball* before returning it behind the ball again. This bit of mumbo jumbo seemed utterly ridiculous until the day I saw two-time U.S. Open champion Julius Boros do the same thing on TV.

That was my father's method on that Saturday at Blue Hill and every other time I saw it. For all his heterodoxy, however, he was a decent player. He wasn't a long hitter, but he generally kept the ball in play, and his low-flying tee shots could sneak out near the 250 mark. On a good day he'd shoot in the low to mid-80s, and I think he actually broke 80 a few times, presumably on baked-out fairways where he could exploit his potent ground attack.

I suppose I found that first day at Blue Hill vaguely interesting, but I certainly wasn't smitten with golf. Indeed, forty years later, my most vivid memory remains the sixteenth hole, a short par 4 where the second shot played over a marsh. While pulling Dad's cart over the wooden bridge that crossed the marsh, I spied an odd diaphanous ribbon dangling among the reeds. It was about an inch wide and nearly two feet long and had spots all over it. From a distance it looked like a cheap belt made of faux leopard.

"What's that?" I asked my father.

"That's a snakeskin," he said. Then he pulled his driver from the bag, reached out and plucked it off the reed, and delivered it to me. I'd learned about how a snake sheds its skin, but this was the real thing. It was like getting a Mantle rookie card. Almost.

I caddied once or twice more for my father and swatted at balls a few times, but it would be another year before I played my first round of golf, and my debut took place in the most unlikely of places: Davenport, Iowa. The occasion was the twenty-fifth reunion of my father's Palmer College of Chiropractic class. With my brother a year from college graduation we decided to make this our last family vacation.

By the time it was over, none of us wanted another one. My brother had broken up with his girlfriend and was in a foul mood on departure day, a mood that quickly became immeasurably fouler when, roughly half an hour after departure, my dad's Chevy Bel-Air broke down and we had to send for our backup car: my mother's 1960 Corvair.

One of America's original "compact cars," the Corvair boasted perhaps six cubic feet of trunk space, and that was filled by Mom's and Eric's golf clubs. Thus it was that we roped our luggage to the roof of the car, Dad and Eric jammed their ample butts into the front seats, and Mom and I crammed in back for a two-thousand-mile journey, knees at our noses, with an assortment of carry-on items across our feet, laps, and shoulders. This in the car Ralph Nader would later declare *Unsafe at Any Speed.*

Day two was sufficiently unsettling for yours truly that I left a 250-mile daisy trail of vomit splotches across the hills of Pennsylvania and Ohio. But the worst came on day three, when the ropes gave way and our six suitcases blasted off the top of the car and into the middle of the Ohio Turnpike.

Somehow we made it to Davenport, where my father attended three days of chiropractic seminars while Mom, Eric, and I paid three visits to the Duck Creek Golf Club. Duck Creek, I learned many years later, was owned and operated by Jack Fleck, the journeyman pro who had come out of nowhere to tie and then beat Ben Hogan in the 1955 U.S. Open.

Maybe it was that old Fleck magic, but in those three days I fell irreversibly in love with golf. I still remember my scores: 147, 126, 112—just the sort of steady improvement that leads a kid—or anyone—to believe he can master the game.

I suspect that almost every golf addict can point to a personal epiphany, a single swing or shot that yielded more than just club-to-ball contact, more than flight, bounce, and roll— something that brought addiction to the game. Mine came in round three at Duck Creek. It was an 8-iron—my first shot hit smack in the center of the sweet spot. Instead of darting forward along the ground, it arced into the sky, soared a hundred yards or so, and plopped softly onto the green five feet from the hole. It was a sight, sound, and feeling I wanted to reproduce again and again.

By the end of that summer golf was the center of my universe. I'd gotten a ragtag collection of clubs, memorized a couple of instruction books, and put myself into the rabbit-caddie ranks at Blue Hill. I'd also started watching golf on TV—not the weekly tournaments (few of which were televised in those days), but the prepackaged predecessors of our current "silly season" events: shows like *All-Star Golf* and *The CBS Golf Classic*—wherein various pros and pairs of pros squared off in carefully choreographed matches.

My favorite was the since-revived *Shell's Wonderful World of Golf*. From the distinctive theme song to the banter between hosts George Rogers and Gene Sarazen, even to the shamelessly shilling visits to far-flung Shell refineries, it was a classic. For sheer fan appeal, however, there was nothing like *Big Three Golf,* the series masterminded by agent Mark McCormack to showcase his three biggest clients: Arnold Palmer, Gary Player, and Jack Nicklaus. Like everyone else, I pulled for Arnie each week.

Those shows, combined with voracious reading of *GOLF Magazine* and *Golf Digest,* plus a hundred or so hours of postdinner carpet putting, got me through the winter. Then, as spring approached, a most serendipitous event occurred. A new golf club had been formed near our home, and the Pepers were invited to join.

Its name was Broadacres. Of the thousands of golf clubs in the world, surely not one was ever constructed in a more unlikely place: within the confines of an insane asylum. The Rockland State Psychiatric Center, one of the largest such facilities in New York, was run by a good friend of my parents' named H. Underwood "Undy" Blaisdell. He was an avid golfer who one day got the inspiration to convert sixty or so acres of his rolling, tree-clad grounds into a sporty little nine-holer.

Blaisdell gained state approval by suggesting that the construction, operation, and maintenance of his course would provide ideal recreational therapy for the patients, at least those sufficiently nonaggressive to be entrusted with picks and shovels. None of the patients were allowed to actually play the course—an acknowledgment, no doubt, that intense or prolonged exposure to golf can cause even a stable person to froth at the mouth. So the early Broadacres golfers were basically shrinks and hospital staff, plus friends of Undy's.

And me. The course was more than five miles from our home, but I managed perfect attendance during the summer of '64, thanks to my mother, who had joined the ladies' league. Mom was actually a pretty fair player, with a strong and solid swing, due perhaps to her sadly remarkable resemblance to Patty Berg. From the ladies' tees at Broadacres she was rarely over 50 and was a perennial dark horse for the ladies' championship. Mom played only once or twice a week, but good-naturedly ferried me to the course and back every day. She could see what was happening between her boy and golf, and I guess she liked what she saw.

Except for Wednesdays (doctors' day off) and the occasional ladies' function, Broadacres was a virtual ghost town until about four o'clock, when the staffers began to drift over. A fast player, I'd usually knock off two or three nines before lunch, grab a sandwich, and then head out for another two or three nines before Mom picked me up. One day in late June when I was feeling particularly energetic, I buzzed through seven circuits of the course—sixty-three holes. Not exactly the Boston Marathon, but an enduring if idiotic source of pride nonetheless.

My golf companions were few and far between. Most days

it was just George, a few scampering squirrels, and a few certified nuts. Generally, they stood in the woods, leaning on rakes and smiling quizzically at me, as if I were the crazy one. Now and then, one would skulk over, offering a handful of used balls at a quarter apiece. When I had caddie money, I stocked up. In general, I was terrified to say no.

Essentially, however, golf at Broadacres, despite its bizarre confines, was no different from golf anywhere else, except for one hole—number 5. It was an unremarkable par 5 of about five hundred yards, but with one unique feature: a building that stretched along its left side—the five-story, white stucco, tile-roofed home to two hundred of New York State's weirdest, wildest, most mentally volcanic citizens.

Each of the patients enjoyed a splendid view of the fifth fairway, albeit through thick iron bars, and in the summer months they weren't shy about expressing their opinions on golf in general and the Broadacres gentry in particular.

One regular seemed to wait for me each morning, always unleashing the same line. At peak volume he encouraged me to be fruitful and multiply, although not in precisely those words. That normally ignited one or two others. There were the paternal types: *"Hey, kid, ain't you got no friends? C'mere, I'll be your friend."* The critics: *"Nice shot . . . at least you won't have to walk far for your next one."* And the natives: *"Oogabooga, oogabooga, oogabooga."* They were particularly brutal on the lady players, who suffered a variety of lewd proposals. Even my mother got the occasional catcall. I just loved that hole.

After little more than a month I wasn't just playing at Broadacres, I was working there, too, three days a week as a soda jerk in the clubhouse snack bar. My boss, Harold, was a terrific old Jewish guy from the Bronx, a lumbering fellow with sad, knowing eyes who did double duty as short-order cook and locker room steward. It was Harold who taught me some of life's essential skills, including how to mix an egg cream, how to spit-polish shoes, and how to shave. By example he also showed me how to be patient and kind to people, even when they weren't showing you the same courtesy. And behind his dour mien was a playful sense of humor that favored lewd knock-knock jokes and Yiddish puns. Harold's wit and wisdom made my workdays pass easily, and over that summer he became as close a friend as I'd ever had.

Around Christmastime that year my mother got a phone call. "That was Mrs. Blaisdell," she said. "Harold died today."

"No," I said, struck by the news.

"Yes, it's a shame. You know, he'd been at Rockland for over thirty years."

"But the club is only one year old . . ."

"George, didn't you know? Harold was a patient, an alcoholic. He was admitted back in the thirties, and he just never left."

For days it troubled me, my first encounter with the fine line that separates sanity from dementia. Harold had seemed more solid, more stable, than most of the adults I knew. In the end, I decided, each of us is at least a little crazy, a little alone.

Indeed, during that summer at Broadacres my own fateful obsession had found full flower. The hospital had become my surrogate home, and I'd become a fourteen-year-old outpatient, returning daily to battle my demons. I really wasn't much different from many of the other sufferers, except that in my case, the affliction and therapy were gloriously one. Golf had consumed me, and I it.

Like Harold, I'd warmed to the comfort and security behind those big iron gates. Away from the course, I'd come to feel uncomfortable, even estranged. None of my friends played golf, and while I was learning about lateral hazards and flop shots, most of the other guys had sharpened their baseball skills and started pursuing girls.

That spring I'd had my own first foray with the opposite sex. Liz was the prettiest girl in our class, and shortly after we became an item she was named queen of our middle school prom. The night of the prom, when she and I took the floor of the school cafeteria for her coronation dance, just the two of us under a glittering silver ball, I became Prince Charming, for a day.

Two weeks later she dumped me. It was like the Little League tryout all over again, and it probably gave me at least a temporary distrust of close relationships. The truth, however, is that I was always a loner. Essentially an only child, I spent a lot of time by myself, and I never minded it. Throughout my formative years, my idea of a big weekend night was to eat two or three bowls of Rice Krispies while watching six hours of TV. I didn't dislike companionship, I just wasn't needful of it. To this day I generally prefer doing nothing to stepping out. I honestly can't recall looking forward to a cocktail party, and even in golf the only games I truly enjoy are those with the half dozen or so people closest to me. Otherwise I'd rather play alone, or practice, without the forced niceties and small talk. Just me and the game.

I think that's what turned me on to golf. There is a blissful monomania, what three-time U.S. Open champion Hale Irwin called an "onlyness," to golf. Whether you're playing by yourself or in a foursome, you are essentially alone. Only you call the shots and only you hit them. Only you rise to the occasion or fall on your face. There's no coach, no team, no refs, no rooting section, no safety net—nowhere to shirk the blame or share the credit. Only you know whether you hit the 4-iron flush or a hair off center, whether you sank the twenty-footer after a perfect read and stroke or out of luck, whether you obeyed the rules or bent them. Only you.

I liked that. Team play may bring out the best in some people, but I'm not one of them. Although at work I've learned to rely on colleagues, it's not my nature. I'm not sure whether it's ego or insecurity (probably both), but I prefer to take my chances solo, neither buoyed nor fettered by others. When all goes well, I enjoy the pat on the head, and when it doesn't, I like knowing that only I will suffer, that I haven't let anyone down. Alone, I'm a risk taker who loves getting out on a limb. I figure I have enough guts, talent, and luck to prevail. But not when others are with me. Then I tighten up. With six seconds on the clock I'm not the go-to guy.

In golf there are no others—just you and the game. Yes, she is a jealous mistress, intolerant and demanding. You don't enjoy the full measure of her charms unless you give yourself to her completely—and even that is seldom enough. On many days she willfully breaks your heart. But she will never leave you.

By the fall of 1964 I'd become good enough to shoot consistently in the mid-80s. Professional golfers—the guys who could spot me a stroke a hole—had become my heroes, while other athletes had lost their luster. They were all too reactive and seemed to lack the completeness—the complexity, control, and courage—the PGA Tour players showed.

There was surely some sour grapes in this assessment. I'd never had the physique for football or the stamina for basketball, and whereas I still enjoyed baseball (and had progressed a bit past my ignominious debut), the game had lost its hold on me. When Mickey Mantle finished the '64 season with 111 RBIs and led the Yankees into the World Series for a fifth straight year, I couldn't have cared less. My year had peaked in April, when Arnie won his fourth Masters.

Watching golf tournaments had also given me the urge to compete, to test my game on the road, or at least outside the hospital, and there was one logical first step: the school golf team.

Now, despite being a small town, Pearl River had one of the finest golf teams in the New York area. For years they'd dominated the Rockland County Public School Athletic League, and they usually contended strongly for the state championship. The reason for this was elusive, but probably had something to do with the town's proximity to Blue Hill, where the caddie pen always seemed to spawn just enough kids to field a solid squad.

Eight or nine players made the team, and six started each match. The number one and two guys were usually near-scratch players, the next two or three were 80 to 85 shooters, and the last spot and alternatives were wild cards who might post anything from 80 to 100. Freshmen seldom qualified for the team, but I knew I had an outside shot.

During the winter I focused on that goal, hitting plastic balls across our frozen front yard, lobbing chips over the foot of my bed and softly onto the pillows (or violently into the wall), and especially by practice-putting. In the twenty-foot-long hallway separating my room from my brother's, I honed my touch with a drill that called for me to stroke the ball with just enough force so that it settled in the doorjamb, on the six-inch-wide strip of bare wood that separated the hall carpet from each bedroom's carpet. Back and forth I went for hours at a time, hitting four balls—one for Palmer, one for Nicklaus, one for Player, and one for me. The first guy to stop ten balls on the wood won. Despite the stiff competition, Peper notched an impressive list of victories.

My zeal got the better of me, I'm afraid, on the day when, in need of a facsimile putting cup, I took a kitchen knife and carved a four-inch-diameter disk out of my bedroom carpet. Since it was under an end table, I figured no one would notice, but I hadn't accounted for my mother's weekly visit with the vacuum cleaner. She wasn't pleased.

Generally, however, my parents suffered my golf infatuation with good humor. In fact, on Christmas that year they spoiled me with my first full set of clubs: Wilson Strata Bloc woods and Dynacraft irons. I'll never forget the thrill of removing them, one by one, from that big red and yellow box, hefting them, waggling them, running my thumb across the gleaming faces of the irons. They were gorgeous.

Needless to say, I couldn't wait to hit a shot. It was about twenty degrees outside that morning, but there was no snow on the ground, so as Mom and Dad began cleaning up the wrapping paper, I slipped out the front door for a quick test launch.

I needed a target, and our front yard had only one obvious landmark: my father's shingle, suspended smartly from an eight-foot pole. "G. W. Peper, Chiropractor" it read in black letters on a pane of frosted glass that could be illuminated for his evening hours.

I'm not sure what perverse spirit impelled me, but for my inaugural shot I took dead aim at that shingle. There I was in slippers, pajamas, and bathrobe, hunched fifteen feet from my target and tweaking the blade of my pristine pitching wedge minutely back and forth until I was sure it pointed directly at the capital *P* in Peper.

Tiger Woods could not have played the shot more purely. It made direct impact, shattered the glass, destroyed the fluorescent bulb, and worst of all, lodged annoyingly within what was left of the sign, eliminating my hope of running to my parents with an eyewitness account of the crazed yuletide drive-by shingle sniper.

I told my mother first, knowing I was simply delaying the inevitable. She rolled her eyes and issued the dreaded directive: "Go tell your father." At the time, she was in the kitchen standing ominously beneath the "Home Sweet Home" sampler-cum-switch-holster.

Realistically, however, I knew I had a couple of things going for me. Number one, it was Christmas, and number two, Dad, after all, was a golfer.

"Jesus, Max, and Joseph!" was all he said. This was one of several epithets he favored, but one of the milder ones, and it immediately positioned my transgression in a less-than-dire light. To my surprise he didn't even garnish my allowance to pay for the new sign. I guess he figured he was partly to blame—it had been his idea to arm me with new weapons.

By spring I was swinging them well enough to be ready for the golf team tryout. A dozen or so guys came out, and in the end it boiled down to me, a sophomore, and a junior for the last spot. Since we were all virtually equal in ability, the coach, who was actually not a coach at all, or even a golfer, but an art teacher who happened to possess the one indispensable asset of any high school golf coach—a station wagon—couldn't make the call. So on the eve of the first match he decreed that the three of us would play nine holes to decide things. One player would make the team, and the two others would be alternates.

I don't remember much about that day except that it came down to the last hole. One kid had shot himself out early, and Frank Davidson and I were all even, about five over par as we went to the ninth tee. On that hole we both choked like dogs. I three-putted for a double-bogey 6, and then Frank settled over a six-footer to tie me. When it slipped past the hole, fortune smiled on me in a big way.

My mother was waiting in the parking lot. Although it

never occurred to me then, I realize now that she must have been a nervous wreck awaiting the news. When I told her, we were two very happy people. I'll never forget the sight as we drove away: Davidson alone in near darkness on that ninth green, hitting that six-footer time after time. It had meant just as much to him.

Making the golf team probably did more for my self-confidence than anything I've ever achieved. Twenty-five years later, while writing a book on the golf courses that have held the grand slam events, I came across something Henry Cotton wrote shortly after winning the first of his three British Opens. "I feel very much like a medical student or other person who has passed an exam," he said. "That person is just as clever some months before the exam as he is immediately afterward. But once he has passed that exam, he is qualified. I don't think I am a better player today than I was a week before the championship, but I am qualified."

At last I was good at something. For that brief moment and in that narrow area of skill, I was better than anyone in my class. I could walk through the halls of the school and the streets of the town knowing I was finally something more than the kid who had beanballed out of Little League and been jilted by the prom queen. I was now the golf kid—and not just a kid who was bonkers about the game but one who could damn well play it!

Granted, in the mid-1960s, golf was still something less than cool, and golf team members were unquestionably the lowest form of life on the interscholastic athletic phylum. Also, I still had a few rampantly nerdy entries on my résumé: marching band, French club, literary magazine. But as my occasional golf exploits gained notice, my classmates and teachers began to look at me in a new way—or at least I satisfied myself that they did. By senior year I was the team captain and num-

ber one player, and we'd won the county title with an unde-
feated record. I'd also managed to get accepted at the college
of my choice, and even found a girlfriend, my first since the
prom queen. Essentially, I'd managed to navigate the minefield
of high school on the wings of golf.

Throughout those years my father had remained a sort of
spectral presence in my life—there but not there. I can't
remember a time when the two of us just sat down together
and talked. I can't remember him looking me in the eye and
saying what he really felt. I always sensed his love, but that's
all. In contrast to the overt displays of affection he showed my
mother, he never touched me, physically or otherwise. It just
wasn't his way. Or mine.

We never played golf together, just the two of us, either. A
couple of times after my brother had graduated from college
we managed a family foursome, but that was all. By the time I
got out of college Dad was an arthritic sixty-nine-year-old
whose days on the fairways were numbered. A few years after
that he lost interest in golf and just about everything else,
when my mother died unexpectedly.

At Mom's funeral an elderly woman approached me. "You
don't know me," she said, "but I feel as if I know you well,
George. I'm a longtime patient of your father's." Then she proceeded to recount for me the salient events of my life. I was
astonished.

After my father's death I had similar encounters with other
former patients, people I'd never met who could quote my golf
scores and SAT scores, who knew I played the piano by ear,
had been editor in chief of the school newspaper, and had
scored a hole in one at age fifteen. One fellow even knew I'd
smashed the shingle. "Your dad was very proud of your short
game," he said with a smile.

All those years, he'd been sharing with his patients the

feelings he couldn't share with me. Such encounters always left me in an emotional muddle of embarrassment, gratitude, pride, resentment, longing, and frustration. Above all, however, what I felt was a sort of retroactive bear hug from my father. Dad, I came to realize, had never been guilty of anything except being himself. He had been the best father to me that he could be.

Moreover, wittingly or not, my father had given me the most important gift possible when he'd introduced me to the game of golf. It was he who took me along to Blue Hill that first day. It was he who equipped me with a collection of used clubs and then a set of new ones. It was he who joined a private club so that I'd have a place to pursue my passion. He had expressed his love and support in a manner other than I'd wanted him to, but he'd managed to express it all the same.

Our golf days together were unjustly few, and as I look back on them now, I think not only of what was but of what might have been. Because we couldn't find time for each other, I missed the joy of measuring myself against my father, of first seeing my drive roll past his, of finally beating him for eighteen holes. And he never got the kick of watching his son grow in the game, watching him grow up in golf.

Oh, how I wish I'd been less self-absorbed, how I wish we'd both been less self-conscious. Golf could have been the key that opened and deepened my relationship with my father. If only he'd been younger, if only I'd been older. All we'd needed was a little less time between us, a little more time together.

2

The Whole Dad-Lad Thing

Half a millennium of recorded history supports the notion that golf makes great intergenerational glue.

Ask a golf nut to name the first famous father-son duo, and the answer will be Old and Young Tom Morris, the St. Andreans who won a combined eight British Open titles. But the dad-lad thing goes back further than that—much further— to the late fifteenth century and the seat of Scottish royalty, where a father and son became golf's first villains.

It was James II in 1457 who put the game in print by issuing a decree that golf be "utterly cryit doune and nocht usit." The reason? National defense. The Scots were at war with England at the time, and it seems the Scottish soldiers were neglecting their archery drills in favor of golf. Ironically, James's zeal for weaponry would get the better of him when he died as a result of a gunpowder explosion from a cannon. But James III took up his dad's cudgel with another Parliamentary Act in 1471 that again condemned the playing of golf.

It would take one more generation for the Jameses to get their priorities straight, when James IV not only declared a truce with the Brits but married Margaret Tudor, the sister of England's King Henry VIII. With the war over, golf began in earnest, the visionary IV becoming the first of a long line of royal golfers. James V played, as did his famed daughter, Mary, Queen of Scots, and families regal and otherwise have been passing the game forward ever since.

Organized golf in America didn't begin until 1888, and for the first fifty years or so the game was played largely by the wealthy. Those not born into golf generally discovered it only one way: as caddies. Although Bobby Jones came from the Georgia gentry (he once asked his father, "Dad, what do people do on Sunday who don't play golf?"), Ben Hogan and Byron Nelson hatched, incredibly, from the same caddie program, at the Glen Garden Country Club in Fort Worth.

Over the past half century, however, as the game has democratized and the caddie ranks have thinned, the main pipeline of golf propagation has been the American family— from fathers (and increasingly, mothers) to sons (and increasingly, daughters).

The stories from the pro ranks are legion and legendary. There's Arnold Palmer, learning the importance of a sound grip and an even temper from his "Pap." There's Charlie Nicklaus and thirteen-year-old Jack, stopping midround at Scioto Country Club to rush home for a quick supper with Mom and then rushing back to the course in near darkness so that Jack can finish with an eagle and break 70 for the first time. There's the Miller home near San Francisco, where in the winter of 1966 eighteen-year-old Johnny hits hundreds of balls into a basement net under the watchful eye of his dad, then emerges in June to finish eighth in the U.S. Open. There's the home in Kansas City where an insurance man plays "the National Open game" with his sixteen-year-old boy, drilling him until he can match each year with the correct champion, neither of them dreaming that one day the answer would be "Tom Watson." And, of course, there is the single-minded Green Beret Earl Woods, molding his prodigy into a bulletproof golf genius.

More important, however, are the countless untold stories, of fathers and sons of all ages and abilities learning and competing and growing together through golf. When in 1980 I learned that my wife of two years was pregnant, I hoped it would be a boy, a golf buddy. At the same time, I began to wonder what sort of golf story he and I might write.

Gerhard Peper had been just an okay father. George Peper, I resolved, would be a good one. Happily, I had a few things going for me that my dad had lacked.

The first was timing. In the thirty years I'd been alive much had transpired. The prosperous, tumultuous era from 1950 to 1980 had wrought major sociological change in America, and the millions of us who came of age during that time were both agents and beneficiaries of that change.

A generation earlier the American father had been burdened with the one-dimensional role of provider. Dad's job was to feather the nest, to work hard, and provide the material comforts for his family. As a consequence fathers rarely participated closely in the lives of their children. Nurturing was left almost exclusively to Mom. As removed as my own dad was, he was far from unique, and better than many fathers.

Indeed, many of the hardworking dads of the postwar period were not just emotionally and psychologically absent, they

37

were physically absent much of the time. *The Hite Report on Male Sexuality,* published in 1981, involved a study of more than seven thousand men of my generation. One of its principal findings was that virtually none of those men had a close relationship with their fathers.

Ironically, however, actual biological fathering hit fever pitch in the two decades following World War II. The world was at peace, the economy was at full throttle, and the returning G.I.'s were at stud. In all, 76 million children were born between 1946 and 1964—the baby boom generation. Their sheer numbers, combined with the flourishing circumstances under which they were raised, caused this to be the most powerful, pampered, and demanding generation the world has ever seen. They wanted it all and wanted it now.

Numerous social changes arose from the vocal boomers, and none were more important than the feminist movement. Just as men had been typecast for generations as providers, women had been shackled to the hearth as housewives, and in 1970 they decided they'd had enough. Spurred by the rhetoric of Kate Millett, Betty Friedan, Gloria Steinem, and others, they demanded equal rights in jobs, education, and family life, and on the heels of NOW, ERA, *Roe v. Wade,* and Title IX, they gained a large degree of the liberation they sought. As two-paycheck households became the norm, the role of the American male also underwent a change, with Mom moving boldly into the workplace and Dad edging tentatively back home.

It was into that world that I took my first steps as a father. Theoretically, at least, I welcomed the kinder, gentler father role—the idea of sharing more of my time, more of myself, with my kids than my father had with me. My father had never admitted to frailties. I would. My father had never shown his thoughts and feelings. I would. My kids, I decided, would not know the father hunger I'd known.

After all, a few other factors were on my side. For one thing, I would enter fatherhood at an earlier age than my father had. When Elizabeth Marshall White and I married in 1978, I was twenty-eight and she was twenty-five. There would be a generation gap between me and my children, but not a forty-six-year chasm. Second, I was a first-generation American. No foreign influence—no Germanness—would hobble me or my kids. And finally, thanks to the blessings of my unbringing and the economic climate of the day, I would not have to work the long hours my father had. Granted, I'd inherited his Protestant ethic—my habit was to leave for my job in New York City at 6:00 A.M.—but I did that so that I could leave the office no later than 5:00 P.M. in order to get home at a reasonable hour for dinner.

Women's lib had helped, too. As a talented freelance illustrator, Libby made good money while staying at home. Essentially, we were a couple of classically privileged yuppies, ready, willing, and able to be perfect parents.

That said, I began my paternal journey with some baggage. Number one, I had no role model to draw from. I wanted to do a good job, but I really had no idea how—it wasn't going to come naturally to me. The things I never knew how to ask for as a son, I now had to figure out how to give as a father.

Most men seem to share this emotional clumsiness. Studies have shown that when a baby cries, the blood pressure and heart rates of Mom and Dad increase equally, but it is invariably the mother who responds first and who knows what to do or say. Men have it within them to love and care and nurture; they just aren't sure how to do it.

Number two, I'm selfish—even for a guy. For the better part of thirty years I'd cared only about me. Me and golf. Golf in fact had become both my avocation and my vocation. At age twenty-six I'd joined *GOLF Magazine* as an associate editor, and less than two years later I'd found myself in charge of the editorial operation. It was a dream job, but a demanding one, and I'd thrown myself into it.

When I wasn't working in golf, I was playing it: twice every weekend as a bachelor and almost that often after marriage. For the first two years, Libby had suffered more or less silently, but when her temper did flare, the cause was almost always my golfcentric behavior. And she was, of course, right. Although both she and I are independent types, from the beginning she gave twice as much to our marriage as I did. I knew she'd be just as giving to our child, but I honestly wasn't sure how I'd react.

At my five-year college reunion I'd bumped into one of my old roommates. I was still single, while he was married with two tots in tow. I expressed incredulity at his transformation from frat boy to family man and asked how he was handling it. "It's really not so bad," he said, bouncing a baby on his knee. "But I don't think you're ready for it yet—kids aren't your type."

Ready or not, I was about to find out. Like virtually every couple at that time, Libby and I attended Lamaze classes, but neither of us was sold on the concept. Moreover, in contrast to most of my male contemporaries, I had little zest for attending a birth. Blessed event or not, the thought of sitting in the front row as my wife writhed in pain while being pried and poked at by medical professionals held no appeal for me. Maybe because of that, I was a less-than-enthusiastic breathing coach. After one of the sessions Libby informed me that I was more hindrance than help. "Show up in the O.R. if you want," she said, "but if the pain gets bad, I'm going to ask for an epidural."

The Lamaze course was six weeks. We played hooky on weeks three and four, and her contractions started on week six. Our obstetrician entered the delivery room, approached me, and said, "You completed only half the course, but if you'd like to take part, I think it would be all right. Your call."

I sat in the waiting room. Ominously, my first act as a father was to be absent.

Our child was born on the afternoon of October 4, 1980, just moments after the Yankees had clinched the Eastern Division of the American League. He was a perfect, healthy seven-pound boy who would change our lives forever and for the good. Given his birth date, I briefly suggested we name him Broderick Crawford, after the star of the old *Highway Patrol* TV series who ended every conversation on his squad car radio with a gravel-voiced "Ten-four." Instead, we settled on Timothy William, stealing names from Libby's family and mine.

Libby instantly became the ideal mother, giving Tim all the love and care a child could ever want. Just as quickly, I assumed a passive, bit-player role. Oh, I changed a few diapers and did some bottle-feeding, but I can't remember being present for any wee-hours meals. Partly, this was because Libby so embraced her maternal duties that there was little room between her and Tim, but just as surely, it was my less-than-aggressive posture as a father—and my selfishness. I knew I could get away with doing the minimum, and so I did.

On the few occasions when Libby did lateral the caretaking ball to me, I fumbled it. One Saturday morning she was busy cooking and asked me to dress our son for the day. I selected a snappy ensemble that included a multicolor-striped cotton shirt and a pair of red corduroy OshKosh overalls. Mission accomplished, I carried my little prize back to Mom, who took one look at him and burst out laughing.

"You've put his overalls on backwards," she said. Sure enough, the OshKosh label was on his back, and instead of the high bib front, he had a racy low-cut look. But Tim didn't seem to care, and neither did I, so he spent that whole day in back-to-front bliss.

Libby later accused me of being purposefully inept. "You figure, 'If I do a lousy job, she won't ask me to do it again.'" I'm afraid I wasn't that devious—just congenitally incompetent—but the thrust of her remark was sadly on target. I had little appetite for parental chores.

Over time, Libby and I settled into a sort of tag-team arrangement that I suspect is not untypical. "I supply the maintenance," she said, "and you provide the entertainment." She cradled Tim—soothed and sheltered him—while I tossed him in the air—stimulated and enthralled him.

At the same time, I enthralled myself. Few things in the world are more fun than playing with your kid, whether it's patty-cake or Ping-Pong. During his first year Tim and I played through a procession of rattles, stuffed animals, pull toys, and assorted plastic, acrylic, and rubberized challenges to his motor skills.

One Saturday morning in the spring following his birth, we were playing in the living room. Tim had reached the stage where he could just about walk on his own, and we were on a tottery tour, Tim holding my finger with one hand as he staggered along the perimeter of the room, the way a novice skater hugs the railing of the rink.

When we reached the windows that looked out on our front yard, Tim suddenly stopped, pointed into the sky, and uttered his first word: "birdie."

Birdie! The first intelligible utterance from my son's lips, and what is it but the sweetest sound in golf! Granted, he was referring to the robin perched in our magnolia tree, but that wasn't the bird I heard. To me this was a moment of prophecy. A message had been sent from above. My kid was a golfer—a natural!

As soon as his footing was sufficiently steady, I went to the closet in the nursery and hauled out the set of plastic golf clubs I'd bought (probably on the day I'd learned Libby was pregnant), and Tim and I went out to the backyard for golf lesson number one. I took a couple of swings with one of my clubs, then handed him his weapon: a blue-gripped, yellow-shafted mid-iron with a red clubface the size of a cauliflower.

"Go ahead, bud, give it a swing," I said, demonstrating what I meant. And he did. In fact, he gave several. When I then set down an enormous plastic Day-Glo orange ball, he swung at it and batted it a few feet along the grass. The swings were, of course, rudimentary, but what struck me was that he'd made them all left-handed. A lefty! Weren't Bobby Jones and Ben Hogan reputed to be converted left-handers? What a moment this was: Tim was not only a natural, he was a natural lefty! I couldn't wait for the games to begin.

But other things would come first. The truth was, I didn't want to rush or push my son into golf. I was determined to follow the prevailing golf-dad wisdom, which was to let the game come to the boy. I'd wait for the right moment, give him a nudge, and hope for the best. Every aspect of his golf germination would be handled with consummate care.

And so, for the first few years of his life, Tim played other things, from Lego and G.I. Joe to tee ball and soccer. At the same time, I became progressively less a participant and more a spectator in his playtime and his life.

Part of this was a natural process, as Tim began to find playmates his own age. But just as surely, I removed myself by making some poor decisions.

Just as I was absent for Tim's birth, so was I absent for his first birthday. The publisher of *GOLF Magazine* had asked me to accompany him on a string of advertising sales calls in Colorado. Our trip culminated in Vail, where we'd been invited to join several golf dignitaries, including President Gerald Ford, for the opening of a new course. It was one of those quasi-legitimate trips—equal parts work and fun—that I might easily have declined, especially considering the timing, but I accepted.

On October 4, 1981, Ford hit the first golf ball at the Beaver Creek Golf Club, and that evening I was privileged to sit next to him at dinner. When I came home two days later, I brought with me a unique item for my son's scrapbook: a handwritten birthday message from the president. It was special, but it was also forty-eight hours late, and as I think back, it was probably a symbol of the kind of father I would be to Tim—there yet not there, unsettlingly like my own father.

I had an excuse, or so I told myself. I was in a high-pressure job. At age twenty-seven I'd become the youngest chief editor of any national magazine, and I'd had a lot to learn. The first few years my workdays not only began early but often ran late. The publication I'd inherited was in need of substantial repair. Our arch competitor, *Golf Digest,* was beating us soundly in advertising and had a circulation nearly three times the size of ours. In the year prior to my becoming editor *GOLF Magazine* had lost over a million dollars. The company was looking to me to turn things around. But many fathers can point to similar stories. There's always an excuse.

In any case, as I carved out my career, I cut off my son. And from April through September, when I wasn't working at *GOLF,* I continued to play golf. The enlargement of our family had not really curtailed my trips to the links—once a weekend always and often twice. Oh, I'd play in the early mornings, in order to be home by noon or soon thereafter, but then, after some perfunctory attention to the family, I'd retreat to my den to work on a freelance assignment or watch the weekly Tour event on TV, leaving my wife and son to find their own diversions. I continued this general pattern even after our second son, Scott, was born, four years after Tim. Although I refused to recognize it at the time, I was behaving inexcusably, taking my wife for granted and thinking of no one but me.

Libby would tolerate this treatment for long periods—longer, I suspect, than many women would—but eventually, she'd explode. Each time, my response was to plead guilty, improve for a while, and then go back to my self-absorbed ways, depriving two sons of a fully committed father.

Ironically, or perhaps appropriately, my neglect of Tim bore its first bitter fruit at the same moment that I'd felt my own father hunger—baseball season. As Tim came of Peewee League age, I shuddered with memories of my trying tryout of 1961 and hoped he would not suffer anything similar. Thankfully, as it turned out, there were no tryouts for the younger kids, and Tim was placed at random on one of the half dozen or so entry-level teams.

After a game or two into the season, however, a couple of things had become clear. While Tim had been placed at random, many of his teammates had not. The Baseball Dad culture was alive and well, and in our little town a kind of syndicate had formed in which the team managers carefully controlled the distribution of kids, each Dad building a nucleus around his son and his son's friends.

Since we lived on the edge of town, Tim didn't attend the same school as most of these kids, and therefore he knew no one on his team. Strike one. He was tall for his age but slight of build, and while not the worst athlete on the team, he was far from the best. Strike two. Although all of these kids were baseball novices, several of them—notably the B.D. favorites—had had some schooling in the rudiments of the game. Tim, thanks to his minimal-participation father, had not. Strike three.

Tim made the starting nine, but he played the position of infamy—right field—a situation that probably bothered only me. And while he held his own as a hitter, generally avoiding strikeouts while slapping out a fair number of singles and doubles, he paled in comparison to the quartet of Billy, Brad, Bobby, and Ben—christened the Killer Bees by their coach, Bobby's father. These boys were beefy, talented, handpicked draft choices, while Tim languished with two or three others whose names the coach could barely remember.

As I watched the games from the stands, I seethed at seeing my son relegated in this way. And yet, whose fault was it but mine? If I'd played a few more games of catch with him, if I'd coached him a bit more on batting, if I'd inserted myself into the Baseball Dad world, things might have been different. The coach hadn't mistreated Tim. I had.

To his credit Tim suffered less than I did. Although the Killer Bees rarely gave him the time of day, he bonded with the team's other nonstars and came to enjoy the rambunctious camaraderie of Little League. He played three years, graduating from right field to second base, and over that time he saw his share of moments as both goat and hero. Ultimately, however, he baled out of baseball, just as I had.

He'd abandoned soccer in the same way, after a couple of promising seasons as a speedy midfielder. So, with a void in his athletic life, the time was ripe, and I was ready. The question was, could I pull him into golf?

There was nothing I wanted more. Here was a chance for me to show my love for him by bringing him into the activity I cherished most. No words would be needed. I could bridge the gap, tap into his emotional world via shared physical activity.

Just as toddlers sit side by side and engage in parallel playing, each with a different toy, so do golfers make their way through eighteen holes, happy to be together and apart. In golf, being "there but not there" somehow works. I could give and take at the same time, pursue my passion selfishly while reestablishing the connection with my son.

I'll never forget that first spring afternoon. Tim was building a Lego castle in his room when I walked in and said, "Hey, I'm gonna go over to the club and hit some practice balls—you wanna come along and hit a few, too?"

"Okay," he said in his best attempt at nonchalance. His eyes, as wide as saucers, could not hide the excitement, the thrill of entering Dad's world. Moments later we were heading out the door. Tim, with Mom's help, had lost his jeans and T-shirt uniform and suddenly looked like a miniature Polo ad in khakis and a Masters green cotton shirt. Over his shoulder was a plaid kid's golf bag, with a half dozen or so clubs—right-handed clubs. Those lefty swings he'd taken as a toddler had proved to be misleading.

We started on the putting green, with one-footers. My hope was that the sight and sound of the ball clanking into the cup would give him positive reinforcement. Gradually, we backed off to three-footers and then longer putts. I gave him only one point of advice—a visual image from a cover article Ken Venturi had done for *GOLF Magazine:* "Pretend your wrists are in a cast." If the resultant stroke was a bit rigid, it at least succeeded in keeping most of the balls on the green.

Although Tim tolerated this foreplay, we both knew that what he really wanted was to take some full swings, so after a few minutes we headed for the range. As we set our bags down next to a bucket of balls, I think I was just as excited as he. Say what you will about the kick of slugging a line drive to center field or swishing a thirty-foot jump shot, there's nothing to equal the visceral pleasure of a solidly smacked golf shot. I desperately wanted Tim to have that experience.

Again, my instruction was minimal, and this time I stole from Johnny Miller, telling Tim just to "brush-brush": brush the grass with the bottom of the club going back, and brush it again coming through. No pointers on grip, posture, alignment, or swing. Just brush-brush.

His first few swipes produced the predictable assortment of whiffs, fats, and tops. Then, on about the fifth or sixth ball, Tim experienced that triumphant moment that every new golfer has known: a beautiful little 5-iron that jumped straight from his clubface, carried sixty yards or so in the air, and bounded to a stop just short of the hundred-yard marker. "Yes!!" he shouted, pumping his fist and jumping into the air. His joy was exceeded only by mine.

As I watched him that afternoon, myriad thoughts, dreams, and fantasies raced through my head, but they all boiled down to one solemn prayer: "Please, Lord, let him love this game as much as I do."

On the way home in the car, I waited for Tim's assessment of the day, hoping for a "That was fun, Dad, when can we do it again?" But it never came. I could see he was lost in thought about something, however, and I finally asked what was on his mind.

"The next time, can we go on the golf course?" he asked.

As my heart leaped, I said, "Sure, we can go on the Lower Course." (Our club is blessed with a third nine holes, comprised of five par 3s and four par 4s, that's perfect for beginners, especially kids.)

"Good," said Tim, "and can we take a cart?"

"Uh . . . yeah, I guess so." His true motivation had been revealed.

That summer we enrolled Tim in the club's junior program, a series of clinics, group lessons, and lighthearted competitions geared to teach the kids and entertain them at the same time. By September he'd developed a sound, free-flowing swing, and thanks to his long arms and legs, he'd shown above-average power for a nine-year-old.

Over Labor Day weekend he and I won the club's Parent Child Championship, an alternate-shot competition over the first three holes on the Lower Course (a par 4 and two par 3s), scorching the field with a score of 13. To be honest, it was a weak field. We beat only three or four other teams. But that did not diminish our pride and pleasure when on junior awards night the Pepers were called up to receive their trophies. Also on that evening, Tim was given the sportsmanship award for junior golf.

I was skeptical of that one. Not that I doubted Tim, who had always been a well-behaved, remarkably considerate kid. It's just that in many circles sportsmanship is a euphemism for "good loser." Such awards invariably go to the kids who are incapable of winning anything else—kids with good attitude but little aptitude—who know how to lose gracefully. Did this mean he had no talent?

No, it meant something worse. It meant he had no interest. Although I'd done my best to deny it, the truth was that Tim kept an even keel, never became upset, and never tried because he really didn't care whether he played well or not, whether he won or not—indeed, whether he played golf or not. He had picked up the game, but it hadn't grabbed him.

I'd gotten an inkling of this on a day he and I played nine holes together on the Lower Course. A club rule held that no child could play unaccompanied on the main eighteen-hole course until he or she had posted a score of 49 or better (average double bogeys) on the nine-hole course. Tim had tried a few times but had never put it all together for nine holes—he always seemed to have a double-digit disaster hole along the way.

On the day in question, however, he'd played beautifully, starting with a pair of solid bogeys that had me projecting his next scores and calculating his chances. After five holes he'd taken only twenty-five strokes, and with two par 3s in the last four holes, he was well on his way to a sub-50 score.

At the sixth, a long uphill par 4, he gave back some ground with an 8, but at the next hole, a downhill par 3 of two hundred yards, he came back with a brilliant par. Thirty-six strokes, two holes to go! All this time, Tim was blissfully unaware of his impending feat—his score never concerned him much. Meanwhile, I was hanging breathlessly on his every swing, applying backseat body English to every putt.

At the par-4 eighth more trouble struck—a 7—and that was after Dad stretched the definition of gimme to "any putt inside the leather of a ball retriever." Tim seemed to be losing some interest at this point, so at the ninth tee I decided to inspire him.

"Tim," I said, "do you realize that if you can make 6 or better on this hole, you'll be qualified to play on the big course?"

"Really? Okay," he said, and with that he set his feet and took dead aim at the green, 130 yards ahead, concentrating harder than he had all day.

"Just keep it to the right," I said, unable to stifle myself. A thick patch of woods near the left side of the green was the only dire threat on this hole. Tim dutifully aimed at the right greenside bunker, put a fine smooth swing on a 5-iron, and deposited his ball smack in the center of the same right greenside bunker.

He was pin high, but when a kid hits into a bunker, anything can happen, and what happened was the worst—a skulled shot that sailed across the green and deep into the aforementioned woods. Two hacks later he was still not on the green. A decent chip left him with a six-foot putt for a 49 . . . and it missed the hole.

I wanted to cry. I wanted to yell at him for choking. He'd come so damned close and let it get away. It was the end of the summer, and he probably wouldn't get another chance. Not until next year. Tim, however, didn't seem to feel any of my disappointment or anger, or if he did, he wasn't showing it.

"I shot 50, right? That's still the best I've ever done." At a time when I should have been consoling him he was consoling me.

That summer was the last year he played golf. It wasn't that he disliked sports or was unathletic. He would go on to play high school lacrosse, and play it well, making the varsity as a freshman. I was never more proud of him than the day I watched him score three goals. During his high school years he also became an accomplished skier, scuba diver, and rock climber. He ran long distances and lifted weights. But he never became a golfer.

Where had I failed? Why had I not been able to bring him into this game I so loved? Had I tried too hard? Had I not tried hard enough? Did he feel that he couldn't live up to my expectations or that he could never beat me? Did he resent me in some way? Was he abandoning me by not playing because of all those days I'd abandoned him by playing? Or was it just that we were different people, that the golf-fanatic segments of my DNA had never slipped into Tim's genes? It was probably all of those things. But the bottom line was, Tim and I would never find each other on the golf course.

At first this embarrassed me, but for the wrong reasons. When asked by friends, "So is Timmy giving you a run for your money on the links yet?" I'd avoid the issue: "He can hit it past me, I'll tell you that—he has the best swing in the family, and he can just flat bust it." This, I've come to realize, is the standard reply of golf-adept fathers with non-golf-adept sons. We're in denial, too macho to admit that our flesh and blood lacks the talent and/or passion for the game. Other versions of the verbal veer include, "Yeah, he's a pretty good player, but recently he discovered girls," and "He's a natural talent, but he plays so many other sports, he has no time for golf."

It took me a while to learn that it wasn't about golf and my ego. It was about what golf and my ego had done to me and my son. In the same way that my father and I had failed to bond, so had my son and I failed, and this time the fault was all mine.

My biggest mistake was in putting all my eggs in golf's basket. Had I tried harder to know and understand my son, we might easily have found another activity to pursue in each other's company. His list of interests—guitar playing, snowboarding, cliff scaling, and poetry writing—wasn't much in sync with mine, but that was because my own list pretty well began and ended with golf. The closest we came to bonding was our occasional tosses of the Frisbee, something Tim does with great élan and I happen to enjoy.

But somehow Tim seems to have survived childhood despite a lack of paternal nurturing. In the book *Real Boys* Harvard psychologist William Pollack says, "Father absence has been correctly linked to a host of ills for boys: diminished self-esteem, depression, delinquency, violence, crime, gang membership, academic failure and lack of emotional commitments." For whatever reasons Tim escaped those problems. At age twenty-two he's self-confident, resilient, outgoing, and kindhearted. He's strong-willed but broad-minded, masculine without being macho. He has never gotten into more legal trouble than a speeding ticket, drinks only wine and beer, doesn't do drugs (at least as far as I know), gets As and Bs in his college courses, and seems to have quite a knack with the ladies. All of which comes as enormous relief to the negligent father who loves him dearly.

Perhaps best of all, as he prepares to make his way in the world, Tim has embraced a profession that also engages and fascinates me: acting. When as a high school freshman he announced that he wanted to join a local kids' theater program, I was astounded. To me, stepping onstage was the ultimate torture. To this day nothing scares me more than addressing a roomful of people, let alone an auditorium full.

I will admit, however, that when I do submit myself to this ordeal—normally after a couple of stiff Scotches—I manage to cope, and the reviews are usually kind. (In fact, after three drinks I can be downright captivating, assuming, of course, that you've had three drinks as well.) I suppose my fear of public speaking is ultimately driven by a fear of failure. Certainly, I labor over the words I put in speeches much harder than I work at the words I put on paper. I suspect I also have a higher-than-average hankering for adulation: Nothing soothes my soul quite like applause. So maybe somewhere in our genetic recesses Tim and I do share a performer chromosome or two.

Tim jumped into the thespian world without either fear or alcohol, and not simply dramas but musicals, where we discovered he had a fine and strong singing voice. By sophomore year he was the lead singer in the school's jazz/rock program, doing a deft impersonation of Dave Matthews and playing the lead roles in several school musicals: *Grease, West Side Story, Good News,* and *Guys and Dolls.* The summer of his junior year he was accepted into the intern program of the Williamstown, Massachusetts, Theater Festival, where he got his first taste of professional theater, including a scene one-on-one with Vanessa Redgrave. The following summer he auditioned at a local Bergen County repertory theater and got the title role in *Joseph and the Amazing Technicolor Dreamcoat*.

Each time I watch him perform, whether as Joseph or Sky Masterson, the same thing happens. Somewhere in the middle of one of his solos my eyes well up with tears. No song has moved me more than "I've Never Been in Love Before" as he sang it in *Guys and Dolls*. After that performance, when he came out to meet us, I began to cry again and threw my arms around him. It was the first time we'd bear-hugged in years, and it felt really, really good—to both of us. Tim later told Libby he felt prouder at that moment—reducing his old man to tears—than at any time in his life. So did I.

In June 2003 Tim will graduate from the Tisch School of the Arts at New York University, where for the past four years he has majored in drama. As a happy consequence of this process, Tim and I have found ourselves together on a semi-regular basis. For one thing, my office and his classrooms are in the same city, less than a mile apart. When he needs something from home, I bring it to work, he comes by to pick it up, and at the same time we catch up, sometimes over lunch. When he needs to go home—roughly once a month to get his wash done—he calls, I pick him up, and we drive out to the suburbs together.

It is during these commutes that Tim and I have become closer than at any time in our lives. For that, I believe we have the car to thank. Cars may be the only place in the world where two males can pull off the art of chatting. Let's face it: The whole notion of chatting doesn't work for guys. Two women can connect over coffee and prattle on for hours. Men can't. We need an outside agency to ease the process, and there is none better than the front seat of a car.

For one thing, there's the space, or lack thereof. You're packed together in a small, enclosed area that, while in motion, is inescapable, so there's a tacit obligation to be at least civil if not fascinating. Second is the element of time. Almost always, as we enter a car, we have a decent idea of how long we'll be together, whether for five minutes or five hours. This shared awareness influences our choice of subjects. In general, the longer the trip, the deeper the conversation. No one talks religion on a beer run.

Third, most guys know enough to keep the radio on—tuned to a ball game, talk show, music, or whatever—as a fallback when the conversation lags or gets too personal. (My car has a volume control built into the steering wheel, allowing me to orchestrate things without my interlocutor's knowledge.)

Finally—and this may be the best part—there's no need for eye contact. In fact, in the driver's case there's an imperative to avoid it. This allows both sides to say heavy stuff while staring idly out a window. (I'd made good use of this technique back when Tim was twelve or thirteen and Libby forced me to have the "birds and bees" talk with him. My ploy was to take him on a weekend fishing trip and open the discussion while in a bass boat, but instead, I impulsively went for it in the car while driving up to the lake. As I stared down the New York State Thruway for twenty traumatic minutes, I learned to my relief that Tim knew more about sex than I did. He was very cool about the whole chat, but I was so stressed that I drove ten miles past our exit.)

Essentially, when you're with another male in a car, you're alone but together, and you can choose to be as alone or together as you want. In that sense it's a lot like golf. In your time in tandem you can do some serious bonding, or leave each other contentedly alone.

On our city-to-suburb chat trips the topic that has brought Tim and me together is his chosen career. Except for whatever girl he's fixated on at the moment, there's nothing he's more passionate or voluble about than acting, and it's a topic about which I'm equally happy to hear, both as a father and as a movie buff and closet reader of *Entertainment Weekly*.

Usually, we talk about the techniques he's learning. One trip was spent entirely on a discussion of the international phonetic alphabet. Both Tim and I are blessed with good musical ears, and with that comes an ability to mimic sounds and voices. (I've always loved doing high-pitched Jack Nicklaus, while Tim has a killer Apu, the Indian Kwik-E-Mart guy from *The Simpsons*.) At Tisch, however, he learned to understand exactly how those sounds are formed—how humans can make only a dozen or so noises and how all words, languages, and dialects are combinations of those elemental moos, hisses, and grunts. Today he can begin a sentence with a Scottish accent, continue it in Irish, and end in Cockney.

On another trip we talked about the Stella Adler theory, which calls for actors to make themselves blank slates in order to approach their roles without baggage or bias. As I listened to Tim explain this, I was reminded of my own senior thesis in college, which focused on novels wherein the main character was *disponible,* a French word meaning open, ready, available to all influences. "That's exactly it," said Tim, and suddenly we understood each other a bit better.

We still look at the world through very different lenses, but increasingly, those lenses are based on age and generation rather than on noncommunication. For example, once he's out of college, I'm anxious to see him convert his acting skills into a career, preferably in films or television, where the money is. I'd like nothing better than to be father of the next Tom Cruise or Brad Pitt. But Tim dismisses most movie stars as nonserious, semicompetent philistines. "Those guys know how to play themselves," he says, "but most of them don't have much range."

For Christmas two years ago I gave him what I thought was a special gift: a framed copy of the first check he'd earned as an actor, for a Sprite commercial he'd done the summer before entering college. His reaction on opening it was less than I'd hoped for, and I asked him about it.

"It's not that I don't appreciate it, Dad," he said, "but every time I get a check for that commercial I'm reminded of what a scab I was, breaking the picket lines of the Screen Actors Guild strike. I'm not proud of that."

At some point soon he'll have to start earning a living as an actor, and I suspect it will be about as easy as earning a living as a professional golfer. The odds are steep, and only a handful of candidates succeed. But at this point, at least, Tim isn't focused on the race for recognition. During one of our car chats I asked him, "If it's not the money or fame, then what is it that drives you to be an actor?"

Without hesitation he said, "I want to change the world. Through my acting, I want to make people see and feel things deeply, maybe look inside themselves and find something new." Youthful idealism? Sure, but it was good enough for me. After all, to love what you do, and also feel it makes a difference in the world, well, what can be better than that?

Ironically, because of my propensity to be remote, I've become closer to Tim, maybe even closer to him than is Libby, whose very need to know everything about his life often makes Tim reticent to share too much. Make no mistake: Most of the good that has come Tim's way in the first two decades of his life has been a direct result of the love and care Libby lavished on him. At times, however, that same love and care has caused her to choreograph his life, to become his director as well as producer, and Tim has now reached an age where he wants to make his own decisions. He knows that when he shares something with his mother, he risks having her analyze it, interpolate and extrapolate things he never intended, and agonize over imagined consequences. As a result, I think he now shares some things more readily with me, knowing there's less risk of internal combustion.

Yet it is Libby, thank goodness, who still has the guts to confront Tim head-on, to draw things out of him in a way I'd never dare. Not long ago we had an argument. The subject couldn't have been further from parenting, but in the heat of a tirade she dragged us there, and as a coup de grâce she reminded me caustically of how absent I'd been as a father to Tim.

It was a blow that struck me deeply. For a few moments we both sat in silence. Then Libby, sensing my pain, looked at me and uttered the three most blessed words I've ever heard: "Tim forgives you," she said. "He says you did the best you could."

Ultimately, I've realized that, as different as Tim and I are, we have one important thing in common. We both survived inattentive fathers. The difference is, Tim grew up more quickly than I did.

3

Mulligan
Boy

I'd love to be able to say that with my second son I atoned for all the sins I'd committed in raising—or, more accurately, *not* raising—Tim, and became a model father. That wasn't the case. Although I learned a few lessons from my first years of fatherhood, I learned them slowly. If there was a difference in the relationship I formed with son number two, it had little to do with the person I was and much to do with the person he was.

Scott Peper was born on November 2, 1984. His full name was Christopher Scott Peper, and we had every intention of calling him Chris. But a decade or so earlier my brother had named his only son Chris, and when my sister-in-law heard we'd chosen the same name, she reacted strongly. "You can't do that," she said. "We already have a Chris Peper in the family." And so our Chris became known as Scott.

That was fine by me. It had an urbane, literary ring—C. Scott Peper—perfect for the cover of his acclaimed first novel. Besides, Libby and I had chosen the name "Scott" because it evoked a place close to our hearts.

In 1978 my boss at *GOLF Magazine* had surprised me with the best wedding present imaginable. "Go to the British Open," he said, "and take your bride with you." I'd never been to the British Open, Libby had never been to Scotland, and we couldn't have drawn a more idyllic event than that one, where the venue was the Old Course and the champion was Jack Nicklaus. By the end of that week we were almost as in love with St. Andrews as with each other.

Five years later I returned to Scotland on a business trip that enabled me to get in a round of golf on the Old Course. At the eighteenth hole that day my tee shot sliced grotesquely over the white fence that separates the course from the town, and bounded along the row of gray stone buildings lining the hole. I never found that ball, but what I did come upon was a For Sale sign. Incredibly, a seven-room furnished residence, comprising two full floors of one of those buildings, was available with a price tag of just 45,000 pounds—less than $65,000.

At the time, I didn't have that kind of money, but thanks to an advance on a book I'd just contracted, I did have $13,000— just enough for the down payment—and when a friend from Scotland said he'd help me secure a mortgage, I called home and convinced Libby we should go for it.

Three months later the two of us returned to St. Andrews for the closing. When Libby first set eyes on the apartment, she burst into tears. It was, I must admit, an unmitigated dump. The previous owner, an elderly woman, had died nearly a year earlier and the place had been abandoned for months. Scraps of wood, plaster, and linoleum were scattered everywhere. The tattered Victorian furniture was thick with dust and mildew, and the whole place smelled like a long-unflushed toilet. Libby was convinced I'd squandered our life savings on a Scottish pigsty.

"Don't look at what it is," I said, "look at what it can be, and for pete's sake, look out that bay window." Our view from the second floor encompassed the first and eighteenth holes of the Old Course, the noble sandstone clubhouse of the Royal and Ancient Golf Club, and a broad sandy beach, lapped by the gentle waves of the North Sea. For those who know and appreciate the origins of golf, there is no more inspiring vista.

"We can take our time getting it in shape," I said. "Once it's habitable, we can rent it out to faculty or grad students from St. Andrews University during the school year to help with the mortgage payments. Meanwhile, in the summers we'll have a cheap place for vacations." By evening she'd started to warm up. In fact, I'm pretty sure Scott Peper was conceived in that apartment.

Whatever his point of origin was, Scott was an entirely different package from his older brother. The wrapping was similar—both babies came into the world with blond hair, brown eyes, fair skin, and a full complement of fingers and toes—but the two young men they became bore little resemblance to each other.

Physically, Tim developed a lithe, broad-shouldered swimmer's body, while Scott, initially at least, took on a fleshier, slightly rounder build—more a floater's body. On the height and age chart at the doctor's office, Tim consistently led his peer group and Scott always lagged. Although their faces said they were brothers, each a down-the-middle meld of Libby's features and mine, their head shapes were completely dissimilar, Tim's long and narrow and Scott's more spherical. In fact, Scott's head always seemed a bit large in proportion to his body, especially during the generally hairless first year or so of his life, when he bore an alarming resemblance to the Peanuts character Charlie

Brown. Once his hair began to grow, however, it grew with a vengeance—dense and coarse, with the tensile strength of Brillo and far thicker than his brother's. (Unfairly, Tim the aspiring actor may be forced to battle the same follicular exodus that has laid waste to his father's pate, while Scott appears to have been granted a lifetime exemption.)

In terms of personality the contrasts between the two boys are astounding. This seems to be the case more often than not with siblings, but it's nonetheless remarkable to see completely divergent personae emerge in your own two offspring.

Almost from the beginning we could see a different look in Scott's eyes—an impish look, full of curiosity. It seemed that before he could put together sentences, he could form questions, most of them beginning with the word "why." And those whys invariably came in nettlesome succession.

One evening while we were watching TV together, I caught him studying my face. Sensing the onset of an interrogation, I made a preemptive first strike.

"What's on your mind there, bud?"

"Why do we have ears, Dad?"

"So we can hear."

"But we hear from inside our heads, right?"

"Yeah."

"So why do we need ears?"

"Well, by ears I meant the inside part, too—the inner ear—we need that."

"If I couldn't hear, would I die?"

"No, but life would be different for you."

"How?"

"You'd have to use your other senses—your sight and smell and touch and taste—to make up for your ears, and that would be hard."

"Can people do that?"

"Sure. In fact, millions of people do it every day."

"They do?"

"Yes."

"Then why do we need ears?"

Another time, after a visit to the doctor, he asked, "Why are we hot when it's only eighty-five degrees outside?"

"What do you mean 'only,'" I said. "Eighty-five is a high temperature. We're supposed to feel hot."

"But our body temperature is 98.6 degrees, right?"

"Yeah, thereabouts."

"So if we're 98.6 degrees inside, why do we feel hot when it's only eighty-five outside?"

"We just do, okay!"

Tim had rarely challenged me or Libby in this way. He was a generally docile, happy toddler, without undue questions, requests, or complaints. Scott was relentless with all three. By the time he was five I'd nicknamed him Annoy Boy.

Clearly, he had a mind that worked quickly and intuitively. But there was also a devious side to him, a tendency to tweak and exploit those around him. Where Tim showed a congenital kindness, Scott had a puckish edge.

The contrast was perhaps clearest in the divergent ways they treated the family dog, a golden retriever named Sandy. Dogs, of course, are the quintessence of unconditional love, and golden retrievers have a well-deserved reputation as the most tolerant of all breeds. When Tim played with Sandy, he gave her the same kind of affection she showed him, whether in tossing a toy for her to fetch, rolling around the floor with her, or just petting her for hours in front of the television. Scott did all these things, too, but not without moments of vexation for Sandy. Instead of just tossing the toy, on every third or fourth throw he'd fake the toss and hide the toy behind his back, leaving the dog to search in befuddlement. (Okay, I'll admit he learned that one from me.) Instead of lying next to her on the floor, he'd board her like a cowboy and bounce in the saddle a few times. Instead of simply stroking her back, he'd occasionally pinch her ears or pull her tail, just to see what sort of reaction he'd get.

None of this behavior was sufficiently demonic to alarm Libby or me. It simply showed a shadowy side in Scott that we hadn't seen in his brother. Scott seemed to need more attention—from us, from the dog, and from the world.

In time his personality came into clearer focus, his sharp mind matched occasionally by an equally sharp tongue. He was, in fact, a bit of a wise guy. And yet behind the brio was a shyness. Scott, we came to see, was self-centered but self-contained, aggressive but insecure, broad-minded but set in his ways, inquisitive but introverted.

Moreover, by the time Scott and Tim were six and ten years old, respectively, one thing had become abundantly clear to Libby and me: Although Scott had little in common with his older brother, he was a budding clone of his father.

Maybe it had something to do with the fact that we were both second sons in families with two boys and no girls. Maybe our respective mothers lavished more attention on our older brothers and then, having learned that kids don't need unrelenting vigilance, left us more to ourselves. For better or worse, Scott and I share a strange sort of shy self-assurance.

Certainly, neither of us drew any confidence from our physical presence. Throughout grammar school, I was small for my age, allegedly because I was a picky eater (at least that's what my mother told me). On top of this I battled chronic asthma, my face was perpetually as white as a Bremener wafer, and my nose seemed to be on tap. Those years, touchingly documented in photos of little George sitting next to his vaporizer, little George wiping his schnoz on his bathrobe sleeve, and little George in bed staring pathetically at a bowl of soup, are referred to within our family as my Wan Period. It ended the day my tonsils were removed. For the past forty years I've been a hearty eater and conspicuously unthin.

Happily, Scott was not cursed with most of my preadolescent frailties, but he did inherit the slow-to-grow syndrome, along with the appetite of a lovesick sparrow. By school age his menu of acceptable foods (other than sweets) could be printed on a postage stamp: pasta, pizza, tacos, chicken nuggets, fried shrimp, and Chinese takeout. It was a sad situation, given that Libby's talent in the kitchen is equal to that of any four-star chef.

What's more, given Scott's stubbornness, additions to the approved list occurred about as often as lunar landings. Libby still loves to remind him of the day he kicked and screamed until she had no choice but to shove down his throat his first bite of cinnamon toast.

What young Scott lacked in physical prominence, however, he made up for in mental skill—the same sort of mental skill I flatter myself as having. I'm sure that sounds conceited, so let me clarify. My wife is far from lacking in intelligence. She thinks more deeply and broadly about things—myriad things—than I ever could, and has an uncanny ability to grasp and unravel complex issues, whether fiscal or philosophical. She also sees quickly the qualities and foibles in people, has a highly tuned bullshit detector, and is the best judge of character I know. When it comes to the really important things in life, Libby is far smarter than I am. The truth is, I don't know where I'd be today had I not had the quarter-century benefit of her wisdom.

However, even she will admit that I'm *cleverer* than she is. A sort of Cliff Notes acuity has allowed me to slip through life far more easily than I should have. I can't always—even usually—handle grand notions or heavy thoughts, but I can get to the headline and bottom-line issues with reasonable speed and accuracy. Moreover, when it comes to minutiae, my brain has the retentive power of a pest strip. For whatever reason (maybe a broad hairless pate aids absorption) I house within my cranium an appreciable archive of useless crap. I can't tell you a damned thing about Marxist doctrine, but I can name all four Marx Brothers and most of their movies.

In the comments section of one of Scott's first report cards the teacher wrote, "Scott is an absolute sponge. His capacity to soak up information is remarkable." At home we'd noticed this in his ability to recite the things he'd seen and heard. While riding in the car or sitting at the dinner table he would suddenly burst into the jingle from a commercial he'd seen on TV. Lots of kids do this—usually ads or theme songs from the Saturday morning cartoon shows—but Scott at age six or so could repeat, word for word, the sales pitch for everything from Alpo to Ziploc. At other times, in a quirk he displays to this day, he'd utter random words, usually mellifluous names of prominent people that had somehow embedded in him and at that moment needed to come out: Wolf Blitzer . . . Isabella Rossellini . . . Hakeem Olajuwon . . . Norman Schwarzkopf. In most cases he barely knew who these people were, and didn't care. He just liked saying their names, enjoyed the lingual lilt. Like me, he wasn't much of a reader, but he loved words.

We therefore weren't surprised, a couple of years later, when his scores on the ERB exam, the standardized test that projects levels of intelligence in a wide range of disciplines, placed him among the top 1 percent in the country in verbal ability. What surprised us was that his scores in the quantitative area—the math side—were even higher. The kid was clearly smarter than his parents.

But Scott was far from faultless. Whether because of his mental agility or his laggardly physical development, he showed an early leaning toward his father's most egregious fault: impatience.

Granted, he had a way to go to reach my insufferable level. No one has less time tolerance than yours truly. Every day of my life I cut people off, both in conversation and in traffic. I have no patience for the long-winded of the world, and I become borderline homicidal when jammed up at the George Washington Bridge.

A few years ago a colleague told me that at *GOLF Magazine* editorial meetings there was a universal fear of "the eyebrow," my signal that my internal tachometer had reached its redline with the discourse of a coworker. I never insult or belittle the perpetrator. I don't need to because the eyebrow tends to induce vocal paralysis. It's particularly mortifying for the younger editors. I wish I could expunge this authoritarian tic—likely a vestige of my Teutonic roots—as it's not only intimidating to those around me, it's hugely egocentric, a sort of "out-of-my-way" attitude that is anything but charming. But I can't—or won't—and I guess that's part of my problem.

However, should any of my beleaguered coworkers ever become sufficiently frustrated, the good news is that I'm an ideal target for assassination. My workday movements are as predictable as the Solunar Tables: awake at 5:45, out of the house at 6:15, in the office by 7:00, lunch at the desk from noon to 12:15, back in the car at 4:45, home by 6:00. Every day. As for meetings and engagements, I'm actually quite flexible. I'll wait ten minutes for anyone, eleven minutes for no one.

Much of my personal life is similarly regimented. Before we go to a movie I purchase the tickets by computer so we don't have to stand in line. When we go out to dinner, I order the check along with coffee and dessert, so all the waiting is done by the waiter. Happily, Libby tolerates this modus operandi. The truth is, she drives almost as fast, has almost as little time for fools as I do, and isn't much of a lingerer herself. Nicest of all, she's blessed with a naturally beautiful face and soft youthful skin and is therefore in the tiny sorority of women who need no makeup—and thus, no time—to get themselves together. Both of us can transform from jeans and sneakers to formal wear in about fifteen minutes.

Libby, however, suffers the brunt of my impatience in other ways. She tends to speak in a circuitous syntax, several ideas jousting for prominence within the same sentence. She can thus be tough to hang with when you don't know where she's going, and even tougher when you think you do. Often I make no secret of mentally bailing out on her, and when I do, she calls me on it. Stopping in midsentence, she'll glare at me and say, "I know I'm boring you, but if you don't give me your full attention, I'll keep talking even longer—*is that clear?*" According to my wife, I do *everything* too fast. Yes, everything.

A few years ago I helped actor Bill Murray write *Cinderella Story,* a book about his life and times in golf. Now, in all the world there is probably no personality more opposite to mine than Murray's. Bill's life follows almost no schedule, he withholds commitments to engagements until the last minute, and his idea of advance planning is to inhale before exhaling. Yet somehow we're friends.

On the book I was billed as coauthor, but Bill did all the writing. I served as sort of caddie-cum-constable, relentlessly beating at him to hit the deadline. He did, but only after several extensions and a desperate all-nighter in a New York hotel where we convened with the book's editor to produce the last four thousand words. Literally the next morning those words went into production, and two weeks later *Cinderella Story* appeared. Incredibly after all that, it made the *New York Times* best-seller list and stayed there for two months.

Somewhere in the middle of that final night a bleary-eyed Murray looked at me over the top of his laptop and said, "You know, George, I've figured it out. You've gotten where you are by being the first guy on the plane, and I've gotten where I am by being the last." He nailed it.

Scott, I could see, was another of those first-on guys. In the way he raced through homework, the way he drummed his fingers and played bongos on his thighs, and in the constantly jittery knees at the dinner table, I could see the beginnings of a type A personality.

Highly trained home psychologist that I am, I can attest with absolute certainty that congenital impatience leads to a decidedly nongregarious nature. Maybe it's the impatient person's smug delusion that nobody can keep up with him. Whatever the reason, I'm not particularly interested in bonding with most of the people I meet (I suspect the feeling is mutual), and sadly, I saw the same attitude in Scott.

Environment surely had something to do with all this. Because my brother, eight years older than I, went away to a private school, I was raised essentially as an only child. No kids my age lived within a mile of us, so there was no neighborhood gang. Similarly, both Tim and Scott traveled ten miles to school every day. Tim, who transferred to the school at age twelve, was able to retain a group of homeboys, but Scott began in the first grade. As such, he had no playmates within easy reach. And even with his schoolmates he was too shy and insecure to be the inviter, the one who phoned cheerily and said, "Hey, can you come over to my house?" Just like me.

During my early childhood years I had no close pals, but I did have imaginary friends, whose names I can remember better than those of my kindergarten classmates. My pillow, a flimsy, feather-stuffed thing with a plain white case, was named Pillow Cloffat. Although we spent a lot of time together, she—don't ask me why she was a she—also had a life of her own that included shopping trips, lavish lunches, and the occasional movie. For a pillow she was highly active. At the same time, she was an ideal confidante, exactly the sort of bosom buddy I needed in my postweaning years.

Then there was the stuffed monkey I got one Christmas. He came wearing a pair of oversize elastic suspenders that allowed him to bounce up and down. For no particular reason I named him Charmie Hankas. I recall Charmie as an ebullient fellow, as full of life and mischief as you'd expect from a monkey with elastic suspenders. For a good time I called Charmie.

But my closest friend was surely Botchelinga. A living, breathing figment of my imagination, Botchelinga was an African American gentleman of indeterminate age who sold colorful helium balloons from a cart that he pushed around the streets of New York. Although an exceedingly wise, warm, and generous man, he had absolutely no family or friends, except for me. In time my own family members grew to love Botchelinga almost as much as I did—despite never meeting him—and my parents were clearly pleased when I assured them that, each time we left home for an extended period, Botchelinga beamed himself up from the city to house-sit until moments before we returned.

I'd forgotten about my imaginary buddies for years until Scott caused me to cultivate another make-believe menagerie. By the time he was age three or four his bed was inhabited by a wide assortment of stuffed animals acquired by his brother and him. One night I sat on his bed, picked up one of the teddy bears, and began talking in my best teddy bear tones.

"Hello, Scott—I'm Mr. Bear. I bet you didn't know I could talk, did you?"

"No," said Scott, instantly enthralled with the idea of connecting with Mr. Bear.

"Well, I can—and I know all about you. Would you like to know all about me?"

"Yes!" he said, his eyes dancing. Scott and Mr. Bear went on to have the first of numerous conversations on topics that would range from baseball to broccoli, nightmares to Ninja Turtles. It was not long before other members of the bed-spread community began to chime in.

"Talk that guy," Scott would say, and I'd come up with a new voice to fit the designated duck, bunny, puppy, or other cuddly acrylic creature. The core group included Rabbit Guy, a close friend of superstar Bugs Bunny; white-furred Christmas Bear, who could spin yuletide magic year-round; the unpredictable Fuzzyhead; and the world-wise Old Ranger. For a year or so they were as close as any friends Scott had.

Or needed. Tim had always been gregarious and needful of friends and constant action. He enjoyed being on teams and loved summer camp, and today as an actor he thrives on the cooperative dynamics of a theater troupe. By contrast Scott showed an early distaste for organized athletics, hated camp almost as much as I did, and tended to keep things, both mate-rial and emotional, to himself. Friends, if they made them-selves available to him, were fine, but he was just as happy hanging out in his room for a weekend.

He seemed to know the virtues of onlyness.

And so in the summer of 1990, after ten-year-old Tim had left happily for a month at sleep-away camp, it was with great hope and optimism that I issued my invitation: "Hey, you wanna go hit golf balls?"

As with Tim I remember vividly the outfit Scott wore for golf day number one: a pair of khaki-colored shorts and a red miniature golf shirt. I'd found him one of my baseball-type golf caps, which, when tightened to the max, fit nicely on his larger-than-the-average-six-year-old's head. He was armed with the same plaid minibag of six clubs Tim had used. As we left the car, he slung it proudly over his shoulder—backward—the clubheads facing behind him. I wasn't about to correct him.

Indeed, I gave him no direction that first day—just let him swipe at balls, and swipe he did, with a rapid-fire cross-handed move that produced a rich assortment of glancing blows. Only once or twice did he make flush contact, unleashing a shot that resembled a sort of power pitch-and-run. But in his demeanor there was an eager aggressiveness and a determination that suggested he was enjoying the challenge. The small bucket I'd placed beside him held perhaps thirty balls, and in less than five minutes he'd dispatched them to all points on the compass.

I took him out a few more times that summer, and he also attended one or two junior clinics put on by the club—just enough to get his hands switched back to their rightful positions on the club. Toward the end of the summer the two of us ventured onto the course a few times for a hole or two. On such occasions the cart proved to be the main attraction for Scott, as it had for his brother. For Scott, however, it wasn't the only attraction. He was clearly fascinated with the challenge of getting his golf ball into the air and into the hole.

Traditionally, the club championships at our club are played on Labor Day weekend—*all* the club championships, including the boys' peewee division, for ages eight and under, and in September 1990 one of the leading contenders turned out to be six-year-old Scott Peper.

Having failed to qualify for the men's championship, I had time on my hands, and there was nothing I wanted to do more than watch him compete. At the same time, I didn't want to spook him, so I left him in the good hands of one of the assistant pros and surreptitiously stationed myself in a nearby stand of trees. (This would become my spectating modus operandi for the decade to follow.)

The championship test for the boys' peewee was a straightforward, no-nonsense layout—one hole. A 135-yard par 3, it played slightly uphill to a midsize green flanked by a pair of bunkers. Scott strode purposefully to the tee with his bread-and-butter weapon—a cut-down Ping Eye2 5-iron—and as I held my breath, he striped out a career tee shot of eighty yards. Clearly, his swing was in the groove.

For shot number two he made a wise club choice, the same 5-iron, since this was the stick with which he'd played 90 percent of his lifetime golf. (Besides, the only other clubs in his bag were a wedge and a putter.) Incredibly, he flushed it again—a string-straight burner that bounded and rolled all the way to the front of the green. He'd just hit the two best back-to-back shots of his life—and in the heat of a tournament. Somebody call Dick Vitale—we have a diaper dandy here!

Compulsively competitive as I am, I'd checked at the pro shop and determined that the peewee leader in the clubhouse was another six-year-old lad with a score of 16. Scott was now a lock to beat that!

With the pin at the center of the green he faced an uphill putt of about forty feet. "The way he's going," I told myself, "he might just slam-dunk this for par!"

Unfortunately, he only slammed it. The powerful wrist release that had helped him reach the green in two remained fiendishly resident in the stroke he put on his approach putt. With a thunderous lash he launched his TopFlite up the slope of the green. As it passed the cup, it was still gaining speed, and it did not stop until the back fringe. On in two, off in three.

Still ensconced in my arboreal hideaway, I chuckled softly as Scott half ran, half skipped to his ball. As far as he was concerned, that turbo-putt was just another well-struck golf shot. Hitting the ball and hitting it hard was, after all, the fun part of golf. And so he hit it hard again—and again and again and again, crisscrossing the green repeatedly as his marker, a female member of the club's junior golf committee, dutifully notched each mighty blow.

As all this unfolded, my amusement waned and three things occurred to me. Number one, in our golf forays together Scott and I hadn't spent much time on the putting green; number two, he was in imminent danger of hockeying himself out of a trophy; and number three, it was time for me to take action.

"What does he lie?" I bellowed, emerging from the shadows with the blustery self-importance of the village constable arriving at a fender bender.

"Oh, hello, George," said his marker with a bemused smile, tapping her clipboard with a pencil as she totted up the slash marks. "Thirteen—Scott current lies 13."

By this time he'd managed to work his ball to a point about six feet below the cup. Somehow we had to get that baby down in two more strokes.

"Okay, buddy, you can do this," I said, striding imperiously onto the green. "You just need to slow it down a bit. Grip the club lightly, set up square to your line, keep your head over the ball, take the blade straight back and straight through, hold the triangle, and don't let your wrists collapse. This putt breaks about two inches left, so start it out to the right a bit."

Somehow, despite that avalanche of advice—all of it in violation of the rules of golf (let alone the rules of parenting)—Scott managed to coax his ball to within a foot of the hole.

"Yes!" I screamed idiotically, eliciting frightened stares from both Scott and the marker.

"All right now, pal, just tap that one straight in—nice and easy."

He tapped it, but it power-lipped out of the hole and rolled five feet away. From there, four more putts were required. His final score: 19. A seventeen-putt 19.

When the championship-tying sixteenth putt failed to find the jar, I had walked off the green, shaking my head visibly enough for him to notice. After he had holed out, he came over to me.

"You had a little trouble with your putting today, didn't you?" I said, unable to stifle my disappointment.

"Yup," was all he said.

"It's too bad, after those two great shots you hit, you came in second."

"How do you know?" he said.

"I checked in the clubhouse."

"Oh . . ."

Now he was bummed out. There were no tears, but he was close. What I didn't know back then was that Scott burned inside with the same competitive fire I did, and in time he would become a far better performer under pressure than I ever was. But in this, his debut, he had faltered, and his father had faltered even more surely.

Why did it mean so much to me? Why at that moment did I feel more anger toward my son than sympathy? Were bragging rights at the junior awards banquet really that important? Did I somehow think anyone's opinion of me hinged on my son's ability to strike a golf ball? Why was this about me at all?

It's hard to explain—and impossible to justify. In that moment I had become the most brutal kind of Little League parent—the Enforcer—perversely imposing his own dreams and frustrations on the fragile shoulders of his child. Scott had done his best that day, and I had done my worst. At a time when I should have hugged him and congratulated him, I'd made him feel he'd failed. There was no excuse for what I'd done.

Well, maybe just one small one. At some level I'd like to think my behavior came directly from golf itself—from its menacing and glorious hold on me, the same hold I wanted it

75

to take on my son. I wanted him to win that tournament because I wanted the game to win him over the way it had won me. What I couldn't see, past my crazed competitiveness, was that golf had already begun to capture my son.

The following summer Scott began drifting to the club's practice range and hitting golf balls—lots of them. By August he had a swing he could depend on, a set of six clubs that served him well, and a determination to win himself a peewee title. This time, playing in a three-hole format, he twirled a snappy 18—one fewer than he'd posted for one hole a year earlier—and won his division by six strokes.

Having learned my lesson, I did not witness the victory. However, another end-of-season event loomed, an event that would give me an up-close-and-personal look at Scott's competitive mettle: the Parent Child Championship.

You may recall that at about the same time a slightly higher-profile team event took place: the Ryder Cup Matches at Kiawah Island, South Carolina. The bitter confrontation known as the War by the Shore, it came down to the eighteenth hole of the final singles match, where Germany's Bernhard Langer needed to hole a six-foot putt to beat Hale Irwin and give Europe a 14–14 tie in the match, enabling them to retain the cup they'd held since 1985. In front of the 25,000 fans at Kiawah's Ocean Course and millions of television viewers around the world, Langer narrowly missed it, and the U.S. won 14½–13½.

In the opinion of many, that six-footer was the most pressure-packed putt in the history of modern golf. Well, they are wrong. The most pressure-packed putt in the history of modern golf was the three-footer I'd faced three weeks earlier on the final hole of the Sleepy Hollow Parent Child. There is only one situation more terrifying than having to sink one for your country, and that's having to sink one for your seven-year-old.

It was the same event Tim and I had entered and won four years earlier: a three-hole Pinehurst competition wherein both players hit tee shots, then player A hits the second shot from player B's tee shot and vice versa, after which they select the better of the two results and finish the hole with that ball, alternating strokes until the ball is holed. The low score for the three holes wins.

Ever the canny competitors, we requested a late tee time in order to know the score we'd need to post. The magic number was 12. With a 350-yard par 4 followed by two par 3s of about 150 and 100 yards, I determined we'd need to go 5-4-3.

At the first tee, Scott made a more confident swing than I did, but he didn't exactly flush his shot, and after I hit a 4-wood second from his ball we still hadn't reached my drive, so when his solid 5-iron advanced my ball another fifty yards, we stayed with it. I hit a wedge to the front fringe, Scott stroked his fifty-foot putt about forty-two feet, and I managed to slobber it home for the requisite opening bogey. So far, so good.

Moments later, after we'd both foozled our tee shots, I found myself in the center of an immense rhododendron to the left of the second green, hunched over and advising my son to smack at my ball with a putter as hard as he could. He did so magnificently, bouncing it under the low-hanging branches and up a grassy bank, just short of the green. I chipped to three feet, and Scott, bless his preadolescent nerves, slam-dunked it. We had our 4 and were still on track.

Hole number 3 at our course surely ranks among the most formidable assignments in intergenerational golf competition. It's an annoying little downhiller in which the implausible assignment is to hit a full shot as short as humanly possible—just enough to carry a bunker yet somehow hit and sit on a green the size and firmness of a manhole cover. For me, it requires a 60-degree wedge, teed high and struck with a convulsive Frisbee-flicking lurch.

For Scott at age seven it was a smooth 5-iron, and on this day he played a beauty that floated over the bunker, hit on the front edge, and stopped on the back fringe of the green. With the pressure temporarily off, I managed to get my ball onto the green. I then chipped Scott's ball to about three feet, after which he putted mine to about the same distance.

Decision time. Do I chicken out and ask him to putt, or do I step up there like a man? Whoever misses will feel awful, and as competitive as Scott is, I know he'll never forgive me if I choke on mine. Still, I know I'm a more reliable putter than he is. Visions of that seventeen-putt 19 still danced in my head.

I agonized for a moment or so, postponing the inevitable. Then, feigning confidence, I waved my son aside and stepped up to the plate, telling myself, "After all, you haven't had the yips in years."

Until then. The instant I stood over that ball, my knees locked, my vision blurred, and my mind raced in a thousand ugly directions as I experienced a ghastly recollection from my darkest decade of golf: that unmistakable boiling up of blood, sweat, adrenaline, and estrogen that starts in the fingertips and courses through the forearms with a single pulsating message: "Don't even try to make this putt, you gutless chump."

Crouched in this stance/trance and staring numbly downward, I became aware of an additional agent of intimidation: A few inches from the ball, and pointed directly at me, was a pair of size 5 white Reeboks with Day-Glo orange laces. The situation was clear: I knew I was gagging, Scott knew I was gagging, and I knew Scott knew I was gagging. Never have I felt as naked, alone, frightened—or needed—on a golf course. Suddenly, being a good father and being a good golfer all depended on negotiating the same thirty-six inches.

Somehow it went in. Scott and I high- and low-fived each other all the way back to the clubhouse, where I bought him an ice-cream sundae that must've tasted almost as good as my double Macallan twelve-year-old on the rocks. At one point, when Scott looked across the table at me, with an ear-to-ear chocolate-sauced smile, I thought, "Golf just doesn't get any better than this."

4

The Great Divide

We were married in a church named St. Andrews. My best man was the current executive director of the USGA. As a wedding gift I gave my beloved a matched set of Lynx Tigress woods and irons. Our honeymoon took us to the finest course in the Caribbean, and two months later we flew to Scotland and watched the world's best player win the world's oldest championship at the world's most venerable venue.

None of it worked. Libby hated golf in 1978, and she hates it just as much today. Probably more.

It's not that she finds the game inherently distasteful. It's not that she doesn't understand it or can't play it. No, Libby hates golf for a much bigger reason: She hates it because I love it. For twenty-five years the game has come smack between us.

I blame it on Johnny Miller. In fact, even Libby might agree that our great divide began with the Golden Boy, the Desert Fox, the kid in plaid polyester who shocked the world with a 63 that stole the U.S. Open at Oakmont.

No, he didn't make a pass at my wife. (In case you haven't noticed, this book isn't about those kinds of playing partners. Besides, Johnny is a Mormon whose practice doesn't include bigamy.) Back in the mid-seventies, however, Miller was the dominant player on the PGA Tour. Between 1974 and 1976 he rang up fifteen victories—six more than even Nicklaus— including the British Open at Birkdale in 1976 to go with that U.S. Open he'd won in '73.

During the same period, Johnny was one of *GOLF Magazine*'s marquee attractions, part of an elite group of tour players we touted as our staff playing editors. (The roster also included Gary Player, Lee Trevino, Ben Crenshaw, Tom Weiskopf, Nancy Lopez, Jan Stephenson, and, of course, Chief Playing Editor Arnold Palmer.)

Now, the title "playing editor" may be the greatest misnomer in the history of magazine mastheads. Johnny et al did plenty of playing but not a syllable of editing. Essentially, their role was to spend an hour every so often in the company of one of the magazine's junior editors, who fired questions at them until enough material was gathered to create an article, usually on some aspect of how to play the game. The designated in-house grunt then wrote the piece, attempting to mimic the voice of the player in question. (As the low man on the totem pole back then, I did several such pieces. I was fond of sprinkling my Trevino articles with "podnahs," my Player pieces with "mateys," as in "Matey, on short putts it's absolutely vital that you give the ball a firm rap.")

Sadly, this has always been the modus operandi in the golf-writing trade. Arnold Palmer may have a dozen how-to books to his credit, but, in the words of one of his operatives at IMG, "not only has he never written them, he's never *read* them." Ditto Tiger Woods. During the 1980s I coauthored two instruction books with Greg Norman, an output of nearly 100,000 words. How much face time did the Great White Shark give me for these two opuses? Less than eight hours. And back then Norman was on the *GOLF Magazine* staff. Absent such enforced loyalty, cooperation vanishes completely and the scribe is reduced to panhandler, shuffling pathetically along the Tour's practice tees, tape recorder in hand: *"Buddy, can you spare a quote?"*

In any case, after Johnny won the British Open, I was assigned to work with him on a piece for *GOLF Magazine*'s July 1977 issue, previewing his title defense. "Terrifying Turnberry" it was called, in honor of the ruggedly testing Ailsa Course on the west coast of Scotland that would be holding the championship for the first time.

Miller and I got together at one of the Florida events, I sent him a first draft of the article, and by late April I was awaiting his corrections, but expecting none.

It was at this time that I met the woman who would become my best friend for life. Elizabeth Marshall White, a petite gamine of a brunet with bright brown eyes and a heart-stopping smile, enchanted me the moment I saw her. In contrast to the other sweet young denizens of Manhattan's fashionable Upper East Side—the assistant buyers at Bloomingdale's, trainees at Bankers Trust, and junior editors at Condé Nast—Libby was something different and something special.

Born in San Francisco and raised in Kansas City, the daughter of a nuclear physician and the granddaughter of a banker, she had enjoyed a privileged upbringing, attending K.C.'s best private school for girls (in the same years that Tom

Watson played quarterback for K.C.'s best private school for boys). She shared all the social graces of the debutantes sashaying through Manhattan, but more important, she shared none of their mindless pretensions. In Libby there was an in-your-face honesty and a disgust-cum-distrust of the trust-funded swells with whom she was often grouped.

She knew how to earn her way and preferred it that way. One summer while in college she got herself a job as a truck stop waitress, to the shock and dismay of her family, just to gain some financial independence. After graduating from Skidmore in three and a half years, which included a semester at Stanford, she headed straight to New York City to seek her fortune as a commercial artist.

She had guts—more guts than I. She was giving but demanding, compassionate but confrontational. Her standards were high, her views of the world sharp and unshakable. She challenged me, asked me questions I'd never asked myself. She was, and remains, the most real person I've ever met.

On the other hand, we didn't have much in common. She liked to read, I watched TV. I was a morning person, she could sleep until noon. I loved Streisand and detested Baez, and she felt just the opposite. She had no taste for pasta, and pasta was my favorite food. But somehow there was a chemistry. We believed in the same things, laughed at the same things, and most important, she laughed at my jokes.

We'd met at a wedding shower. Libby knew the bride, I the groom. By the end of that party I had matrimonial thoughts of my own. Our first date was not really a date. Libby and her roommate were moving into a new apartment and, legendary Good Samaritan that I am, I volunteered to help them transport a three-cushion flower-print sofa bed to their fourth-floor walk-up. My fee for the job was dinner with Libby. The appointed time was a Thursday evening, just after work.

Which gets me back at last to Johnny Miller. Just as I was about to leave the office that day, the phone rang. It was Miller's agent, calling to alert me that in one hour—six o'clock EST—Johnny would be calling me with corrections to the Turnberry piece. (Big-name Tour pros don't keep regular business hours and don't particularly care whether you do.) Rather than cancel my sofa-moving appointment, I gave the agent the number of Libby's apartment.

One hour later I was in the middle of the first flight of stairs, couch on shoulders, when the British Open champion summoned me to the phone. It was a lengthy call—nearly an hour—so the heavy lifting fell to Libby and her equally diminutive roommate. Just as I signed off with Johnny, they heaved the couch through the apartment door, sweating and swearing.

Golf had come between us for the first time—and far from the last. For the next twenty-five years the game would pull me physically, mentally, and emotionally from my wife.

Golf would give us many things, but it would also take things away. Most of all, it would take me away—to work and to play. In all the years we've been together I have never cheated on Libby, never strayed, never touched another woman. However, I have nonetheless been criminally unfaithful to her, through my fatal attraction to golf.

Our first "sleepover" date was in July of that year. I'd been invited to spend the weekend checking out the refurbished golf facilities of one of the venerable Catskill Mountain resorts, a couple hours north of New York City, and I asked Libby if she'd like to join me. When she said yes, I suspect we both wondered what the weekend would mean to our relationship.

The answer was nothing. As it turned out, this was the week of that British Open at Turnberry, where Tom Watson and Jack Nicklaus would battle head-to-head down the stretch in perhaps the most dramatic major championship ever. And so, after spending Saturday and Sunday mornings on the golf course, I immediately repaired to the hotel room, where I became so entranced with ABC's tape-delayed broadcast of the historic encounter between Tom and Jack that I suspended interest in the historic encounter between Libby and George.

Libby showed little interest in either match. You know your weekend tryst is a flop when the highlight of Saturday night is ninety minutes of stand-up by David Brenner.

Somehow our relationship survived, and on Thanksgiving we became engaged. After our wedding the following spring, we settled into an apartment on East 74th Street, and golf again began to rear its ugly head. Libby's dowry had included one very attractive item: a 1975 Ford Pinto station wagon. (Her job as a medical illustrator in Douglaston, Queens, involved a "reverse commute" out of Manhattan each morning.) Transportationally challenged since the day I'd arrived in New York three years earlier, I was now suddenly mobile. That meant a big change in my weekend lifestyle. Until that time, Saturday and Sunday mornings had routinely begun with a dash to Grand Central Station, where I hopped the IRT subway line, the last stop of which was a sub-six-thousand-yard public course called Mosholu Park. There I lined up with fifty or so other desperate dew sweepers for the pleasure of a five-hour round on hardpan fairways and punchboard greens.

With a car the entire metro area was my oyster. In short order I got myself accepted as a junior member of the Rockaway Hunting Club, a stone's throw from JFK Airport on Long Island, where, by the first summer of our marriage, I became a dawn-patrol regular. That meant I'd leave the apartment just after six virtually every weekend morning, play my round, and then battle back home through the Long Island Expressway, arriving at the apartment by midafternoon. As I think back upon this, it was brutally insensitive treatment of my bride—a far cry from a honeymoon. But she suffered it with good grace.

Down deep, I guess I knew then that I was getting away with something, taking Libby for granted, but I blotted that out in my blind pursuit of golf gratification and justified it with the notion that I was letting my dearest catch up on sleep. My addiction was simply too strong. Besides, I was new to this marriage stuff: I'd been a golfer for fifteen years, a husband just a few weeks.

Fortunately, some nice perks came with the golf entanglement, and they served to mitigate my disappearing act. Our first few years of marriage took us to Scotland, Ireland, India, New Zealand, France, and Hawaii, all in the dubious name of editorial research. But even those trips brought unwanted baggage for Libby. At Gleneagles I talked her into playing the Kings Course with me, despite the fact that she'd never unsheathed her nascent skills in public, then betrayed her, revealing her horrendous scores on holes 1 and 2 in a column entitled "The 18-12 Overture." After the one round she played with me in Ireland, I did it again. The first paragraph of my piece read: "It was at the 18th tee of Ballybunion, high above Ireland's Cliffs of Moher, that I experienced my most terrifying moment in golf. Well, not exactly terrifying—more like mortifying." From there I described the humiliation of being forced to walk rather than play the final hole, having lost—with Libby's abundant help—all twelve of the golf balls with which we'd begun the round.

In India, while I was playing the Delhi Golf Club, she was hit on—horrifyingly—by a seventy-year-old houseboy. In Hawaii, while I was playing in the Kapalua Pro-Am, she was hit on— although far less horrifyingly (to her at least)—by a legendary professional golfer. Such episodes tended to dampen the holiday mood.

Approximately two years into our marriage I put down simultaneous deposits on our first house and our first child. Out of Manhattan we went—Libby never to return, I to return five days a week on the Metro-North commuter railroad. The main trade-off for my hour-plus trip to the office—aside from fresh air and chirping birds—was a short hop to numerous fine golf courses.

Within moments of our move I dropped my Long Island membership and joined the Tuxedo Club, a onetime enclave of the elite (and the place where the tuxedo was born) that had been forced of economic necessity to lower its standards sufficiently to admit the likes of me. It was just twenty minutes or so from our new home in Nyack, New York. I may have let up a bit in the first summer or two as a homeowner—probably playing an average of 1.3 rounds per weekend instead of 2—although I wouldn't be surprised if it was closer to 1.8.

In any case, Tuxedo turned out to be too difficult a course for me. In two years there, despite a strong attendance record, I never parred the first hole, a hilly, tightly wooded par 4 that doglegged left, in complete disrespect of my irreversible fade.

It was at my third club in five years—Sleepy Hollow—that I found my golf home. Perched high above the east bank of the Hudson River, twenty-five miles north of New York City, Sleepy Hollow is arguably the most scenic parkland course in the metropolitan area. For several years it was the site of the Commemorative, one of the first events on the PGA Senior Tour, and in 2002 it played host to the U.S. Women's Amateur Championship. It's also one of the area's best family clubs, with fine facilities for swimming, tennis, squash, paddle tennis, and even horseback riding.

But I joined for the golf.

Within a short time I'd found a regular group: three guys of my own age and in roughly the same financial and familial straits. All fast players, we made a point of securing a crack-of-dawn starting time each weekend so we could be back home in time for lunch. One Saturday I was pulling out of the parking lot when another member caught up with me.

"How the hell do you guys get done so fast?" he said.

"It's easy," said I. "We have little kids and big wives."

In retrospect, it wasn't the bigness of the wives as much as the smallness of us husbands. And I was the smallest of all—often invisible. In the early 1980s I was on the road more often than not, making sales calls with advertising reps, attending industry trade shows and major tournaments, and generally doing whatever was necessary to get *GOLF Magazine* noticed.

Among my promotional forays was a day of golf in 1981 with Ben Crenshaw and two executives from the Metropolitan Golf Association in which we played "the Dream Course," eighteen magnificent holes on different courses in the New York/New Jersey/Connecticut area, starting at dawn with number 14 at Shinnecock Hills and finishing at dusk with the fourth at Baltusrol. Our trek, which included fourteen ups and downs in a helicopter, produced a six-column story in the *New York Times*. About all I can recall from that day is feeling constantly airsick and watching Ben one-putt seven straight greens across three states.

In an effort to top that stunt, in 1983 I enlisted Bobby Clampett, his business manager, Hughes Norton, and golf photographer Brian Morgan for a marathon in which we played St. Andrews, Winged Foot, and Pebble Beach in the same twenty-four hours. We teed off on the Old Course at dawn's early light, about 4:15 A.M., finished in about three hours, then hopped a puddle jumper from nearby Leuchars air base to Birmingham,

England, where we joined up with the Concorde (which was bringing several U.S. Tour players back from the British Open), raced through Winged Foot in a little over two hours, flew across the country, and putted out at Pebble at roughly 7:30 P.M.—twenty-three hours and fifteen minutes after we'd started.

When I told that story to Greg Norman, competitive Aussie that he is, he suggested a more ambitious jaunt: five courses on five continents in five days. To make it worthwhile, I placed a call to Bryant Gumbel, then host of the *Today* show, who liked the idea and lobbied his producers to do a week of live remote reports from Los Angeles, Melbourne, Tokyo, Morocco, and London. We were all set when, four days before takeoff, Gumbel called me back.

"I can't do the trip," he said.

"Why not?"

"I have to stay in New York that week. Gorbachev has decided to pay us a visit."

So that one's still on the table.

Back then, it seemed, when I wasn't on the road, I was on the course. To be truthful, I liked the travel. Curtis Strange, whose two sons are about the same age as my boys, once shared with me the dilemma he felt as a Tour pro: "When you're on the road, you wish you were home," he said, "and when you're home, you wish you were back on the road." To a degree I felt that way. Libby knew it and, quite rightly, resented it.

One January I called home from the golf industry's annual trade exposition, the PGA Merchandise Show in Orlando. The day, as it happened, was both my birthday and Super Bowl Sunday, and the moment I chose to call was halftime of the game. I was at the Bay Hill Club, where *GOLF Magazine* was hosting a party for the Ben Hogan Company, then our biggest advertiser. I'd had a few beers, and I was in a great mood.

Libby wasn't. That morning our boiler had broken down. Simultaneously, an ice storm had hit the Northeast, so the temperature in the house was fifty degrees and plummeting. On top of that, three-year-old Tim had come down with a virus, and after giving him a spoonful of children's cherry-flavored Tylenol, Libby had left him for a moment, returning to discover that he'd consumed the entire bottle. She had just finished dosing him with ipecac to induce vomiting when my call came through.

"Happy birthday," she said sweetly.

"Thanks," I said. "Are you watching the Super Bowl?"

"No, I've been a little busy . . . but I hope you've had a nice day," she said, now suspiciously sweet. "By the way, don't bother to come home. I've changed the locks on all the doors." *Click*.

When my repeated attempts to call her back were fruitless, I wondered what I'd done, what she'd discovered that had led her to such wrath. After all, I had had no affairs, there were no incriminating letters in my desk, no gay porno tapes under the mattress. I was not a closet member of the mob, the Klan, or the CIA. Where had I sinned?

I hadn't. I hadn't done anything, and that was precisely the problem, as I finally learned late that night when she tearfully recounted her travails. All day long she had filled the roles of both mother and father—as she had on so many other days—and she was sick and tired of it. I would either have to improve my ways or find someone else to take for granted.

I promised to improve, and I tried, but I made only minimal progress. Within a few months there was another incident, another rebuke, another promise. Again I inched forward, until the next time, when the process repeated again.

And for two decades it has continued that way. On one level our marriage has been a chronicle of golf-widow abuse and its consequences. But I think I've gained at least a little ground.

I gather, at least I hope, that we are not atypical. Women are givers, men are takers. Women feel myriad things that men don't. I think, however, that Libby and I may be extremes of our respective species. Thoughtfulness seems to be second nature to her.

"Libby is constantly making mental notes about everyone," one of her closest friends once told me. "Do you know why you have Equal sweetener in your kitchen?"

"No, I hadn't noticed we had any sweeteners at all," I said. "Nobody in our family sweetens their coffee."

"Well, I do," she said, "and Libby noticed that at our house we use Equal. You guys used to stock Sweet 'n Low, but you're now Equal people, simply because Libby wants to make me comfortable when I drop by. She's always doing things like that—random acts of kindness."

Especially when it comes to the kids. Libby knows exactly how to nurture them: love and punish them with equal ease and passion. Call it maternal instinct or whatever you want, but somehow she knows precisely what to say and do—how to give guidance and encouragement—whether it's a kiss on the forehead or a boot in the butt. Countless times I've marveled at her ability to come up with the perfect mix of words and actions.

By contrast I'm all thumbs and stammers. I'm not sure whether, universally, fathering comes less naturally than mothering, but I know it does in our family. Libby claims that my ineptitude stems partly from my Germanic roots, a heritage of impassive detachment where the national lust has always been for lebensraum—living space—rather than closeness. There's probably something to that. Certainly, I've always been semi-detached in my dealings with friends and colleagues. I have affection and respect for them all, I'm just not in the market for confidants.

In any case, I prefer this "irreversibly aloof Aryan" theory to the alternative notion: that I don't care enough about my kids to make a full effort. However, Libby also alleges that I'm a less-than-ideal father because I'm a golfer—not because I play golf, but because I'm a golfer. Based on the countless golf addicts to whom she has been subjected during our marriage, she has constructed a rough psychological profile of the golf-obsessed American male. "Golfers are essentially nice guys," she says, "but they're insensitive. They need to be beaten over the head with things. Once they understand what it is that you want or need, they're like big loping dogs, only too eager to please. But until then they're clueless, so absorbed in themselves and their game that they're oblivious to everything else."

I don't particularly enjoy this theory, but I suspect there's some truth to it. On the Golf Addiction Scale, I'm surely at least an 8 out of 10. Although I drop the game completely for most of the winter, my mind never strays far from it. I watch the pros on TV, read all the magazines, and fantasize for hours about the first round of spring, the season to come, and how this will be the year I'll cut my handicap in half.

Golf, they say, isn't fun unless you take it seriously, and if you take it seriously, it breaks your heart. In that sense we're all jilted lovers, desperately, eternally seeking a return to the game's good graces. In the most extreme cases, that pursuit leaves others behind.

Libby is one of those innocent victims. If she had an all-consuming passion of some kind that routinely took her from me, I'd resent it and everything about it. That's how she feels about my golf. She feels it most acutely on a personal level, an abandonment, but she expresses her frustration most often and most vehemently in reprimanding me over my neglect of the boys.

The problem is exacerbated, I think, by the differences in our own upbringings. Libby grew up pampered, especially by her father, who made no secret of her being the favorite of his three children. I, while hardly neglected, was left more to my own devices. As a result, we've adopted opposite child-rearing philosophies. She believes in giving our two boys everything, maternally and materially, in order to make them feel secure and confident. I favor a more hands-off approach: Don't protect them too much or give them too much. Allow them some slack, make them take some responsibility, and let them gain self-confidence and self-esteem by finding their own way. I defend this as a "man's way," and she calls it the rationalization of a golf addict.

The truth, I suspect, is that we're both excessive. Libby shows too much interest and I show too little—and as such, neither of us does the best thing for our sons. The boys would probably benefit most from an approach somewhere between our two extremes. She knows she tends to cross the line from mothering to smothering, but she can't change the way she is any more than I can snuff out the selfish lout I am. We can only try.

Rather than beat myself up for underfathering, I console myself with the notion that the boys appreciate the noninvasiveness aspect of my detachment. It's unfair, really. I care less, do less, show less interest, yet I often benefit for that very reason: I'm less on top of them, less questioning, probing, intrusive.

One day not long ago, after seeing the movie *Meet the Parents,* Scott and I were joking in the car.

"You're going to have to go through that someday, you know, bring a girl home to meet us. I can see you warning her: 'My dad's okay, but my mom's kind of crazy.'"

"That's *exactly* what I'd say," he said.

Instantly, I felt a stab of guilt at having thrown Libby under the bus.

"Well," I backpedaled, "you know Mom may seem crazy at

times, but the truth is, she's only crazy about you. I get credit for doing almost nothing, while she gets almost no credit for doing everything. She *lives* for you guys, and she doesn't ask much in return. All you need to do is say thanks once in a while, and neither you nor Tim does it often enough. For that matter, neither do I. Do you realize how happy it makes her when you simply say, 'Thanks, Mom'?"

After a brief hesitation Scott said, "She made me and Tim a great breakfast last night . . ."

"That's what I mean. At ten o'clock at night you ask her to make you breakfast, and despite the ludicrousness of that request she complies. The fact is, there was probably not anything in the world she would rather have done. She was actually psyched when you came into the bedroom, flopped down on the bed, and said, 'Mom, let's have breakfast.' Why? Because she felt needed and appreciated. All you need to do is tell her those things, and in ways more selfless than 'Mom, let's have breakfast.'"

As we rode the next few miles in silence, I congratulated myself on a rare moment of parental effectiveness. Oddly, that same evening, Libby had a distinguished moment of her own.

With Libby, confrontation often escalates into conflagration. In the heat of verbal battle she shouts things, occasionally even throws things. It's a tactic that none of the Peper males particularly appreciate, but Scott, a member of his school's debate team, appreciates it least of all. At dinner that night, Libby began a discourse on the institutions of higher learning to which Scott should and shouldn't consider applying. In the case of one university she was vehemently opposed and would allow no dissent. Her fervor had reached a theatrical quality worthy of Jerry Springer when Scott, surprisingly, cut her off.

"Stop, Mom," he shouted back. "Just shut up and stop for a minute. Can't you just *discuss* anything? Do you always have to scream? You know I value the give-and-take of a debate, where both sides present their cases in the same tone of voice. With you, it always becomes a screaming session. I can't tell you how much that bothers me. It pushes me away so fast. I can't discuss—or even argue with you. It always becomes a fight. And because I hate your screaming, and know I can't win fairly, I just let you rant on, resenting you every minute."

Those were harsh words—hard words for a mother to take—but this time Libby, God bless her, did not come back swinging. She listened until Scott was done and then, in an eerily measured voice, responded.

"Scott," she said, "you are right. My temper often gets the better of me, and I wish it were otherwise. It's a major weakness of mine, and I promise to work on it.

"In the meantime please consider three points. Number one, I'm a woman, and we often resort to emotional displays in a way that men don't. Number two, I know you have a brilliant, logical mind, Scott, and if it comes down to an actual debate, I know I'm going to lose—but the truth is that sometimes no matter how logical the argument may seem to you, you are wrong. Dad and I have seen things, know things, and require things of you, and sometimes we have to win. Shouting simply shortcuts us to that inevitable end.

"And number three, as with your father, the only time I can get you to understand, to do something, to realize how important something is to me, is when I scream. How many times have I asked you nicely to clean up your room—two, three, four? If I allow you to argue that, you'll say, 'Mom, who cares—no one goes in there but me.' And yet you somehow lost three library books in that room last year, and I had to pay for them. So I yell, 'CLEAN UP THAT ROOM THIS INSTANT!'

"So please, Scott, try to understand where I'm coming from, and at the same time, I'll try very hard to control my temper."

It was a quite a speech—brilliantly constructed, compellingly delivered. I was proud of her, and I think Scott was, too.

One point in particular struck me. The "messy room." In the messy house that is my golf addiction, one room has consistently infuriated Libby more than all others: the one occupied by my golf buddies.

She doesn't hate my friends—in fact, the wives of these guys are among Libby's own best friends, which only complicates things. However, she does hate what my golf pals have done to me, the influence they've had on me and the way they've taken me away from the family. My friends—harmless middle-aged shlubs to most of the world—have become Libby's competition, her enemies. In her eyes they take on the personae of street thugs, or more accurately, street whores, beckoning me to a life of male-chauvinist deviance and debauchery.

I'll admit that I have warm feelings for these three or four guys at my club with whom I play most of my golf. Our backgrounds and personalities are as diverse as can be, but there's a love through understanding—of the game and one another— that we share. In the eyes of nongolfers, particularly golf widows, this bond, this need to spend golf time together, is hard to understand and even harder to abide.

Libby suffered for several years with only the occasional mild protest—the equivalent of asking me nicely to clean up my room. In fact, initially she actually defended my friends, albeit in a backhanded way. "When someone is away from home for business as often as you, he doesn't have the same rights as the guy who's home all the time," she'd say. "Larry and Dan and Tom and Richard don't travel anywhere during the week, so they're more entitled than you are—especially because, when you go on a trip, you usually play golf!"

Then, when my weekend golf failed to slacken, she exploded. The trigger came the day I returned from a round at the club and announced that my foursome was planning a golf trip to Scotland. In no uncertain terms she let me know what she thought of my friends and the excessive time I spent with them. Then she proceeded to recount the many specific occasions I had played golf when I should have been there for my family, especially for Tim: The time I didn't go with her to pick up Tim at the end of summer camp, and he said, "Where's Dad?" The day Tim left on a school trip overseas and I was unavailable to see him off at the airport. The three straight spring jazz concerts, where Tim was a featured singer, that I'd missed because each one had coincided with the week of the Masters.

The equivalent of "Clean up your room this instant" came in the strongest antigolf ultimatum since James II's "utterly cryit doune" edict of 1457: "You will not go to Scotland with those guys this year or any other," she said. "At least not while we're married. Choose them or choose your family."

It wasn't a choice at all. My friends would always be there, waiting to play. My sons would not. And so a few years ago I began to back away from golf with the guys. In my nonconfrontational way I chose not to make an announcement or tell them directly in any way; I just started becoming a bit less available on those weekend mornings. They've gotten the message, and they understand. In golf, as in life, there's buddy bonding and there's son bonding, and the latter comes first— or should—for as long as possible.

Meanwhile, I turned to my sons. It was time for me to become more a part of Tim's world before he became a part of the big world. And it was time for me to become a real father and friend to Scott. Tim and I would have to build our relationship without the aid of an outside agency. In Scott's case there would be a blessed intermediary. Ironically, the same demon that had so brutally separated me from my wife would bring my son and me firmly together. Scott and I would have golf.

5

Addiction

It was on a hot, humid afternoon in August 1993 that I realized my life was about to change. Eight-year-old Scott and I had just finished playing eighteen holes of golf. It was the second or third time we'd gone out together, just the two of us, and he had played well, hitting determinedly from the ladies' tees en route to a score somewhere in the 120s. His day had been highlighted by a par 3 at the seventh, where he'd popped his driver 160 yards to within ten feet of the cup, and a well-crafted bogey at the home hole, an uphill par 4 of 390 yards. We were walking off that green, my arm on his shoulder, when he looked up and asked, "Dad, now can we go chip and putt?"

It was a straightforward question, asked without intonation or guile. Yet it filled me with such emotion, I was barely able to blink back the tears. For it wasn't a question at all—it was an answer, a declaration. My son had just assured me he was certifiably hooked on golf. He had felt the pull—the pull of the shot, the need to put club on ball, to test a thought or a theory for its ability to improve the strike, add a few yards, tighten the shot pattern, drop more six-footers. It's the pull that overcomes you—the need to see and feel golf. This was the moment when I knew that Scott and I would be linked eternally by something far more powerful than genealogy. The great game had snared us and paired us in its interlocking grip.

That evening after dinner, as Libby and I lingered over a glass of merlot, Scott rattled through the back door, his little red-plaid golf bag over his shoulder.

"Dad, I want to clean my clubs," he said solemnly. "What should I use?"

"Just good old soap and water, pal. Here, I'll show you," I said, reaching under the kitchen sink for a plastic bucket and some Ivory liquid. "Check under the cabinet in the pantry and you should find a wire brush. That'll help you get the grass stains off."

As the bucket filled with warm water and Scott began extracting his weapons from the bag, I decided to share one of the game's tribal secrets.

"Yup, soap and water does the trick for just about any club," I said, "except, of course, for those beryllium-copper Ping irons I used to play."

"You still use the L-wedge, right?"

"Right, and you'll never guess what gets those clubs shining."

"Car polish?" he said, always ready to test his savvy.

"Nope."

"The stuff Mom uses to clean her paintbrushes?"

"You mean turpentine? Nope."

"Windex?"

"Nope."

"What, then?"

"Coca-Cola."

"No, really, Dad, what?"

"I'm serious. Coca-Cola. For some reason, if you leave those copper irons in a bucket of Coke overnight, by the next morning they're shining like brand-new."

"Wow, that's cool. Can I try it on your L-wedge?"

"Sure. I think all we have is Pepsi, but that should work just as well."

As Scott hoisted the sudsy bucket into the dining room, Libby joined the conversation. "Do you have to do that inside?" she said. "You're gonna get grass and gunk all over the carpet."

I could tell from her tone that the objection was halfhearted, bordering on facetious—Scott could, too—and when I offered no support and he no compliance, she dropped her line of questioning. Libby knew something good was happening, and although for different reasons, she was as delighted as I was.

As we watched our boy scrub the faces of his half dozen junior-length clubs, I began to daydream about the golf future starring Scott and me. It was a dream I'd occasionally let myself conjure in the past, but until that evening I'd never dared to dwell or expand on it. Now I let myself go—to the tournaments we'd play, the trips we'd take, the courses we'd battle, the shots and holes and rounds and matches we'd share: all the idiotic ups and downs that only golfers know.

By the time I returned to consciousness Scott had talked his mother out of a dish towel and was buffing the blades and shafts of his weapons, a sight that shifted my reverie rearward, to my own days as a greenhorn golfer. I was a few years older than he, but the infatuation ritual was similar, as it is for so many golfers first smitten.

It was like falling in love for the first time, a time when every aspect of life is infused with a glow and when only a moment or two passes before one's mind and heart leap back to the object of affection. When you're not playing the game, you're practicing it, and when you're not doing either, you're thinking about it: plotting, planning, preparing, and dreaming about golf.

What Scott didn't know as he buffed those blades and shafts was that I had embraced precisely the same ritual, three decades earlier. By the time I was thirteen, golf clubs had replaced baseball cards as the most prized possessions in my life. The many hours I'd spent arranging and rearranging teams and rookies and all-stars into neatly rubber-banded packs were now directed to the ceremonial soaking and scrubbing of every item of my golf equipment. The neat's-foot oil I'd slathered on my Kubek Trap-o-Matic glove was now lavished, preposterously, on my leather grips (the then-legal Wilson "reminder" grips, where the top portion of the left side was flattened to help you rest it in the palm of your left hand).

I used only top-of-the-line products, courtesy of the family linen closet: Lemon Fresh Joy in my pail water, Pledge furniture polish on my Strata-Bloc laminated woods, Kiwi saddle soap on my tasseled white shoes, and terry-cloth towels to wipe everything clean.

Even my golf balls got a warm soaking bath. (The balls, after all, were a fragile, endangered commodity, especially under the assault of my youthfully unrestrained swing, and they required both maintenance and renewal. Since in my precaddying days I'd had no source of income beyond a meager allowance, I'd ball-hawked relentlessly. One day at Broadacres, when play was unbearably slow, I spent the afternoon stealth-raiding the large forced-carry pond that crossed the second fairway at about the 150-yard mark. After each group passed through, I emerged from the trees and waded in waist-deep, using my feet as feelers to pinch up as many Titleists, Dots, and Maxflis as I could before the next group arrived. By day's end I had three hundred pellets of varying vintages. It was like raiding King Solomon's mines.)

The final step in my club-cleaning sacrament involved the bag. After all, what's the point of stowing pristine equipment in an impure receptacle? So before restoring the clubs and balls, I inverted the bag, pockets open, and shook out the resident assortment of tees, pencils, ball markers, Band-Aids, shriveled gloves, and other treasures, along with a pound or so of dried grass and coagulated mud that always managed to accumulate. On particularly ambitious days I saddle-soaped the leather trim and used Mom's Electrolux to suck-clean every pouch and pocket. The whole process was as cathartic for me as it was for my gear. The next morning, when I hoisted my spick-and-span sticks to the first tee, I almost felt as if I had an unfair advantage.

These days I keep my equipment in a comically crummy state. My clubs are never in their proper slots, balls and gloves lurk at random throughout the pockets, which are perpetually unzipped—even the one that happens to house my wallet—and I emphatically eschew head covers. (To me, head covers in the age of metal woods are an utter scam.) I never wash a golf ball except with my own spit. When a caddie offers to wipe it clean for me, I reply, "No thanks, I prefer a little texture on the surface." Over three decades I've begun to sense that the condition, cleanliness, and general order of my equipment have almost no bearing on the quality of my shots. (Of course, my inborn need to sanitize hasn't vanished, just transferred, as these days all cleansing rituals are reserved for my midlife-crisis convertible. When I get that baby shining, she moves like a gazelle.)

Ironically, for someone who has spent more than half his life trying to convince people to read a magazine based on golf instruction, I had almost no early interest in printed how-to. However, my early courtship did include a fling with *How to Play Your Best Golf All the Time,* a classic by Tommy Armour

103

that was recommended by both my father and my brother, and *The Master Guide to Golf,* a large-format A-to-Z tome illustrated with hundreds of line drawings. Its author was the same guy whose autograph was stamped on my Wilson golf clubs, Dr. Cary Middlecoff, the Memphis dentist who in the course of his career had pulled a few iron shots and putts but nary a tooth. For what it's worth, I doubt Cary did much of the lifting on the *Master Guide* either.

But if Middlecoff didn't really write the book, that's okay, because I didn't really read it, just dipped in and out whenever I needed to unreverse my pivot or check the technique for the bump-and-run. The truth is, I wasn't much of a reader as a kid, and thus I wasn't surprised to see that Scott was similarly blasé (just a bit hurt when the objects of his nonaffection included *GOLF Magazine*). Several studies have shown that teenage boys don't read magazines (although teenage girls do), and my gut tells me that most teenage boys don't read much of anything. Each June, Scott's school has sent us a lengthy "summer reading list," and typically, Scott dives into it around Labor Day weekend, and only then after a torrent of maternal harassment. His brother, Tim, was the same way, and so was his father, George.

When it came to off-season golf, however, Scott didn't need to read. He had available to him something that was not around when I was courting and sparking the game: the computer. By the early 1990s Microsoft, Nintendo, Electronic Arts, and others had exploited the addictive power of golf by issuing games that allowed us to simulate the experience of playing the world's best courses. Scott, who'd mastered the mouse and joystick at about the same time that he'd learned to walk, took to these games immediately, spending hours in cyber-competition against not only his friends but an international assortment of anonymous bartenders, barristers, stockbrokers, and surfer dudes, all linked through the Internet.

"I played Bay Hill today," he said matter-of-factly one fall evening. "The finishing holes aren't as hard as you said. I was twenty-two under for four rounds—that's better than the pros."

"Yeah," I said, "and with all that walking you did, not to mention the crowds, the wind, the TV, and Tiger breathing down your neck . . ."

On another evening he was behind closed doors in his bedroom, which abuts ours. I was about to nod off to sleep when a scream of anguish came from Scott's room. I shook it off, as did Libby, until another pained howl pierced through the wall.

"He's having some sort of major problem with his homework," Libby said. "I bet that damned computer's crashing again. Go help him."

"Libby, I don't think that's it. He's—"

"Go help him *now!*"

As I tramped dutifully down the hall and knocked on Scott's door, I suspected exactly what I found: Scott, on the virtual back nine of the TPC at Sawgrass, was leaking oil as he toggled through the difficult finishing holes.

"I was three under coming to 17," not even looking up from the screen, "and then I missed that stupid island green with two 9-irons. Faded 'em too much trying to go for the pin on the front-right."

"So choke down and punch an 8," I said. "Then get to bed."

Of course, for the true golf addict—software savvy or not—winters are never totally golfless. You make do in and around the house. The staple is carpet putting. You can buy one of those automatic ball-return gizmos if you want, but such extravagance isn't necessary when a plethora of splendid alternatives is in situ, including table legs (every limb of my mother's dinette set had impact marks), soup cans (full and upright or empty, topless, and toppled), and shoes (set in a vee, heels touching, toes apart). And if you're really dedicated, or looking for a quick divorce, there's always that hole-in-the-carpet option.

The short game also may be honed in the winter months, through a regimen of over-the-couch flops, onto-the-bed pitches, and into-the-stuffed-chair chips. For most of these, Wiffle or Nerf balls are recommended, although the truly intrepid (and/or unmarried) may want to use the real thing.

One winter in the mid-1970s, while living as a bachelor in New York City, I waged a series of furiously contested short-game contests with my similarly golf-crazed roommate. Since we were apartment renters, we didn't exactly leave the course in the same condition that we'd found it, but we were at least respectful in the choice of our designated hole: a wastebasket. That may seem like an ample target, and it is until you consider the difficulty of actually holing out in the maw of a standing receptacle eighteen inches high. Most of our shots were played from a distance of less than a yard, with the result that, by the end of that winter, we'd both reached world-class skill at the quick-rising, short-flying flop shot. (By the way, like me, my roommate turned out to be incapable of keeping golf out of his career. When in 1976 I went to *GOLF Magazine,* he took the job I'd had—communications director of the Metropolitan Golf Association. From there he went to the USGA, where today he is, among other things, the guy who sits in the TV tower at 18 to explain Rules situations during the U.S. Open, Executive Director David Fay. And by the way, he still plays a wicked flop shot.)

My point is, where there's a will to play, there's always a way. And so in his first winter of golf deprivation Scott crafted a fine three-hole course through the ground floor of our home. We are blessed with an open floor plan, ideal terrain for indoor golf, and his design took full advantage of natural contours and elevation changes. My own favorite hole was the third, a bruising yet strategically designed par 3 that traversed three rooms and called for a full measure of shot-making skill and savvy. A double dogleg, it began at the northeastern edge of our dining room, from a tee hard by the kitchen door. Two options were offered on the tee shot: either a safe fade into the center of the entrance hall or a more courageous route, a stinger over the dining room table, under the hall chandelier, and across the open top of the baby grand piano to a small patch of sea-green Dupont Krylon at the west edge of the living room. Pull off that shot, and you had a fifteen-footer for birdie.

With two chandeliers, four table lamps, and a dozen windows constantly in play, Nerf golf balls were our ammunition of choice. Also, as at most in-home courses, the one-club rule was in effect, Scott favoring a sand wedge, while I used either an L-wedge or an 8-iron depending on how I was striking the Nerf that evening. With the 8-iron I could occasionally burn a low draw that carried not only the table and piano but also the couch guarding the green. On one glorious evening I made that triple carry, got a fortuitous bounce off a bookcase, and trickled into the hole for an eagle. It remains one of my greatest moments in golf.

Still, when your outdoor golf days end shortly after Labor Day and don't begin again until April, the off-season can seem like purgatory. It was thus on Christmas 1993 that I gave Scott a special present. After he had opened all his gifts, I said, "Okay, I have one thing more for you, but first a question: What golf course would you like to play more than any other in the world?"

He thought for a moment. Scott was hardly a student of the world's great courses, but he'd seen enough televised tournaments and played enough computer games to know what was good. He'd also listened to my opinions.

"Pebble Beach?" he said, to my great delight.

"Okay, then I have good news for you. You and I are going to go out to California and play Pebble Beach."

"Coooool!! When?"

He had asked exactly the question I had hoped he would.

"Tomorrow," I said.

I have never been as excited to deliver a word, or as delighted to see the reaction, as when I uttered that "tomorrow." A longtime *GOLF Magazine* friend and Top 100 Teacher, Dick Farley, had started a father-son tournament, running from December 27 to 30 on the Monterey Peninsula. It included three rounds—at Poppy Hills, Spanish Bay, and famed Pebble—plus four nights at my favorite place in the world, the Lodge at Pebble Beach. And the best news: As part of an advertising trade-out with *GOLF Magazine,* the magazine was accorded one free father-son entry. All I'd needed to come up with was the two plane fares.

Well, actually there was another cost—and money was only a part of it. Months earlier, when I'd broached the idea of the trip with Libby, her reaction was immediate: "That's fine for Scott—and you. Now what are you going to do for Tim—and me?" She wasn't looking for a treat for herself, just a way to protect Tim from my favoritism, and she was, of course, right.

The ideal solution was for me to come up with an analogous trip that Tim and I could take. In the two years or so that Scott and I had developed a closeness through golf, Tim and I had begun to drift apart. And while I regretted this more than anyone will know, I'd also done little about it. Sadly, Tim and I didn't share an interest or activity that brought us naturally together.

About all I'd done was make annual July trips to the sleep-away camp he loved, for fathers' weekend, and those weekends—just Tim and I hacking around in the Massachusetts woods for forty-eight hours—remain some of the best, most significant, and most memorable experiences of my life. On the other hand, I'm not much of a camper, so just plain self-ishness prevented me from scheduling a two-man retreat.

Besides, Tim, now aged fourteen, had begun to show other interests—in acting, rock climbing, lacrosse, and girls—and I wasn't quite sure how to parlay any of those into a meaningful dad-lad experience, at least not one that was legal. Therefore, Libby and I agreed that instead of my promising Tim a trip later in the year, she and Tim would go somewhere at the same time that Scott and I went to Pebble. From there the answer came quickly: a ski trip. And so, as son #2 and Dad headed to California, son #1 and Mom flew off to Montana for a week on the slopes.

On the plane, as Scott happily punched at his new Game Boy, I sipped a Bloody Mary and daydreamed of the fun we were going to have. It would be our first real tournament, the first extended time we'd spent together, and we'd be doing the thing we loved doing most: golf. What's more, we'd be playing the course that, in my view, is hands down the finest in the world.

We'd arisen that morning before five in order to make the first flight to the coast, and by the time we arrived at the reception desk of the Lodge, I suppose we both looked a little haggard.

"Welcome, Mr. Peper . . . and Master Peper," said Melanie, the cheerful desk clerk, as she took my American Express card. "Is this your first stay with us?"

"Not for me, but yes for Scott," said I. "We're here for the father-son tournament that starts tomorrow."

"You are?" she asked somewhat incredulously, looking again at Scott. A small ten-year-old, he could not have weighed more than seventy pounds. As he stood at my side, his shoulders were about even with my belt. "Well, good luck to you," she said, smiling down at Scott. "I have a feeling you're going to have a great time."

"Me, too," said Scott, and off we headed to our room. And

oh, what a room it was. Scott had never seen anything like it. Two big poufy double beds, a wood-burning fireplace, a TV with a hookup that offered not only in-room movies but video games as well, and a minibar stocked with five kinds of soda plus potato chips, Slim Jims, and candy bars. There was even a camera in there, and why not: From our balcony we had a panoramic view of Pebble's famed eighteenth hole.

As Scott was getting the feel for the game controller, there was a knock at the door. It was a bellman carrying a tray.

"I have a delivery here for Master Peper, from the front desk," he said with a smile.

"Wow," said Scott as the bellman set the tray on the coffee table in front of the fire. There, with a note of welcome from the staff, was one large glass of milk and a plate of warm chocolate chip cookies. Yes indeed, we were going to have a great time.

That evening at the opening reception we got to meet a few of the nearly one hundred dad-lad teams in the tournament. Most were twenty or thirty-somethings with their elder pops. Scott was by far the youngest player in the field. Going in, I was afraid that we might be a burden to the teams with whom we'd be paired, since Scott's Sunday punch rarely reached two hundred yards. But the tournament organizers had done their homework, made a few phone calls, and paired us with three of the world's kindest and most tolerant father-son duos.

Pebble Beach in round one proved to be more than Scott could handle, and although he made a few bogeys, it was a long day for him, with his first case of jet lag adding to the rigors. Still, there was nothing to match the widening of his eyes as we got to the tee of number 6 and began the most awesomely beautiful stretch of golf terrain in the world. At 7 he was as mesmerized by the sea lions basking on the rocks below as he was by the little par 3 itself, a hole he reached with a smartly spanked 5-iron and two-putted for his first par of the trip. And even as the big course progressively revealed the rust in our games, we both smiled most of the way.

Spanish Bay introduced Scott to something he'd never seen: deer on the fairways. But the repeated forced carries from the tee of over 150 yards made it difficult for him. Day 3 at Poppy Hills turned out to be our best, for two reasons. Number one, I made an executive decision to forget the competition and allow Scott a reasonable chance to score by playing from the ladies' tees. Number two, we were paired with one of golf's most gregarious and generous men, Joe Mayernik. A highly successful Cincinnati businessman, Joe and his twenty-two-year-old son, Geoff, had been playing the father-son circuit for years and were also old hands at Pebble Beach, where Joe was among the resort's most loyal corporate customers. He's also a fine low-handicap golfer—he and Geoff were among the leaders going into the final round.

"We Pepers aren't exactly lighting up the scoreboard," I said as we shook hands at the first tee, "and I hope we won't be holding you back."

"Nonsense," said Joe. "Dick Farley told me about young Scotty, and I've been looking forward to this round all week. Let's go out and have a good time."

And so we did. Scott, in fact, summoned some of the best golf I'd seen him play. On each of the first two days he'd managed to make two pars. Now, knowing he was on the front tees, I gave him a challenge I thought would spur him. "You know that Nintendo game you want? If you can make me four pars today, you've got it." (It wasn't the noblest of incentives, but hey, I know what works for my kid.)

Poppy Hills features five par 3s, and on those holes that day Scott scored a 4, three 3s, and a 2! The 2 came on the last of them after his 5-wood tee shot of 120 yards stopped two feet from the hole. It was the first birdie of his life.

"I don't think I've ever been so nervous as when he stood over that two-footer," said Mayernik, who had just birdied the hole himself. Joe by this time had all but adopted "Scotty." I will be forever grateful to him, not only for the warm welcome he gave us that day but for all the kind things he did for my boy.

That night at the closing banquet we sat with Joe and Geoff. As dinner arrived—a surf and turf combination that held little appeal to Scott's finicky palate—Joe excused himself for a moment. Fifteen minutes later, as we were finishing our steaks, a waiter arrived with a covered dish, set it in front of Scott, and lifted the top to reveal one mammoth chili dog with fries. Joe had phoned the head chef at Pebble with an emergency order and had made himself Scott's friend for life.

Since *GOLF Magazine* was a cosponsor of the event, I was asked to say a few words.

"We may not be among the prizewinners this evening," I said, "but I can guarantee you this: We were the only team in the field to visit the Monterey Aquarium, hit the local theater to see *Dumb and Dumber,* eat three straight dinners at Cafe Napoli, and use the in-room Spectravision for nothing but Mario Brothers games." Then I told anyone who was still listening the story of my young partner and his performance that afternoon on the Poppy Hills par 3s. "Partner, stand up on your chair and take a bow."

With surprising speed he did just that, and waved proudly to the applauding crowd, his smile smeared with chili. It was a moment I hope neither of us ever forgets.

6

Coeducation

Late in the summer of 1994, as eighteen-year-old Tiger Woods roared back from four holes down in the final match to win the first of his three consecutive U.S. Amateur Championships, nine-year-old Scott Peper took his own first step toward immortality, firing a 47 on the par-31 Lower Course at Sleepy Hollow Country Club. For each of them it was a defining moment, Tiger ascending to the center of the public stage, Scott qualifying to play unaccompanied on the big course.

The trouble was, "unaccompanied" was usually the way he played. None of the other kids his age had managed to post the sub-50 score required for access to the club's 6,600-yard, par-70 layout. There were a few older boys, but like most older boys, they were less than enthusiastic about bonding with a squirt. Furthermore, club rules forbade juniors from playing on the eighteen-hole course except at narrowly prescribed times, generally after 3:00 P.M. on weekdays. Now and then, one of the assistant pros would take pity on Scott and scoop him onto a cart for a quick nine, but basically he was like a traveler with a passport but no visa.

Scott's best shot at a playing partner in his full first year as a big-timer was his father, but I wasn't there for him as often as I should have been. Looking back, I know I could have sneaked out of work early on a few more of those long summer days, Protestant ethic be damned. And I certainly could have cut back on my weekend rounds with my buddies. But I chose not to, rationalizing that my friends and I played in the early morning, when kids weren't allowed to tee off anyway. Besides, the four of us had played together for years. My relationship to those guys, while hardly father/son-like, was close to brotherly, and I couldn't bear to be the one to bust up the foursome.

The shameful truth, however, was that I just flat preferred playing with them. Although I derived undeniable joy from golf with Scott, it was easier to hack around with the guys. Scott, I told myself, hadn't grown up enough to play regularly with me.

In reality it was I who hadn't grown up enough.

So thanks to his underage status, an undersupply of pint-sized peers, and an underindulgent father, my son's earliest golf consisted of little actual play. Instead, he spent long days on the practice tee. While some golfers—and most kids—would view this as hard labor, Scott loved it. Six-hour sessions were the norm, and eight-hour days were not uncommon, as he batted out bucket after bucket of balls, then chipped and putted until he'd worn furrows in the practice green. He was one lucky kid to have a high-quality facility at his disposal (and

I was one lucky father to belong to a club where the annual dues include unlimited range balls).

When he wanted to test his skills, Scott still had the club's nine-hole course at his disposal. During the week it was largely deserted, so on many days he used it as an extended practice area.

"I made a hole in one today," he announced at dinner one night.

"What?" said I, incredulous at his nonchalance.

"Well, sort of," he said with a smile.

"What do you mean 'sort of'?"

"At the third hole of the short course—you know, the little ninety-five-yard par 3—I dropped a bunch of balls on the tee to practice my wedges, and on my eighth shot the ball went in the hole."

"That's not a hole in one," I laughed, "that's a hole in fifteen!"

That summer on his own turned out to be a watershed year in Scott's education as a golfer, for it was the year he began to get his style—everything from the shape and rhythm of his swing to his pace of play, approach to course management, and match play mettle.

Of course, the core quality is the swing itself, and on that subject I'm afraid I've always had a rather fatalistic view, which I first expressed back in my golf-writing debut, a forgettable little instruction book I wrote in 1974 called *Scrambling Golf*. On the very first page of that book I staked my position: "Most of us, after a year or so of golf, should abandon the search for the perfect swing. For once having learned the basics of the grip, stance, and hitting motions, we develop a swing-style that will probably never change in its essential character, no matter how much we fiddle with it."

Yes, each of us is stuck with his or her swing. The particularized manner in which we orchestrate the motions of our ankles, knees, hips, shoulders, arms, and wrists took shape almost the moment we began playing, and after just a few rounds, the die was cast—our swing was our swing for life.

Oh, there are exceptions to this rule—players with generous supplies of the four Ts: time, talent, tenacity, and tutelage. But in my experience they are extremely rare. Personally, I can think of no player—professional or amateur—who has made a substantial change in the essential tempo and motion with which he applies clubface to ball. I've compared photos of my own swing from thirty-five years ago and now, and except for a loss of flexibility (and hair) there's almost no difference. I make the same desperate lunge today that I made as a teenager. On the other end of the scale I've heard Jack Nicklaus crow more than once about a momentous swing change he's made, then compared a sequence of that swing to one from the 1960s, and once again, except for a shortened backswing, it's basically the same leg-driven, high-handed, downward-slamming blow that made the Bear golden.

Due to this cynical view, I was more paranoid than the average golf-absorbed father, more determined to see my son adopt a low-maintenance, high-efficiency, compact yet powerful, on-plane, effortless, classical pass at the ball. Kids being natural imitators, he needed a good model to copy. Indeed, if there was a noble aspect to my steering clear of Scott at this formative moment, this was it: I knew the importance of sheltering him from my own horrific move.

The only element of my game that I foisted on Scott was my grip. I'm an interlocker: The pinkie of my right hand slides between the second and third fingers of my left. This is not the game's most popular grip; the Vardon, where the pinkie overlaps rather than interlaces, is. Although no reliable statistics exist, my guess is that about two-thirds of the world of golf overlaps, perhaps a quarter interlocks, and the rest use either a ten-fingered (baseball) grip or some unorthodox clench they're convinced works for them.

If you believe conventional wisdom, the interlock is for small-handed individuals, a fraternity to which I do not belong. I interlock for one reason: because my father interlocked, and it was he who taught me how to hold the club. But I like the fact that I share my father's grip—and now my son's—and someday in the future I'd be entirely delighted to have a grandson who interlocks.

Besides, we Pepers have some impressive company. The brotherhood of interlockers includes both Jack Nicklaus and Tiger Woods. Growing up, I always felt a proud grip-kinship with Jack, and I wouldn't be surprised if Scott feels the same with Tiger.

Happily, however, when it came to the golf swing itself, Scott was in hands other than mine, and superb hands they were. Our head professional at Sleepy Hollow in the early 1990s was Jim McLean. The owner of a picture-perfect swing, McLean had played on the University of Houston golf team with Bruce Lietzke, Bill Rogers, and John Mahaffey and would have undoubtedly been a success on the PGA Tour had he been even an average putter. But the flat stick drove him crazy and he turned to teaching.

By the time he arrived at our club McLean was already one of the best teachers in our area. But he had ambitions beyond that, and he knew the right moves to make. Immodestly, I will suggest that one of those moves was to ingratiate himself to me. From the start I was one of Jim's closer contacts at Sleepy Hollow, and from our friendship a business relationship grew. Back then, *GOLF Magazine* was expanding its roster of staff teaching professionals, and Jim became one of the first of them. Over the next several years he would appear numerous times on our cover, most notably with a groundbreaking story called "The X Factor," wherein we used computerized measurements of Tour players' swings to show that a key to power is maximizing the shoulder turn while restricting the hip turn.

Largely because of the recognition that such exposure brought him, Jim became a hot property in the world of golf instruction, expanding his teaching in a series of books and videos as well as a regular gig on the Golf Channel. Eventually, he became too big for our private club and moved on to the Doral Resort in Miami, where he started one of the nation's most successful golf schools.

But fortunately, Jim was very much in residence when the youngest Peper needed him. The club had given him a mandate to develop a strong instructional program, and he did just that, hiring a pair of young assistants, Mike Lopuszynski and Jeff Warne, both of whom would go on to rank among the Top 100 Teachers in America. Their first focus was the club's juniors, and so, along with young John and Matt McLean, Scott got just about the best grounding in the fundamentals that a kid could have.

And therefore, I suppose what I saw on that summer afternoon in 1996, the first round Scott and I played together that year, should not have been too big a surprise. Still it came as a revelation. My little ball-beating worm had magically transformed into a sweet-swinging butterfly. A miniature Ernie Els he was, with a smooth, simple, free-flowing back-and-through move that made me simultaneously proud and envious.

He wasn't perfect—his plane was extremely flat, and I blamed myself for that. Although I'd equipped Scott with junior clubs, over the winter he'd unearthed my set of graphite-shafted Callaway S2H2 irons in the basement and decided he liked them better because they gave him more distance. I hadn't dissuaded him, despite the fact that the shafts were about a foot too long for his sixth-grade frame. Even after gripping down to the metal, he stood a long way from the ball in relation to his height and thus had little choice but to swing almost horizontally around his body.

On the practice range, as I watched him bang out a series of crisp but low shots, I rationalized my mistake with the notion that flat wasn't all that bad. After all, Ben Hogan and Gary Player had flat swings. Besides, I've always thought of the flat swing as rather classy, with a British under-the-wind quality that produces controlled draws rather than those oafish banana balls that most Americans battle. Yes, I'd surely done my lad a favor.

More troubling was the way those heavy clubheads tugged on his spindly forearms and wrists as he reached the top, adding a floppy foot or so to his backswing. Happily, however, he was able to keep control of the club, thanks to that astoundingly syrupy tempo, a tempo with which I was not familiar.

As we stepped onto the first tee that afternoon, one of my fellow club members walked by.

"Aha," he said, "looks like a big match. Has he beaten you yet, George?"

"No, but I suspect my days are numbered," I said as Scott teed up and, with a minimum of fuss, pumped out a dead-straight beauty of nearly two hundred yards.

"Whooooeeee!" crowed our observer. "What a gorgeous golf swing. That's one acorn that fell a mile from the tree. His mother must be a natural athlete."

"Not really," I muttered before slapping a ball into the right rough. It was the first time Scott's and my swings had been juxtaposed in the arena of that opening tee, and I wasn't sure how I felt about it. After all, I'd spent the better part of three decades trying to ignore unsolicited reviews of my spasmodic warp-speed lurch (former PGA tour commissioner Deane

Beman once likened me to a rocket launcher) and now suddenly I had this mini-icon for comparison.

Happily, Scott seemed oblivious to our divergent styles. He was just glad to be out there. On the second tee I happened to get all my vectors aligned and nailed a big high one down the center of the fairway.

"Wow!" I heard from the side of the tee. That was all he said—"Wow!"—but never had I heard a syllable uttered with more reverence. Certainly, no drive of mine had ever earned such sincere praise. I loved it.

I loved the whole day. On a real course, with real golf clubs and a real swing, Scott had suddenly become a real golfer. Indeed, within a short time I came to realize he was the best of all playing partners, a golfer bereft of psychological baggage.

There was no hidden agenda, no rivalry. Oh, we played a match. I gave him three strokes a hole (two strokes on the par 3s), and we both played hard to win. But there was no undercurrent of rivalry. We shared each other's joy in the good shots, disappointment in the bad ones. I felt none of the competitiveness that always bubbled under the surface with my buddies, none of the shameful furtive glee I drew from their sculled irons and missed putts. For the first time, the old line "Every shot makes someone happy" didn't apply. I was playing with my son.

My greatest joy was in seeing how much he loved just playing the game, hitting the shots. When his ball flew long and straight, a look of pure euphoria spread across Scott's features. I knew that look well. All golfers know it.

The golf cart was still a kick for him, but no longer as an amusement. Now it was simply the fastest way to reach his next shot. When playing alone, with the bag on his back, Scott's leg speed couldn't match his eagerness to get from shot to shot. Even in the cart with me he'd often pop out when we reached my ball, grab a club, and dash to his ball like a base runner stealing second. This warmed my heart because I also like to cover a course at hurricane speed. Together, we played a game that resembled polo. With no one in front of us Scott and I routinely finished eighteen holes in under two hours.

The only problem with such rounds was that they ended too quickly. Although I'm surely among the two or three most impatient humans on the planet, some of my fondest early memories of golf with Scott involve late-afternoon rounds when we teed off on what had appeared to be a wide-open course, only to hit a logjam on the inward nine. On such days, with no groups pushing us from behind, we'd hang in back of the traffic, killing time with chipping and putting contests, or playing crazy flips and flops from all kinds of lies.

I'd sometimes use these moments to impart a bit of golf knowledge to my son—almost always on the short game. He'd learned the basics of chipping and pitching from McLean et al., but the subtleties had been left to me. Happily, the short game is one area where I have a degree of competence and confidence, and just as happily, eleven-year-old Scott was an eager and precocious pupil.

One afternoon we were hockeying around a green when he said, "Dad, you know that little chip you like to play—the one that pops over the fringe and rolls real slowly—how do you hit it soft like that?"

"Well, first you need the right lie," I said authoritatively, nudging a ball into position. "Ideally, you need to be in heavy fringe or light rough so you can slide the club under the ball. Just open the face a few degrees—that adds loft. It also lets you hit the shot like a putt, coming through the ball pretty flat rather than chopping down on it. That way the ball sort of slides up the face of the club and pops into the air instead of jumping forward."

My demo shot, blessedly, came off as planned and stopped about a foot from the cup. Then Scott propped a ball into position, set his wedge as directed, and executed his first pop shot to perfection, the ball rolling six inches inside mine. His face lit up. For father and son it was a moment of pure bliss.

The only other tips I offered were of a nonmechanical sort—on course management, especially on using imagination to "see" all the possible shots before choosing one. Since Scott hadn't made many trips around the big course, I had a few tricks to show him. One afternoon his tee shot stopped about ten yards short of our seventh green, a downhill par 3 with a redan-style green that slopes severely from back to front and left to right. With a hundred feet or so to the pin, Scott blithely pulled out his wedge and lofted a shot that caught the downslope twenty feet short of the hole and then bounded and rolled another fifty feet, almost off the back-right of the green, much to his displeasure.

"You actually hit that shot perfectly," I told him, "but this green is kind of squirrelly. The best way to get close to that pin is to sort of sneak up on it, by running some kind of low shot up near the left bunker and letting it roll down to the flat. Here, watch this."

I took a ball from my pocket and tossed it at the front-left edge of the green, at an angle almost ninety degrees left of a straight line to the hole. It took one bounce and then began rolling, slowly at first and then faster and faster in a swooping rightward arc until about ten feet short of the hole, where it slowed again, drifted a few inches back to the left, and miraculously dropped into the center of the cup. Harry Potter could not have played it better.

There's nothing to describe the feeling when your kid looks up at you with wide-eyed wonder, as if you have powers beyond those of mortal men. For that one brief shining moment I think I was his idol, or at least a very cool father. Whatever he felt about me at that moment, I know I felt exceedingly good about me!

Late one Sunday afternoon, on one of those hang-in-back-of-the-pack rounds, we came to the hole listed on the score-card as "Panorama," number 16. A 150-yard par 3 that plays slightly downhill and due west against a backdrop of the Hudson River, it is the signature hole on our course and one of the most photographed holes anywhere. On this afternoon in September, with the sun setting over the red-faced cliffs of the Palisades beyond, it was particularly beautiful.

As I sat in the cart, waiting for the group ahead of us to fin-ish, Scott remained on the fifteenth green just below and to the right of the tee, relentlessly chipping and putting. I watched him for a moment, then gazed out at the river and began to muse on my good fortune: to have been born in the time and place I was, to have had a normal childhood and sup-portive parents, to have found a terrific job and a loving wife, to have been blessed with a pair of healthy, handsome sons.

And now, on top of all that, to have been granted this young partner with whom to share my life's passion. No one deserved the munificence I'd drawn as my lot in life. What's more, with Scott and golf, the best was yet to come. So many experiences awaited us, so many shots and holes and rounds and tournaments, so many courses to play together, victories and losses to share.

My reverie took me decades forward, to a time and place where three generations of Pepers were sharing a day of golf. I was on a windy hillock somewhere in Scotland, demonstrat-ing a tricky pitch shot to my young grandson when the spell was broken.

"Why are your eyes all watery, Dad? You look like you were crying or something," said Scott, a look of concern in his eyes.

"No," I said, hopping quickly from the cart. "Must be from staring into that sunset."

That winter was a long one for Scott and me, with televised tournaments and our indoor Nerf games weak substitutes for the real thing. By March we were hitting chip shots off the still-frozen lawn and watching daily for the open sign to appear at the local driving range. When finally it did, we were among the first to hit the mats.

Six months of hibernation had left my muscles stiff and uncooperative, but Scott stepped up and hit ball number one of 1997 as if he'd never let go of a club. There was only one difference: He hit it much longer. I wasn't surprised. According to the most recent pencil mark on the door casement of our bathroom—the area that serves as the Peper family growth chart—Scott had added nearly two inches over the winter. He had entered an important new stage in his evolution as a golfer, and many aspects of his play and demeanor were about to change.

With a tee shot that sneaked out to the 225 range, he was now able to reach all but a couple of our course's holes in regulation. The added power had brought an improved ability to spin the ball from tight lies and extricate it from thick ones. The Official USGA Handicap Index he had debuted with a year ago—38.6—was about to plummet precipitously. In the first few rounds I played with him that spring, I was reminded of the observation made a century earlier by venerable essayist British Amateur Champion Horace Hutchison: "The happiest golfer is the man whose game is improving."

It's odd the way one's game can affect one's demeanor. I will admit, rather pathetically, that at any given moment a large measure of my happiness and self-esteem derives directly from my most recent round of golf. In the hours following a score in the low 70s I feel ready to cure cancer and secure world peace while simultaneously writing a symphony and dancing the tarantella. After an 85 or higher every aspect of my deportment says, "Keep Back 500 Feet."

By contrast my dear wife, on the rare occasions she plays, never gets upset, no matter how poor her performance. Once, after watching her comprehensively scuttle a fourth consecutive iron shot, I asked how she was able to contain her legendarily volcanic temper.

"Well," she said matter-of-factly, "I've never hit a really great shot, so I don't know what it's like to feel that rush of excitement and happiness you like to crow about. Therefore, I don't miss it—and I don't get angry when I fail. All of my shots are at the same low level. The slightly better ones don't turn me on, and the really bad ones don't upset me."

As usual, she'd gotten to the core of the matter. As beginners we may hit only a few solid shots per day, and when we do, we're delighted. At some point, however, every committed golfer crosses a major border, a point where the good shots become less affecting than the bad ones. We stop reveling and start reviling.

Once we're serious about the game, we enlarge the unit by which we measure ourselves. Good shots become less important than good holes. The higher handicapper seeks strings of bogeys, the better player pars, the best players birdies. Ultimately, our yardstick becomes the eighteen-hole round, as we seek a consistent ability to break our scoring barrier, be it 100, 90, 80, or par. The Tour pros take this to an even higher level, striving for consistency over the four rounds of a tournament, and then from tournament to tournament. And the very best players in the world—the Hall of Famers—are able to stay at top form for years, even decades.

By the summer of '97 Scott had moved beyond the shot-euphoria stage and become focused on scoring. By August he'd broken 100 several times, his handicap was into the low 20s, and his goal was to break 90.

In our head-to-head matches, instead of giving him two or three strokes per hole, I now gave him just one. And instead of intentionally misplaying a shot here or there to keep those matches interesting, I found myself bearing down. Suddenly, I had a worthy opponent who was getting worthier every day.

We weren't yet equals, but I could see that day coming. Likewise, our relationship had begun to mature, as we interacted less and less as parent and child and more and more as fellow golfers.

How do golfers interact? Minimally, in terms of conversation. On the course serious golfers don't talk about anything but golf, and *really* serious golfers don't talk about anything. The conversation rarely strays beyond "Nice shot," "You're away," and "That's good." Bear in mind, however, that there are half a dozen ways to utter "Nice shot," and they carry meanings that range from "I'm delighted to see you're striking the ball so well" to "You're a lucky son of a bitch." All true golfers know how to deliver—and decipher—these messages.

But golfers communicate constantly in nonverbal ways, particularly when there's a match or tournament on the line. Consciously or not, they tweak and test one another, looking for a clue to competitive mettle. Body language can convey myriad and complex messages, and body English can be downright dynamic.

Even the pros use it. Back in the 1980s *GOLF Magazine* used to convene a Tour players panel during the Wednesday night of the Players Championship in Ponte Vedra, Florida. We'd assemble a half dozen or so of the game's best players, ask them a provocative question or two, and let them talk. We found that, once one player opened up, the others started to come forth with insights and stories they might not have shared one-on-one with a reporter. Our topics usually focused on the dark underbelly of the game—stuff like choking and cheating.

One year we got on the subject of gamesmanship. Ray Floyd told a Gary Player story, Greg Norman chimed in with one on Lee Trevino, and then Seve Ballesteros, who had been sitting quietly at the end of the table, suddenly jumped up and told this beauty on his fellow European Tour player Bernhard Gallacher.

"You know how, when you hit a tee shot that starts out to the right, you lean your body to the left to make it turn back? Well, a couple of years ago I am paired in the final round of a tournament with Gallacher. It is a very close competition between the two of us. On one of the finishing holes I push my tee shot right, toward the out-of-bounds. As I am leaning hard to the left, out of the corner of my eye I see Gallacher behind me. He is leaning hard to the *right!*"

The story may lack something without Seve's playful reenactment, but you get the point: Golfers can communicate both clearly and cruelly with their bodies.

Twelve-year-old Scott's body language told me he was growing up. For one thing, there was no more running from shot to shot. A year earlier, when he'd hit his 5-iron and 7-iron roughly the same distance, there was not much point in deliberating over club selection. Now, with a growing gap between his clubs and a more-than-occasional tendency to underestimate his power, he gave his shots a bit of planning. This included a new practice of pacing off his yardages. Since I'm a confirmed antipacer—for most golfers I feel it's a waste of time—I'm not sure whether he adopted this from the older kids, saw the pros do it on TV, or just decided he liked monitoring his increasing might. In any case, he'd become more deliberate, more focused on his game.

And less focused on mine. Suddenly, no matter how long I hit a drive, there was no "Wow!" from the side of the tee. I did occasionally get a "Nice shot" delivered in a middle tone that, while hardly resentful, was not particularly supportive. Maybe most unsettling was the fact that he had ceased asking me questions. I was no longer a source of golf technique and savvy, just an occasional sounding board.

Our chats had not stopped altogether, but their setting had shifted, from the golf course to the car. That suited me fine. I'm one of those golfers who prefer to keep things relatively quiet on the course. Besides, as I've noted earlier, I'm a confirmed believer in the capacity of an automobile to bring two males closer together.

The twenty-minute drive from our home to the club was just long enough to get into a subject nicely without belaboring it. Typically, on the way over we stayed pretty quiet, each of us privately planning his attack on the course. When we did become verbal, our banter brimmed with the hopeful optimism all golfers feel as they make their way to the tee. Newly embraced swing keys dominated the discussion, along with the occasional resolution to conquer a particular shot or hole that had caused recent suffering.

"I think I may start carrying two drivers," Scott said as we pulled out of the driveway one morning. "I like the Taylor Made Burner Bubble off the tee, but that Callaway—the little-headed one before all the Berthas—has eleven degrees of loft and I can hit it a long way off the fairway. I might even be able to get home in two on 15."

"Hmm . . . what club would you take out of your bag?" I asked.

"I dunno. Maybe the 9-iron. I can just hit a soft 8 or a hard wedge."

I couldn't argue with his strategy. With the par 4s on our

course averaging more than four hundred yards, he had plenty of occasion—and lots of incentive—to swat that driver off the deck. Besides, it was good practice. If you can pick a driver off the deck, you can hit anything.

"Sounds like a plan," I said. I was struck, however, by his glibness on the subject of golf equipment, another sign that he was growing up. When a small child first points into a tree and says "robin" rather than simply "bird," he has gained an ability to define and segregate the things in the world around him, but at the same time he has begun to lose his innocence. So I was both thrilled and saddened to hear Scott talk Taylor Mades and Callaways instead of clubs.

Our return trips from the club to home were reserved for wound licking on the bad days and shameless self-congratulation on the good ones. Scott was not beneath recounting an entire round, shot by shot, and I was not above listening. I actually enjoyed his postmortems.

Occasionally on weekdays Libby would call me at the office and ask if I could pick up Scott at the club on my way home. It meant a half-hour detour from my usual route, but I never minded. In fact, I usually arrived early in the hope that I could sit on the club terrace and watch him play the last hole. If he'd had a good round, I knew I'd hear every shot of it before we arrived home. Such narratives were the highlight of my day.

All golfers have this impulse to share their triumphs with anyone who will listen. Sadly, the population of willing listeners is nowhere equal to the universe of eager narrators. The most rapt audience is the golf-addicted parent listening to a child's hole-by-hole. The least interested interlocutor is the non-golf-playing spouse.

Early in my marriage I learned that Libby was quite happy to remain oblivious to the details of my exploits on the links. Once I came back from a great round of golf and started telling her about it: "I made par at the first, birdied the second, one-putted for pars at the third and fourth, bogeyed the fifth, then made a thirty-footer for birdie at 6, then—"

"Wait a minute," she said, "you've got me confused."

"Confused? Okay, let's see. I made par at the first—"

"No, I don't mean that kind of confused."

"What, then?"

"You've got me confused with someone who gives a damn!"

Happily, it was just the opposite with Scott and me. Another favorite activity on our rides home was stats crunching. For as long as I can remember, I've had a habit of reviewing rounds in my head on my drive home from the course, ticking off the number of fairways I'd hit, the number of greens I'd reached in regulation, and the number of putts I'd taken. It serves no real purpose—just relentless pursuit of the obvious—but it passes the time, and I suppose it does give me a clearer notion of the strengths and weaknesses of my game.

"Generally, I hope for nine or ten of the fourteen fairways," I said to Scott on the way home one afternoon. "You don't count the par 3s. Anything over eight greens is good for me, and depending on the number of greens I hit, I tend to take between twenty-nine and thirty-three putts. If my total of fairways and greens hits twenty, I usually break 80. A friend of mine, Lou Riccio, is a stats freak who is even more into this kind of thing. In fact, he has a formula that he calls Riccio's Rule: Take the number 95, subtract from that twice the number of greens you hit, and the result should be within a stroke or so of your score. In other words, if I hit eight greens, it's 95 minus 16 equals 79."

I could see all this appealed to Scott's mathematical mind, and for the next minute or so he quietly ran his numbers. "I don't think that works for me," he said. "Today I hit four greens and shot 93. I hit eleven fairways, but I took thirty-six putts . . . I stink at putting."

He went silent for a while, then made an announcement. "I'm gonna start making notes of the mistakes I make on each hole—the shots that take par away. Then, for every mistake, I'm gonna do ten minutes of practice the next day."

"That sounds pretty ambitious," I said.

"Yeah, but I have all day, and they don't let kids play until the afternoon anyhow. This way I'll have some purpose to my practice."

"Well, I like that," I said. "You know, practice doesn't make perfect . . ."

"Yeah, yeah, I know, *perfect* practice makes perfect. Anyway, I just figured it out for tomorrow: ten minutes on tee shots, thirty minutes on irons, forty minutes on chipping, and an hour on putting."

"Go to it, my friend. If I were to do that, I'd be out of minutes—and energy—for the golf course."

"Yeah, but I won't," he said, gazing a mile down the road.

We were getting toward the end of summer, and I knew exactly the purpose of this dedication. Scott wanted desperately to break 90 before heading back to school. He'd come within a stroke or two on a couple of occasions but hadn't quite done the deed.

A week later while playing with me, he made the turn in 45. He wasn't hitting the ball particularly well, but his putting had suddenly come together.

On the inward nine he kept the hot blade, saving one-putt pars at 10 and 11 and one-putt bogeys at 12 and 13, the number one and number three handicap holes. A triple bogey at the fourteenth derailed him a bit, but with four holes to go he was still just fifteen over par. Since our course is a par 70, he could bogey the last four holes and still shoot 89.

There was just one problem. A late-afternoon thunderstorm had brewed up and was heading right at us. The fifteenth hole, a par 5, played straight into the swelling breeze, and Scott, still reeling from his triple and undoubtedly trying to get a little extra out of his drive, topped it. He did well to cover the remaining five hundred yards—playing like six hundred—in another six strokes for a double bogey.

Now he needed a par and two bogeys. With a fine 4-iron into the wind, he reached the par 3 sixteenth and sneaked his second putt in the side door for his par, just as the first drops of rain began to fall. By the time we reached the seventeenth tee the sky was nearly black, and thunder and lightning were fully upon us.

But Scott was not about to quit. The father in me said get him to shelter, but the golfer knew we had to finish this round. To speed things along—and stay dry—I sat in the cart and left the stage to him. The seventeenth plays downhill but is 440 yards. With the rain now pelting, Scott managed to get home in three and two-putted for his 5.

Now with just one more bogey 5 he'd reach his goal. But the weather had become absurd, and the whole situation had taken on an eerie resemblance to the scene from *Caddyshack* where the priest and his caddie, Carl Spackler (Bill Murray), fight through a hurricane to finish the ultimate round. The good reverend, you'll recall, meets his maker when a lightning bolt strikes just as his putt is about to drop at 18. I was beginning to fear Scott and I might be facing the same end.

After a solid but unspectacular tee shot on the uphill 405-yard home hole, Scott lost his grip on his 4-wood and topped it just twenty yards or so. The worst part was that this forced him to walk to his ball rather than gain brief refuge in the cart. So sudden and hard was the assault by Mother Nature that a half dozen puddles had already formed on the fairway. It was only six o'clock, but it looked like three hours later, and in the clubhouse behind the final green the lights had been turned on.

On his third shot he again lost his grip, and thinned the ball to a point roughly eighty yards short of the green. The pin was positioned dead center, but we couldn't see it because when Scott addressed his ball, the conditions became even more surreal as the rain changed to hail! Somehow the thunder and lightning also continued. This was, quite simply, the worst weather in which I'd ever found myself on a golf course.

But there was no stopping now, and Scott seemed more intent than ever. With perhaps the finest wedge of his young career, he lofted the ball through a barrage of ice pellets to within four feet of the hole.

Much of the green was under water, but Scott had a clear path and a straight uphill putt. As I took the flag out, I fought the impulse to coach him. He'd never putted on a green this wet and slow, and I was afraid he'd leave the putt short. But I also knew he needed to do this all by himself.

I don't think I've ever wanted a putt to go into a hole more than I did that one. And it did!

"Yes!" we both screamed, and Scott leaped into my outstretched arms. A bolt of lightning could have struck us at that moment, and we both would have died happy.

Scott finished that season with a Handicap Index of 18.3, exactly half what it had been at the start of the year. According to the last of the biweekly printouts sent by the USGA, he was the most improved player in the club. And I was the most proud father.

The return to school, coupled with a hard winter, brought golf to a halt for seven months. All we could do was watch the pros on TV and dream the way golf addicts do about playing the Tour ourselves. In early February we were watching the final round of the 1998 AT&T Pebble Beach Pro-Am when Scott offered a prediction.

"Tiger will win at least seven events this year," he said confidently.

"You think so, huh?"

"How much does the winner get?"

"Eighteen percent of the purse. For a $4-million event, $720,000."

"Tiger will probably win more tournaments than anyone in any year."

"I doubt that. In 1945 Byron Nelson won eighteen; eleven of them in a row."

"No way . . ."

"Way . . . He could play. He was a great guy, too. Still is."

"Do you know him?"

"Yeah, sort of. I've met him a few times. You could probably say he's my golf hero—not for what he did, but the whole way he handles himself."

"What do you mean?"

"He's very modest and gentle. He's kind and patient, nice to everyone, no matter who they are. The qualities I wish I had in greater supply, Byron Nelson has in spades."

"Tiger really dominated last year—he probably was the best in one season since Nelson's era, right?"

"No."

"Who, then?"

"Johnnny Miller."

"The TV guy?"

"Yup, he won like eight times one year in the seventies. Won about 20 percent of the year's total purse that year. I think that's the modern record."

"Wait a minute . . ."

"What?"

"If you only get eighteen percent for winning, how could he win 20 percent of the total year's purse?"

(Pause.) "That's a very good question . . . but he just did, okay?"

I later checked. Miller had taken home closer to 10 percent of the 1974 purse. I never corrected myself to Scott, but both he and I knew he'd caught me. My son was getting older and wiser, beginning to see more, feel more, process more in that nimble brain of his. A teenager now, he was also becoming the other kind of wiser: more cocky and confident—and more willing to take on his parents.

Over that winter he'd also grown another inch or so. He was still short for his age, but he'd at least busted through the five-foot mark, and by spring it was clear he'd added some more distance to his tee shots. But power corrupts. Seeing he could hit the ball another dozen yards had made him lust for a dozen more than that. As a result, by mid-May his once-silky swing had degenerated into a more manic move, marked by a rushed and jerky transition from backswing to downswing. He now hit the ball a fair distance, but he had Mickey Mantle might—power to all fields.

Sadly, this has always been my own fatal flaw. For as long as I can remember, a little man has lived at the top of my swing, a little man who whispers "Kill" the moment my hands reach shoulder height. Now the same insidious gnome seemed to have taken up residence with Scott. It was troubling to see my son lose the best aspect of his golf swing, but I told myself this was an inevitable part of golf maturation. Besides, I drew some consolation from the knowledge that both Palmer and Nicklaus were taught to hit the ball hard first and worry about finding it later.

More disturbing was the blindly aggressive style Scott had adopted: a sort of bulletproof "I can pull off any shot" attitude that caused him to take some very low-percentage chances—Phil Mickelson without the talent.

Should I say something? Not, I decided, on the subject of his swing speed. I had zero credibility there. Maybe on his shot choices, his course management. Granted, kids tend to play aggressively, but all the more reason to have a chat with him. If I could somehow get him to play smart—smarter than most kids—he'd have an advantage over his peers.

On the Friday of July 4th weekend I got my chance. I'd sneaked away from the office early, and it was just Scott and I for a quick eighteen. It was a beautiful afternoon, and Scott, who'd practiced all that morning, had his game in great working order. Although to this point he'd never come close to beating me, even for nine holes, when we walked off the eighth green, we were dead even. More important, we were each just three over par. Scott's best nine holes to that point had been 40, and now he was one par away from a 38.

A lot was at stake on that ninth hole, and Scott came through with his best drive of the day, a clout of nearly 250 yards. However, it left him on the side of a swale in the fairway with an extremely awkward lie, the ball sitting several inches below his feet.

With plenty of trouble between him and the hole, this situation was an invitation to disaster. At least I saw it that way. Scott, without hesitation, had pulled out his 3-wood and was preparing to play what I recognized immediately as an insane shot, the kind of shot that any good father would throw his body in front of before allowing his son to play.

"Wait a minute, bud," I said. "Do you really think that's the best club to hit from this lie?"

"Yup," he said.

"Scott, that's a very risky shot. From that stance you could easily lose your balance and push the ball into the woods. Or you could chunk it or top it or even shank it."

"Shank it? With a 3-wood?"

"Okay, not a shank per se, but you know what I mean. You might hit the ball anywhere with a 3-wood from that funky lie. I'd hate to see you ruin a great nine with one bad shot. Why don't you take out a short iron and just punch it up the fairway, then wedge on and you'll still have a chance at a par, at worst a bogey."

"Dad, I know this shot, and I know I can play it."

"I'm sure you can—maybe one out of ten times—but why take the chance? You want to break 40, don't you? Why risk throwing that away? Do whatever you want, Scott, but I'm telling you, I certainly would never hit a 3-wood from there."

"Well, I'm not you," he said, adding a "thank God" under his breath as I retreated to the cart.

He stood there in silence for a moment, staring at the ground. Then he scowled at me, shook his head once, and came back to the cart, where he slammed the 3-wood back into his bag and pulled out a 6-iron. I was feeling relieved, if also a bit dictatorial. But most of all, I was praying that my strategy would combine with his execution to produce the result we both wanted so dearly.

That didn't happen. Playing with uncharacteristic dispatch, Scott comprehensively smothered that 6-iron, the ball advancing only twenty-five yards or so. Without returning to the cart he stomped forward and whaled at the next shot almost without addressing it. The resulting skull-and-run finished in the right greenside bunker. From there he needed four more, taking a triple-bogey 7 for a front nine of 41.

It was not until the fourteenth tee that he spoke to me.

"You have no idea what shot I intended with that 3-wood," he said. "I was just gonna punch it out. I play that shot all the time. The minute you say something, you get into my head. I feel I have to play the shot you suggest because if I play my shot and screw it up, I'll never hear the end of it. But since I have no confidence in the shot you want, I hit it bad, and then it's worse than ever. Just don't tell me anything!"

There was not much I could say, so I said nothing, and we went another hole in silence, both of us mulling and stewing. I decided to believe that he had indeed intended to punch that 3-wood rather than hit it full, although he may well have added that notion as a ploy to strengthen his argument. In any case, said argument was difficult to rebut: namely, that each golfer has different strengths, and needs to trust those strengths.

The fact that I didn't like a 3-wood from that position had a lot to do with the fact that I don't like 3-woods in general. It's my worst club. But it happened to be Scott's best club, the club he'd been using for his second shots to par 4s for years. For him it was therefore the right choice.

Idiotic as we may sometimes appear to our fellow players, each of us must go with the shot that fits and suits us at the moment of truth—the one that brings comfort and confidence to our own fragile psyche, not someone else's. I can think of at least one example in my own game. From eighty yards or so the shot I'm most comfortable with is a violently slicing, low 8-iron, a banana-ball slap-punch that lands thirty feet or so left of the pin, takes one bounce, and then sucks straight to the right. I know of no other human who would happily choose so perverse a shot. Why do I? Two reasons. First, because four decades of unremitting ineptitude have convinced me that I'm incapable of executing a straightforward wedge shot of eighty yards; and second, because I believe firmly that I'm the best in the world at that violently punch-sliced 8-iron.

Scott was saying essentially the same thing to me. Trying to impose my preferences and convictions on him was a presumptuous idea with little prospect of success. Even if I couldn't bring myself to believe in the way he managed his game—all the choices he made—I at least had to let him believe in himself, let him chart his own way. In golf and in life it was time for me to start showing that I trusted him.

That wouldn't come easily for me. I wanted so much to teach him, to help him become the best golfer he could—a far better player than I'd ever become. No one had ever shown me the subtle stuff—stuff like how to feel out a bunker shot with your feet or read the wind in the trees. No one had told me it's easier to play a draw with a 5-iron than an 8-iron, that hardpan is the perfect lie for an intentional slice, or that you can hit a flyer with a 6-iron but not with a 3. No one had taught me that it's just as dangerous to concentrate too hard as too little, that golf is as much instinct as calculation, and that on some days the most important thing is just to get out of your own way.

Those things had taken me years to learn, to dig out of the dirt, as Ben Hogan put it, and I saw no reason for Scott to wait that long. On the other hand, I had no blueprint, no plan, and no idea how to impart such subtleties with subtlety.

One thing I'd learned was that all dissections of Scott's game needed to be initiated by him. Happily, when he and I were alone together, his golf game was still his favorite topic. He was still asking me for help, just in a more guarded way.

"I don't know why I can't get the feel of the greens," he said on the ride home one Saturday. "Yesterday I couldn't get the ball to the hole, and today I slugged everything way by."

"There's a reason for that," I said, "and it has nothing to do with your putting stroke."

"Okay . . ."

"Yesterday you played at two in the afternoon. It had rained the night before. Also, they don't cut the greens very low on weekdays. By the time you got out there the grass had grown for six or seven hours and the greens had gotten even slower. Today, on the other hand, we were the first ones off the tee at 7:15 A.M., playing on pristine greens that had just been cut low and rolled for the weekend. Yesterday you probably putted on greens that were running at about 8 on the Stimpmeter; today we saw speeds of 11 or more."

When there was no rebuttal, I felt myself on a roll and so launched into a sermonette on putting technique. "You're a rapper, you know—you hit at the ball rather than stroke through it as I do. Rappers tend to putt better on slower Bermuda greens—the kind they have down in Florida—while we strokers prefer the faster bent-grass greens up North."

That's where I blew it. I'd had his attention for the agronomy lesson but lost him with the him-and-me stuff.

"Yeah right, Dad" was all I got, and there was an all-too-familiar hard-edged tone to the "Dad."

Scott had come to view just about everything I said with a skepticism that bordered on disdain. I consoled myself with the thought that it was a standard sort of teenager-parent rebellion. In truth, it wasn't the source of his defiance that troubled me as much as the effectiveness of his opposition. He had begun to display a brutally logical mind along with a knack for debate that allowed him to argue with annoying effectiveness.

"I wasted at least six shots on the greens today," he said after one round. "Did you see me on 13 and 14? A three-putt followed by a four-putt."

"Wasted is probably a good word," I said. "You tend to throw shots away by putting too quickly, especially after you miss a short one. You just get up and Lanny Wadkins it."

"Lanny who?"

"Lanny Wadkins. He's a pro, about my age. Good player

but almost as impatient as I am, and sort of petulant when he plays poorly. He's famous for nonchalantly backhanding putts into the hole, especially after he misses from short range. Just sort of chops down on the ball. Once I saw him hole a two-footer on the fly. Anyway, that's the way you act. If you miss a short putt, you rush the second one and often miss it. What you need is a routine. You need to address and stroke every putt in the same methodical way. Have you ever noticed how Nicklaus and Tiger do it?"

"I don't need a routine, Dad." (The hard "Dad" again.)

"Scott, there are two hundred or so guys playing the PGA Tour. How many of them do you think don't have putting routines?"

"None."

"That's right. And there's a very good reason for that. A routine takes your mind out of the stroke—gives you less chance to have negative thoughts."

He paused for a moment, looked me straight in the eye, and said, "Thank you. That's exactly the reason I just get up and hit it!"

Hmm, I thought, a nimble and well-placed retort, and he also has an interesting point—but I can't let him off.

"Fine," I said, trying to stifle my exasperation. "Make it a *quick* routine."

A few days later, when I came to pick him up at the course, I found him on the practice green. He didn't see me at first, and so I was able to observe him long enough to see that he'd adopted a routine—probably that very day, since he was being very diligent about following the exact sequence of movements putt after putt: feet placement, practice swing, centering of the club, look at the hole and hit.

On the way home I called him on it.

"Was that a putting routine I saw you doing?"

"Sort of," he said. "Brian [one of the assistant pros] convinced me I'd putt better if I tried it."

Neither of us said another word the rest of the way home.

In the course of losing my status as chief counselor, I'd learned that my best hope of getting Scott to try new ideas and techniques was to wrap them either in my own foibles and failures or in the words of famous players—import the instruction from a higher source.

After yet another difficult putting day Scott hopped in the car with an announcement.

"I'm the worst short putter in the world," he said.

"You should be one of the best," said I.

"Why?"

"Because you're thirteen years old. When I was thirteen, I sank everything I looked at. It wasn't until much later that I got bad. By age thirty I had the yips, and they stayed with me for a decade or so. Thank goodness, today I'm in remission. Now the only putts I yip are the ones that really count."

"Yeah, so I've noticed," he said.

"Anyway, it's a matter of getting your confidence back," I said.

"No duh . . . and how am I supposed to do that?"

"By sinking lots of short putts."

"Thanks for nothing."

"No, I mean it—and the only place to do that is on a practice green, to build comfort with ball after ball plopping into the hole."

"I've tried that, Dad—it doesn't work."

"Have you tried the Greg Norman drill?"

"What's that?"

"It's one of the few original things he gave me in the two days I interviewed him for the *Shark Attack* book. It's a practice drill he uses to work on his stroke and his nerves at the same time. He puts half a dozen balls in a circle around a hole, each of them one foot away, and he putts each of them into the hole. If he misses any of them, he has to start all over. Once he makes all six from one foot, he backs off to two feet. If he misses any of the two-footers, he goes back to one-footers. His goal, he says, is to get to six-foot putts and make all six of those. It's not as easy as it sounds, since you begin to feel the pressure. Norman said he'd often be out there for hours trying to finish that drill, but when he finally left the green, he had 100 percent confidence in both his stroke and his nerves."

Had that advice come directly from me, Scott would likely never have tried it. But as the Greg Norman drill, it had credibility and cache, so he gave it a shot. The first few times he used it, he putted like a pro, and so it has become an integral part of his preround preparation whenever a big event is on the line.

But sometimes my name-dropping got the better of me. One of our bitterest confrontations (a battle that lasted two or three years) involved Scott's overreliance on one shot around the green: the least versatile of all shots—the flop. He flopped not only from the rough and over bunkers, he flopped from the fairway and from a yard short of a flat green with the hole fifty feet away at the top of a second tier. The flop is a classic kid's shot, a show-off shot, which, if you're sufficiently talented or practice it constantly, you can pull off with consistency. However, except in situations when you absolutely must get the ball up quickly and/or stop it fast, it's a rather foolish choice.

Scott, however, was good at it, and he practiced it plenty. Conversely, he'd never put much time in on the gamut of ground-hugging alternatives, with the result that when he did try them, he invariably failed, thus thrusting him ever more passionately into an embrace of the flop.

I cringed each time he addressed that shot and seethed each time he pulled it off. One summer day the two of us hit approach shots that stopped side by side in the fairway, about ten feet short of the long and narrow eighth green. The pin that day was at the extreme back center, an assignment that clearly called for a pitch-and-run, and that is what I played, scooting an 8-iron to within three feet or so of the hole.

Scott then drew his sand wedge, opened the face, opened his stance, took a big loopy driver-length swing, and hoisted one toward the clouds. It pelted the green, nearly hitting my ball on the fly, and then stopped dead a foot from the hole. He turned toward me, hoping for paternal approval, but instead found me shaking my head in disgust.

"You'll never learn any other shots, will you?" I said.

"I just put it inside your stupid chip," he said. "I don't need any other shots."

I let that one slide, plotting my retort, which came as we headed to our tee shots on 9.

"You're just like Nicklaus and the pot bunker," I said.

"Okay," he said, skeptical of my oddly titled fable. He knew I was a Nicklaus fan, but he also knew I wasn't about to let the "stupid chip" remark go unpunished.

"Peter Jacobsen told me this story. It happened down at the Players Championship at Sawgrass, several years ago. Next to the practice green there's this huge, deep pot bunker, and one afternoon Seve Ballesteros was in there giving a sort of impromptu clinic on shot making for Jacobsen and Ben Crenshaw. He was just fooling around really, and one of the moves he was showing them was an explosion shot from that deep, steep-faced bunker . . ."

"Yeah . . ."

"With a 2-iron."

"A 2-iron? You're joking. He was hitting bunker shots with a 2-iron?"

"Yup, shots so high and soft they looked like they were hit with a lob wedge."

"How?"

"I really don't know; I only know that he made it look easy. So Jacobsen and Crenshaw each got in there to try it, and they failed miserably until Seve gave them a couple of tips, and they at least were able to hit shots that stayed on the green.

"At about that time, who strolls up but the Golden Bear. He sees these guys screwing around and asks what's going on. Jacobsen tells Seve to get back into the bunker and show some more artistry, which Seve does. Now, Jack, being Jack, does not like to let anyone show him—or show him up—when it comes to golf, and so after watching Seve a couple of times he says, 'Let me give that a try.' He hops in there, sets his stance, takes a swing, and skulls the ball smack into the face of the bunker so hard it buries out of sight. Then he tries again and skulls another one. Then he hits one fat. Then he thins one clear over the green. By this point Jacobsen and Crenshaw are doubled over with laughter, and Seve is just standing there with a smile.

"Jack, realizing that additional attempts will only heighten the humiliation, climbs out of the bunker, hands Seve the 2-iron, and as he stomps off, says, 'Aw, you'd never need to play that shot anyway.'"

"That's pretty funny," said Scott.

"Yeah, and it's exactly the same attitude you have about every shot except your beloved flop. You never need to play them."

"Right. To me they're about as useful as a 2-iron from a pot bunker. I agree 100 percent with Jack Nicklaus."

There it was again: that debater's ability to parry with words.

"You know what I'm saying: Your own ego and denial are getting in the way of your improvement as a golfer."

"Fine. Then I guess I don't need *you* in the way at the same time. I *hate* playing with you."

That line, delivered in cold, measured syllables, without a trace of petulance, stung deeply. It was a line that drew a line, marked a rift—or at least a shift—in Scott's and my relationship, both on the course and off. In what seemed a very short time, my role had transformed: from idol to idiot, from the guy who'd shown the way to the guy who was in the way.

I knew, or at least hoped, that he didn't want to reject me entirely. Much of his behavior, I told myself, was typical rebellion. Still, I couldn't help but ask the questions. Did he really have no further need of my advice, or even my approval? Had I suffocated him that thoroughly? Was this the mothering/smothering syndrome Libby went through, or was it something entirely different? Had golf—the force that brought us together—now somehow pushed us apart?

We continued to play together sporadically through that summer of '98, and those who waved to us across fairways saw the idyllic tableau of father and son, side by side in shared golf passion. Beneath that facade, however, was a relationship far more complex, a boy struggling to grow up and away—trying to please and impress, repudiate and repel his father all at once—and a father wrestling with his own changing role, searching for a way to help rather than hinder.

A complication in all this was my nine-to-five persona as editor in chief of *GOLF Magazine*. I knew more than the average guy about the game and how to play it and thus had more to share with my son. But I suppose that just made me a more ominous authority figure, simultaneously fueling and complicating Scott's quest to renounce me. We'd reached the point where every instructional gem I spouted was fodder for ridicule, and each breathless account of prodigy Woods or Garcia did nothing but add pressure to my son's eagerness to excel.

And so I resolved to take a more passive tack, to go into a holding pattern as to advice and commentary. I would simply watch and listen, keeping my observations to myself. No critiquing, no pontificating. I'd try to teach less and learn more.

Instead of analyzing his shots, I paid closer attention to Scott himself, observed his demeanor before and after each swing. What I saw made me feel immeasurably better: He did indeed still need my approval.

Consider that for the first five years of his golf life I'd reacted verbally to just about every significant golf shot he'd hit, whether it was "Well struck," "Whoops," or "What club did you hit?" I was overly involved, to be sure. But Scott was never in doubt as to my interest. Now suddenly there was silence, with the result that after a particularly good—or poor—shot, Scott cast his eyes furtively, but needfully, my way. He cared whether I cared.

The challenge for me—beyond keeping my trap shut—was to let him know I was still there for him. And so I continued to praise his best shots, but no more effusively than I would have if he were one of my regular golf buddies. A 2-iron to ten feet no longer elicited "Wow, what a shot, I can't believe how well you're hitting it," but simply "Shot."

Such casual interest wasn't easy to feign, either physically (each time he began to look toward me, I'd pretend to be occupied with the cart, the scorecard, or my own next shot) or emotionally, as it belied the life-and-death involvement I continued to feel with each of his swings. But it was the dance we needed to do.

One night after dinner I shared my charade with Libby, and her reaction startled me.

"Scott lives to impress you," she said perfunctorily. Women seem to have factory-installed radar for such things. At some level I suppose I suspected it, too. After all, doesn't Psychology 101 teach that sons yearn to impress fathers? What son doesn't want to show his dad how high he can jump? But being essentially obtuse, I'd never actually seen or felt it. Now, on the golf course, I had, and the feeling was very good.

But during my vow of near silence I noticed other things about my son—and myself—that weren't nearly as comforting. Foremost was the volatile temper Scott had begun to develop. His improved ability had imbued him with higher standards, and when he failed to meet them—whether for a shot, a hole, or a round—he showed his displeasure. The childlike joy of simply playing had been replaced by a burning need to succeed. It was interesting to watch the changes in his deportment during the course of a round. There could be up to five stages.

His first few holes were crucial. With a good start—pars and bogeys—he maintained focus on his game while also chatting freely and amicably, and this mood would last for as long as the solid play continued. After each hole he'd run a quick mental projection of a goal score—first on the front nine, then the entire eighteen—the same waking dream most golfers allow themselves: "Gee, I'm only two over after six. Three more pars and I'll have my best nine ever."

However, once Scott hit a bump—a double bogey or two—stage two began. He'd become noticeably quieter—more despondent than petulant. At the same time, his pace would quicken, both between shots and while over the ball. At this point he was on a slippery slope, trying to get a grip on his game but perilously close to collapsing. The score projecting continued, but by now he'd lost hope of a record—only a reasonable-to-good total could be salvaged.

Sometimes he'd be able to hold it together, but more often he'd have another slipup that precipitated stage three: full meltdown. It would usually occur somewhere between holes 8 and 13, a stretch of tough treelined par 4s punctuated by a par 3 over water. Scott would spray a tee shot into the trees or dump his 5-iron into the pond at number 10, and that would be that.

His shoulders would slump, he'd make an angry windmill second swing before the errant shot came to earth, twirl 360 degrees on one toe, and deliver his clubhead thunderously to the turf. (Blessedly, he had no proclivity for actually throwing clubs.) The flailing pirouette would be capped vociferously with either an *"I stink"* or an *"I hate this game."* The remainder of the hole was played in utter silence, each of his shots executed at warp speed.

By the next tee he'd be into the fourth or cool-down phase, a buffer hole or two of quiet self-pity and introspection during which he surely felt some remorse and shame at his behavior, and just as surely abandoned all interest in the remainder of the round.

At the other end of this tunnel emerged "Happy Scott," a carefree clone of the kid with whom I had teed off. Happy Scott sashayed through the last few holes in a jolly mood, albeit with a tinge of cynicism in his voice. His swings were made without concern for the outcome, and so the home-stretch holes often produced his best golf of the day. In the end his score usually fell within the expected range for his handicap.

After observing three or four performances of this tragi-comedy I began to become concerned. It was one thing for Scott to behave this way while playing with me, but quite another for anyone else to see it. He had reached the age where he was occasionally asked by members to join them for a few holes: older members, lady members, couples. I shuddered at the thought of any of these people being treated to one of his flaming whirl-around club-slams.

For a while I tried a sort of reverse-psychology approach to show my disappointment. After a bad front nine I'd say something like "I can feel the meltdown coming."

More often than not, he would then hold it together for a decent score. After one such occasion—a day when he'd turned a 91 back into an 84—he said, "You know, Dad, one of the reasons I didn't 'melt down,' as you call it, is that you so loudly predicted to everyone that I would."

"Yes," I said, "and the only reason I so loudly predicted you would was so that you'd—"

"Yeah, I know, I know, so I'd try to prove you wrong. Reverse psychology."

"I guess I can't use it again, huh?"

"I guess not."

Increasingly, I sensed that Scott and I had reached another new stage in our coeducation as golfers, a time when playing skills had become less important than life skills. After all, there are so many lessons that golf can teach you—and will teach you over time. Lessons like working for what you get, accepting victory and defeat with equal grace, believing in yourself, being courteous and supportive to others, even when things aren't breaking your way. Having direction and goals, never giving up, never caving in to self-pity, and maybe most of all, behaving with honor.

Scott's aptitude had been fully nurtured. What he needed now was some work on his attitude. And I was the only guy to do it. But how? Exactly how do you teach someone to be a better person?

I'd love to place myself alongside all those omniscient fathers of golf's great champions. If you believe the biographies, the sire of every titan from Jones to Woods has brought about an epiphanous disciplinary moment in the rearing of his son. I'm referring to the moment when paterfamilias says, "Lad, if you throw one more club or one more tantrum, you will stop playing immediately, walk home, and wait for me in the woodshed. I will finish my round, then come home and beat you silly, and after that you will never play golf again." From that day forward the son becomes a flawless golfer and an exemplary human being.

Yes, I'd love to be one of those dads, but for one thing, we don't have a woodshed. For another, I just don't have it in me. There's no transgression I can imagine my son committing on the golf course—short of rape or murder—that could cause me to threaten him with banishment from the game. I love him too much and love golf too much to even threaten pulling them apart. He knows that, and therefore knows that any such threat would be empty. Besides, let's face it: Colonel Bob Jones, Deacon Palmer, Charlie Nicklaus, Ray Watson, and Earl Woods were all just bluffing.

At the same time, those guys at least had the guts to discipline their kids. I'm basically a coward. I tend to avoid confrontation, whether the adversary is my boss, my coworkers, my wife, or my sons. Scott, however, was beginning to test me, in ways I could no longer ignore. I had to show some strength—for both of our sakes.

In particular, I'd noticed that bad language had begun to creep into his displays of temper. "I stink" had become "I suck," and although he hadn't yet embraced the nasty *s* and *f* words—at least not that I'd heard—he was using "shoot" and "freakin'" liberally. I tried to ignore all this as routine boy stuff—borderline acceptable golf-guy talk—but when after a particularly frustrating bounce, he spat out "Son of a bitch!" I couldn't let it go.

So what was my response? "Nice talk, Scott." That's all I could muster. What a wimp I was—afraid to reprimand my own kid. What was wrong with me?

On another occasion, after three-putting, he let out a loud "Jeezus Christ!" It was at that moment that I realized why I couldn't scold him. He had delivered that "Jeezus Christ" with the precise intonation that I do. Scott's sins, to a great extent, were my sins.

How could I ask my son to be a more admirable person than I was? The sad truth was, there were problems I hadn't yet addressed in my own temper, my own demeanor, on the golf course. At age forty-nine I still occasionally acted like a child.

How do you tell your kid to keep his chin up after double-bogeying the first two holes when you know that you yourself would be wallowing in self-pity? How do you hold your kid down when you yourself are seething at the slow pace of play? How do you chastise your kid for bad language when you yourself let the same words fly?

I had no credentials as a teacher, and no lesson plan either. But if I didn't help him with these things, no one would. So I decided I'd wing it. I'd drop in what few pearls of golf/life wisdom I had with whatever finesse I could muster.

The first thing I wanted Scott to understand is that in golf as in life we're all struggling together—we're all what Bobby Jones called "dogged victims of inexorable fate."

One afternoon Scott staged a tour de force presentation of his Five Phases of Immaturity while we played in the company of two other club members. I couldn't let him get away with it, but I held my tongue until the ride home.

"You know, don't you, that you were a pleasure to be with

for the first five holes and a pleasure for the last three holes, but a consummate brat in between?"

"Yeah, well, it's easy to be nice when I'm playing well," he said. "It's also easy after I've given up hope of a good score. What's not easy is to be nice when I'm in the middle of blowing the round."

"So why should you be different?" I said.

"What do you mean?"

"When my game starts to unravel—especially after a good start—I fight the same demons. You have no idea how hard I struggle to maintain my composure and good humor while inside I'm ready to burst."

"You do? You don't show it much," he said.

"I do. Everyone struggles to stay civil—at least everyone who takes this game seriously. Some are just more successful than others."

I doubt that I did much to change his ways on that day, but I at least let him know that his misery had company.

Another tactic I wasn't above using was the "I'm not mad, I'm disappointed" line, a ploy that my dear wife had wielded effectively on me for two decades.

"You were a disgrace today," I told him as we packed the clubs in the trunk after a round where he'd double-bogeyed the last two holes and stomped off without shaking the hands of our two companions. "I want you to remember something. The people you play with for the first time, like those guys today, will take two things away from their encounter with you—the quality of your golf and the quality of your character—and emphatically not in that order. I realize you wanted to play well today, both for yourself and to impress those guys. That's human nature. But remember this: Half the people you play with don't care how well you play, and the other half wish you played worse. That's human nature, too. If you really want to impress people, worry less about the kind of swing and score you show them and more about the way you act, especially on days when that swing and score don't show up. I know it's hard," I said. "As tough as it is to be a good golfer, it's often tougher to be a good person. But try. And please don't ever disappoint me the way you did today."

He was silent for a moment or two after that, and since we still had a few miles to go, I decided to throttle down a bit with a classic family story that fit the occasion.

"Your grandfather was a golfer, you know, and he once had a day of really bad golf and bad acting. It was over at River Vale Golf Club, shortly after he'd taken up the game. He was playing alone one afternoon, and at about the fifteenth hole he caught up with another guy, and they played in together. Well, your grandfather hit it all over the place, and from the way he tells it, he acted worse than you ever have: slammed a couple of clubs and used some really bad language.

"I forget the circumstances, but it turned out that he needed a ride home, and the other guy kindly offered to give him a lift. On the way, your grandfather continued to swear like a drunken sailor as he described his frustration with the game of golf. As they reached your grandfather's house, he realized he'd failed to introduce himself beyond a first name, so before getting out of the car he shook hands with his new friend and said, 'By the way, I'm Gerhard Peper. I'm a doctor of chiropractic, and I have a practice here in town.'

"'Nice to make your acquaintance,' said the man. 'I'm Father Toner. I'm the priest at St. Margaret's Church. I think we're both a little surprised.'"

There was one other notion I wanted to impart to Scott— a lesson that I'd needed decades to learn—and that was on the power of positive thinking. In golf, maybe more than anywhere else, mind triumphs over muscle. I had never really bought into this until an expert on the mental side of the game, Chuck Hogan, put me through a two-day session on concentration and visualization. I learned that simply by visualizing the path of each shot you plan to hit, you can have a profound influence on the path of the ball. The summer following my session with Hogan I sank more chip shots and struck more iron shots close to the pin than ever in my life. On three occasions I holed out with full shots from the fairway. What was scary was that not all of my pin-finding shots were even struck well—a few were flat-out skulled—but somehow they found the target.

For some perverse reason I abandoned that visualization technique, but I continue to believe in its effectiveness. More important, and Tony Robbins trite as it is, I firmly believe that a positive frame of mind—hard as it can sometimes be to muster—always brings better results than a negative frame of mind. Aptitude grows from attitude, competence flows from confidence.

"I'm gonna do lousy here," Scott said as we stepped to the tee of the sixth hole. He was already five over for the day.

"Yes, you are," I said.

"How do you know?" he asked, surprised at my response.

"You just told me. That's your mind-set. You have a very strong mind, and I'm sure it will prevail. You'll do lousy on this hole."

"Right, Dad."

"Why don't you try positive thinking instead, and see what happens?"

"Yeah, like that's gonna work."

"I'll admit, it's not easy. In a way you have to get lucky."

"What do you mean 'lucky'?"

"You have to almost fake it. You have to get up there and pretend you're on a roll, you've just made a couple of birdies, you're really focused and you can't wait to keep the good golf going. That's the kind of attitude you bring to the tee shot. If you're lucky, you'll hit a good one—and go on to make par or birdie. Then you'll try that mind-set for the next hole. If you're lucky, you'll keep it going, and you may just turn your round around. Once that happens a couple of times, you'll realize the power of positive thinking, and you'll start incorporating it into your game. In effect, you'll see that it's not luck at all.

"I'll be honest with you: I wasn't able to do it until a few years ago. If I got off to a rough start, I couldn't turn it around. But by playing mind games with myself I was able to convert a few four-over-par-after-five-holes rounds into 75s, and I've been a believer ever since.

"Someone once asked Jack Nicklaus why, after a poor start, he never seemed unhappy or discouraged. Jack answered that he knew he'd make a couple of mistakes in each round, but he also knew he could expect a few birdies. When the bogeys got out of the way early, he knew the good stuff was still to come. It actually got him into a positive mood about the rest of the round."

"Yeah, well, that's Jack Nicklaus."

"Right, and he's no more intelligent than you are. He's just smarter at golf. I can tell you one thing: Jack has never stepped up to a tee and said, 'I'm gonna do lousy here.'"

He had no reply to that. On the other hand, at age thirteen Scott was hardly ripe for conversion into Norman Vincent Peale. Like most teenagers, he had moments in which he felt the world was against him, and, perhaps more important, he had not yet come to terms with the golf gods.

He began one round with a string of pars and bogeys and seemed on his way to a record score until he buried his approach shot under the lip of a bunker. Rather than take an unplayable or hack it out sideways, he tried to muscle the ball up over the lip, with the result that he bellied it and buried it deeper. A 9 went on his card, and he descended immediately into one of his most profound funks.

"I can't believe that stupid lie I got back on 7," he said. "If that sand hadn't been so soft, I would've had an easy bunker shot, but no, it has to bury—and right under the lip! I had a great round going, too."

"Well," I said, "that's golf."

"That's what you say to justify everything," he said. "'That's golf.' It doesn't explain anything!"

"Well, a lot of what happens in golf is exactly that: unexplainable—a rub of the green. Golf was never meant to be fair or logical. You can make your own breaks to some degree—let's be honest, if you'd hit a better iron shot, you wouldn't have buried in that bunker—but there's still a big element of luck involved. In that way golf is a lot like life. The key is to prepare for the best but be ready to accept the worst."

I have no idea whether such sermons had any effect. The truth is, they were delivered as much for my own sake as for Scott's. What I do know is that by the end of that 1998 golf season I began to get reports, one after another, from members who had randomly joined up on the course with Scott.

"Your son caught up with us the other day and we played the last twelve holes together," said one matronly type. "What a wonderful young man he is. You must be very proud of him."

"I knew Scott was a good golfer," said another, "but I didn't realize what a great kid he is. He was a delight to play with—more fun than most of the adult members."

A third fellow had never even played with Scott. "I've been meaning to catch up with you for weeks," he said after introducing himself in the locker room one Saturday. "I wanted to tell you how impressed I was with your boy."

"Thanks," I said, "that's nice of you to say."

"Well, I'm not just saying it to be pleasant," he said. "Scott did something for which I'll always be grateful. You must know what I mean . . ."

"No, I don't think so," said I.

"I lost my wallet on the golf course. It just slipped out of the bag somewhere on the course. Later that day I was going frantic when the pro shop reported that it had been turned in, by Scott. All my credit cards were in there along with about $300—and everything was intact," he said. "You've raised not only a nice kid but a very honest one."

Scott had never mentioned the incident to me or his mother. I liked that.

But what I liked most were the reports of his on-course behavior. Frankly, I was surprised. On one occasion I pressed the reporter for details.

"Did he play well?" I asked.

"Not as well as I've heard he can" was the reply. "In fact, he struggled through some big numbers in the middle of the round."

"Hmm. And he didn't show his temper, didn't get all silent or impatient or anything?"

"Not a bit. He seemed to take it all in stride."

I was so pleased at that news that I played it back to Scott at dinner that evening. He reacted with words that, I suspect, he'd wanted to say to me for quite a while.

"Dad, you just don't get it, do you? I'm always worst when I play with you. It's the same with Eamonn," he said, referring to his best golf buddy, the fifteen-year-old son of my good friend Bob O'Brien, who had sponsored me at Sleepy Hollow before Scott and Eamonn were born. "Eamonn and I are fine when we play together—we just hack around and have a good time—and we're both okay when we play with the club members, but when he and his dad play together, they're always at each other's throats. Mr. O'Brien tries to tell him stuff all the time, just like you do with me, and then Eamonn usually plays and acts even worse than I do with you. You guys get into our heads, and we hate it."

"Scott, no one wants you to play well more than I do."

"Yeah, and that's a big part of it. I always feel I have to play well, perform, shoot a low score. Playing with you is more pressure than playing in a tournament. I always know what you're thinking. I can hear your thoughts, your judgments. I can't relax when I play with you."

I thought about that for a moment. As Libby had said, he wanted nothing more than to impress me. With me he played harder, tried harder, and when he didn't play well, crashed harder. He was, in truth, playing for both of us, trying to satisfy himself and also satisfy me. He wanted and needed my approval, but at the same time, he wanted and needed to show he *didn't* need me. Scott's game, like everything else about him, had matured and strengthened. At age thirteen, with a rhythmic, free-flowing swing, near fully developed wrists that whipped the clubhead through the ball, and an increasingly deft touch with the wedge and putter, he knew he had some game—and he needed to show me.

"I think there's another similarity between you and Eamonn," I said.

"What's that?" said he.

"You both want nothing more than to beat your fathers," I said.

"Not really," he said, looking downward for a moment. Then he looked up—looked me right in the eye—and with a widening smile said, "Well, maybe."

"Well, let me tell you something, laddie," I said with mock authority. "You can forget about that. You will not beat me the rest of this year and you will not beat me next year, which means you will not beat me this century or this millennium. I will hold you off until at least the first day of 2000."

To which the little smart aleck replied, "The year 2000 is part of the twentieth century, Dad."

"Fine," I said, "you will not beat me in any year that begins with a 1."

"No way!" he said, now grinning ear-to-ear. "You're going down, big guy—and soon."

And so the battle was joined. From that day forward Scott the thirteen-year-old/13 handicap would take on Dad the forty-eight-year-old/6 handicap—even up—in a quest for golf primacy that would dominate our rounds together until the deed was done. It was all out in the open now, and I could see in Scott's eyes that he couldn't wait for the war to begin.

Neither could I.

7

Fending
Him Off

Somehow I held out through the rest of 1998, mostly because, a week after Labor Day, we both hung up our sticks for the season, as Scott returned to school and I set myself to the task of writing a documentary for PBS, *The Story of Golf,* which had been optioned by CBS for broadcast prior to the Sunday telecast of the '99 Masters. My job was to recount the six-century history of the game in ninety riveting minutes, and in the four months since I'd taken on the assignment, I'd done a superb job of avoiding it. So between October and the following March I wrote lots of golf while playing very little.

In my maiden encounter with Scott that spring, however, I got a brisk warning of what was to come. It was the first day of spring vacation, a cold afternoon in mid-March, when Scott put on the best display of ball striking I'd ever seen him stage:

a round of 81 where he hit a dozen greens in regulation. Had he not putted poorly, and had I not had an uncharacteristically strong season opener myself (78), I would have succumbed in battle number one.

Indeed, for most of that round Scott had held the lead, only to give it away by three-putting four of the last five holes. On a couple of those holes, his approach putts had stopped only three feet or so from the cup. The barely thawed greens were hard and bumpy, and I might easily have conceded those knee-knockers. But neither of us wanted that.

Neither of us wanted a tainted victory. In fact, although we never said so to each other, my guess is that on that day neither of us wanted a victory of any kind—not just yet. I wasn't ready to yield my position as number one golfer in the family, and Scott wasn't ready to take it. We both knew the moment was coming—and fast. But for now neither of us wanted to "defeat" the other. I was happy simply fending off my son, but not so soundly as to discourage him. He was eager to dethrone me, but not defame me. It was important to both of us that I receive a proper burial.

"When I beat you," he said, "I want us both to play really well. You shoot 75, I shoot 74."

"Yeah," I said, "I guess I could handle that."

I suppose we were doing a sort of universal father-son dance. Although every boy wants to show his father what he can do—maybe even show him up—what he wants most is his father's respect. Ultimately, he may want to surpass dear old dad—live a more successful and/or admirable life—but what he wants first is to impress him. The same kind of admiration that young boys lavish on their fathers is what they seek in return as young men.

For Scott and me, however, a special irony hovered. He knew he would win a huge measure of my esteem—my golfer-to-golfer admiration—only when he finally and firmly defeated me. Absolute rejection would earn absolute acceptance.

It was a moment that loomed large for both of us. And for me, at least, there was no hurry. I didn't hate the thought of losing the match so much as the thought of losing the joy of being hunted. Once the deed was done, Scott would stand over my sorry carcass and that would be it: nothing left to prove. A large measure of our shared thrill would be gone.

We'd been through this once already, on a different battle-field. For my fortieth birthday my ever-thoughtful wife had given me a pool table, and all three Peper men had developed a mod-est ability when it came to leaning over the felt. One winter, Scott and I had taken to playing nightly after-dinner games. I invited him the first few nights, then one night he said, "So you wanna play pool?" After that we rarely missed a night, no matter how much homework or paperwork either of us had to do.

It was not actually pool that we played, but pocket bil-liards, a game played with three balls in which the object is to use the cue ball to strike the two other balls and thus earn two points. In addition, each time you pocket one of the two other balls you get one point. If you scratch (by pocketing the cue ball or failing to strike either of the two object balls), you lose all the points you've earned during that turn. First man to twenty-one points wins.

I'd played this game since college, so I had a big edge when Scott and I began our matches. Before long, however, he learned the subtleties of caroms, massés, etc., and started win-ning the odd game off me. We always played three games, and after a few months he got to the point where he could occa-sionally win two of the three.

One day he announced that his goal was to win all three games. I immediately replied that my solemn mission was to thwart him. Thereafter, just as in our battles for golf supremacy, we engaged each other with new zeal. Invariably, our most stirring sessions were the ones where he took games one and two and I somehow held him off in the final stages of the third. So many times I'd somehow manage to come from behind in that last game, or he'd somehow scratch away his lead and let me sneak in for the win.

Then one night he won all three games. We never played billiards again.

And so what I yearned for in our golf encounters was a lingering series of well-played, hard-fought ties. Indeed, over the next few months I would go to some lengths—and do some things I wasn't proud of—simply to extend our delicious dance.

My lowest moment was probably the day that I played poorly on the front nine and got so disgusted that I flailed through the back nine using only a 4-iron and a putter. Scott beat me soundly that day. He won fairly, but since I had refused to lose fairly, neither of us could legitimately consider it "the" defeat.

A couple of weeks thereafter we played a friendly match against another father and son. At 18 Scott had a putt of less than three feet to tie our opponents.

"That's good," said the other father magnanimously.

"Not by me it ain't," I said from the back of the green as Scott was picking up his ball. I had just three-putted for an 81, and Scott needed that tiddler for an 80.

"What?" said Scott, genuinely irritated.

"Replace your ball and putt it," I said. "You need that to beat me, and I'm not giving it to you."

Rarely have I seen him so angry—on a golf course or off—as when he replaced that ball, missed the putt, and stomped off the green.

Then there was the day that Scott beat me but didn't know it—and I never told him. We'd played a casual round with a couple of fellow members, not paying much attention to

our father-son struggle until the last few holes, where we battled fiercely to a pair of 78s.

Or so I thought. After the round Scott headed to the practice
tee while I had a beer with the two guys with whom we'd played.
I'd had a bet with one of them, and he'd brought the scorecard
to the table to total up the damage. When he was done, I glanced
at the card, mentally recounting my round. Immediately, I saw
that on the fourth hole my friend had erroneously credited me
with a par when in fact I'd made bogey. I'd shot 79, not 78. Scott
and I had not tied—he'd beaten me by one!

I decided not to tell him. It was too late. Besides, if he'd
known he'd had a one-stroke lead—if I'd known—things might
have gone differently over those last few holes. But most of all,
I knew this was no way for our noble combat to end—not with
an eraser at the nineteenth hole. I didn't want to be De
Vicenzo to Scott's Goalby, and I knew he didn't want that
either. So I tossed that card into the trash. Scott didn't learn
about that round until he read the manuscript of this book.

By Memorial Day Scott had become a bit frustrated with
his quest, and he was to suffer some more aggravation that
weekend. Our home is situated on a hillside about fifty yards
from the west shore of the Hudson River, with the result that
we're blessed with not only a magnificent view but a splendid
natural driving range.

For the last decade or so we've hosted a Memorial Day
weekend ball-beating party for a few close friends. Each year
I'm able to procure a few dozen of my club's worst-looking
range balls—balls so yellowed, nicked, and otherwise abused
that they've become unfit even for practice. Everyone is invited to whack away—even the kids—in a variety of power and
accuracy competitions, until all the balls have found a home at
the bottom of the Hudson. (Note to tree huggers: Yes, I realize

this is an ecologically despicable thing to do, and last year we stopped doing it, okay?)

The traditional finale is the men's long-drive contest, and in the year in question there was a surprise addition to the field: Scott's older brother, Tim. Now, Tim hadn't hit a golf ball in roughly four years—since the days he'd discovered acting, singing, lacrosse, and girls—but despite a general disinterest in the game, he has some natural ability, and on this day, with one mighty, roundhouse, randomly on-plane swipe, he crushed out a beauty that broke the surface of the river fully twenty-five yards past the best efforts of his assembled rivals, including Scott.

On the way to the course the next morning, to goad Scott a bit, I said, "I can't believe that drive Tim hit last night. I wasn't watching at the time. Was it straight as well as long?"

"Yeah, it was straight," said Scott quietly.

"It's really too bad he doesn't like golf. With those long, strong arms of his I bet he could be a helluva player. He has sort of a Tiger Woods body."

Scott thought about that for a moment. "I don't think Tim could ever be a golfer," he said.

"Why not?"

"It's against everything about him. I just tried to picture him saying, 'Do you want to go out and play?' and I'm having trouble doing that."

There was a tone of deprecation in Scott's voice and, I suspect, some morning-after jealousy.

"Well, he's into other stuff," I said.

"Yeah, I guess so," said Scott, feeling the guilt of his thoughts. "Ever since he played Sky Masterson in *Guys and Dolls* at school he's become like an icon. All the girls in my class are in love with him."

Three weeks later Tim gave me one of the best surprises I've ever received. He'd come in late the night before from his weekend job as a busboy and left a note outside our bedroom door. It read: "Dad, if you and Scott are going golfing, I want to play with you. If not, Happy Father's Day . . . and don't wake me up."

Had his triumph in the driving contest somehow ignited an interest in golf? Was he smitten with the notion of more colossal clouts? Or was he just being a good son for Father's Day? I didn't care. I was going to have the best of all treats: a round of golf in the company of both my sons.

Tim, to no one's surprise, hit the ball all over the place that day, but seemed to have the time of his life, exulting in his sporadic good shots and laughing genuinely at his bad ones. His blithe spirit was both a joy and a revelation, and along with my love for him that day came a touch of awe as well as envy of his intrepid cheerfulness.

"Yeah," he said, "on most shots I really don't care, but sometimes, after I've hit a couple of good ones in a row, when I then hit a bad one, it's hard to laugh off."

"Welcome to my world," I said, patting him on the back. Maybe there was a bit of golfer in this lad's soul after all.

Scott, I believe, had been quietly pleased to hear that his big brother would be tagging along for the day. Indeed, I think he saw this Father's Day as a poignant opportunity to finally beat me while simultaneously showing Tim what a player he'd become. But that didn't happen. As Tim laughed his way through the round and I reveled in his spirit, Scott fell into a bogey-filled funk that began to spoil the day.

Midway through the back nine, sensing the need to get Scott back into the party, I announced that we'd be playing a game: guess the total score that the three of us would make on each hole. This succeeded in stirring Scott's competitive juices while diverting his attention from the scores he could shoot to the scores he could predict. (Tim, who has always had a measure of his mother's radar for such things, later told me he knew exactly what I was doing.)

I can't remember who won that game, but I do know we all had a lot of fun from that point forward. Scott even started to give his big brother some golf instruction, and one little lesson became the subject of an enduring joke among the Peper males.

Tim had hit a series of huge hooks off the tee, so as we approached number 17, Scott gave him some advice on ball position.

"Put it off your left foot," he said, the first three words coming in a high-pitched trill that made him sound exactly like a purring pigeon. Immediately, Tim and I purred "Put it off" back at him, producing laughter from Scott. We all purred like pigeons through the last two holes and most of the ride home. Nobody posted a score that day, but in the end I think we all felt like winners. Father's Day golf with my two sons has since become a tradition I hope will never end.

As the summer progressed, Scott played less golf with me and more with his peers. In early July he entered his first competition, a qualifying tournament for the Metropolitan Golf Association's Boys' Championship. I think I was more excited than he was on the morning we drove down to the Suneagles Golf Club in southern New Jersey. A friend of mine, Semo Sennas, had come along, and our plan was to drop off Scott, go play a nearby course, and come back to get him after his round.

Suneagles is an unassuming place, but on this day it had the aura of a major championship site. Officials in long-sleeved white cotton shirts and MGA armbands, a starter with a megaphone at the first tee, a big scoreboard at 18—everything but TV towers and a merchandise tent. I was intimidated, and I knew Scott was, too.

"Good luck," I said as we left him. "Do your best and try to have some fun."

I wanted nothing more than to follow him around all eighteen holes of that tournament, but I knew he wanted nothing less. Still, by the time Semo and I had finished about twelve holes of our own round, I couldn't stand it anymore, and Semo, easygoing soul that he is, happily agreed to my suggestion that we cut over to the seventeenth tee and play in.

At warp speed I drove the ten miles back to the qualifier, ripped into the parking lot, and raced to the first tee to get a read on Scott's progress.

"His group should be at about the fourteenth hole," said the starter.

Out we went, stalking a five-footer in khaki shorts and a green-striped shirt. By the time we caught up with his foursome they were on the tee of 16, a par 3, and I was elated to see that the first to play was Scott. At least his three playing companions hadn't outscored him on 15.

Since I didn't want to spook him, I insisted to my friend that we skulk in the trees. So for three holes we stood behind trunks and peered through branches. I felt like Arte Johnson playing the Nazi soldier on *Rowan & Martin's Laugh-In*.

His tee shot found a bunker, but he got up and down for par, then made a rock-solid, fairway/green/two-putt 4 at 17. Maybe he was actually going to qualify! But at 18, just after we'd nestled ourselves in the arms of a massive spruce tree two hundred yards down the right rough, Scott's tee shot sailed over our heads—out of bounds by only an inch or two. When I reached the ball, I felt a mighty temptation. If my friend hadn't been with me, who knows what paternal felony I might have perpetrated.

Fortunately, he was there, so we scurried to the eighteenth green, positioning ourselves as if we'd been waiting there all along. It was excruciating to watch Scott play that final hole. He'd hit a second tee shot, then duffed his approach and three-putted for an 8. When finally our eyes met, I could see he was not a happy boy.

"How'd it go?" I asked, trying to seem less informed than I actually was.

"Not great," he said.

"Do you know what you shot?"

"Eighty-six, I think."

"That's pretty good, especially for your first tournament."

"Yeah, but I made 8 at the last hole. It could've been 82, and that might have qualified—86 won't."

"Hey, that's okay. You got some good experience, and you made a couple of great pars at 16 and 17."

"You saw those?"

"Yup, from the trees," I said. "We were stalking you."

"You're kidding," he said, simultaneously pleased, amused, and embarrassed at how his father had spent the previous hour.

Most of the one-hour trip home was devoted to a shot-by-shot account of the other fifteen holes, descriptions of his playing partners, and a general vilification of the Suneagles greens, where many strokes had been lost. But there was no mention of nervousness, and I could see one thing: He loved competition and wanted more of it.

That was a big difference between him and me. Generally, under the pressure of a tournament, I shoot half a dozen strokes worse than my handicap. Scott seemed to rise to the challenge.

When the Sleepy Hollow club championship rolled around, as usual I failed to qualify for the championship flight, settling into the euphemistically named "A" flight reserved for myself and assorted other rejects and chokers. Through a combination of good breaks, fortunately timed shots, and extremely charitable opponents, I won that flight.

My victory in the final came over a member whose locker is next to mine, and one of the finer guys in the club, Chuck

Rockefeller. No, he is not one of *those* Rockefellers (although we do have one or two of them as members; their ancestral estate, Kykuit, complete with a nifty eighteen-hole course of its own, is just a couple of miles from Sleepy Hollow), but Chuck has a rich sense of humor, and I'll never forget what he told me on the day we met. "Although we have zero connection to the millionaire Rockefellers, I'm not above leveraging the name. It's a huge help in getting restaurant reservations. But when I call for takeout from Pizza Hut, they tend to hang up on me."

Chuck and I were having lunch after our match when in walked Scott. A day earlier, in a major upset, he'd beaten the seventeen-year-old son of Larry Stewart, a close friend of mine at Sleepy Hollow, in the semifinals of the club championship. Larry Jr.—or Little Larry as he was absurdly referred to, being five inches taller than his father—was a far superior athlete to Scott. He had lettered since freshman year in football (as quarterback), basketball (center), and baseball (pitcher). His drives soared past Scott's by fifty yards and more. But he lacked Scott's dedication to the game—not to mention his wedge game—and Scott was able to score a tortoise-and-hare victory, which was probably more awkward for the parents than the kids. Little Larry, a kid used to winning far more contests than he lost, was a class act all the way.

The junior finals, according to club tradition, were scheduled to tee off that afternoon just in front of the finals of the men's and women's championships.

"So are you ready?" I asked Scott.

"I guess so," he said.

His opponent was Chris Sanossian, a formidable foe indeed. Like Larry Stewart, he was three years older than Scott, several inches taller, and many yards longer off the tee. And Chris was a player; he'd come close to winning a couple of American Junior Golf Association events and sported a handicap of 1 to Scott's 9.

"Do you mind if I come out and follow you this afternoon?" I said.

"No," he said, surprising me. The last thing I would have wanted was my father watching every shot of the biggest match of my life. I wondered whether he really did want me out there or was just showing me he could handle my heat. In any case, I decided to stay away. But an hour later, as he headed from the practice range to the tee, I couldn't resist a few words of coaching.

"Remember," I said, "in match play anything can happen. Just be patient. Plan your shots conservatively but play them aggressively—be confident and committed. And if you get one or two down, don't panic—he's just as nervous as you are. At one point this morning I was four up on Mr. Rockefeller and all I could think about was, 'Gee, if I lose this hole, I'll only be three up.'"

"Yeah, but you're a head case, Dad."

"Granted, but you know what I mean."

"Yeah, I know."

Four hours later the two boys played up 18, before a gallery of fifty or so members. Scott had lost, but he'd given his opponent a great match, playing him even for the first eight holes. Then, after he'd fallen to four down with five holes to go, he'd won three holes in a row, before losing on the seventeenth green. Chris had shot 75, but Scott had stayed close with a 78. He was disappointed, but also proud, and no more than I.

But with the playing of that club championship, another golf season had ended for Scott, a season in which he'd failed to accomplish his goal of beating me. My playful prediction, that he would not unseat me before the year 2000, had sadly come true, as Scott would have no further opportunities to play with me until the following spring.

Or so I thought. In mid-September I received a phone call from a fellow I'd met earlier that year, one of the executives of the Lone Cypress Company, then owners of the Pebble Beach resort. Lone Cypress was interested in increasing the exposure of some of its other holdings, notably the Taiheiyo Club courses in Japan, and as part of that effort they were inviting me to tour Japan and play in the pro-am for the Visa Taiheiyo Masters in November.

I had never been to Japan, and I had little trouble convincing myself of the potential for at least one good article, so with that thin veil of legitimacy as my justification I not only accepted the invitation, I brought Libby and Scott along with me.

Two months later, while ensconced in a business-class seat to Tokyo, I reflected on my good fortune to have had a job that has taken me to so many parts of the world. Jimmy Cannon, the famed columnist for the *New York Post,* may have said it best when he observed that sportswriters are entombed in a prolonged childhood, underpaid and overprivileged.

However, if there is a species on the planet even more coddled than sportswriters, it is surely the children of sportswriters. Across the aisle on that Japan Airlines flight, my son slumbered blissfully, on his way to yet another exotic golf destination. During the past decade or so we'd taken him and his brother on trips to England, Scotland, France, Italy, Mexico, the Caribbean, California, Arizona, and Hawaii.

Scott, by the unworthy age of fourteen, had played ten of the courses ranked by *GOLF Magazine* among the top one hundred in the world—Pebble Beach, St. Andrews, Pinehurst #2, Loch Lomond, Royal Dornoch, Estancia, Cabo del Sol, Casa de Campo, Ocean Forest, and Spyglass Hill—and now was hurtling toward the best courses in Japan.

At the same age I'd never been out of North America. I'd played barely half a dozen courses, all of them public tracks of no distinction, and most of them within a ten-minute drive of my home. Ironically, the first private course I would set foot on was the club to which I now belong, Sleepy Hollow, when the Pearl River High School golf team crossed the Hudson into tony Westchester to take on a team from the Hackley School, a posh playpen for the progeny of Wall Streeters (and I'm pleased to report that we drilled those preppies, 7–1). Now, I'm not one of those guys who can remember every shot he's ever hit, but I must say I can recall a good number of strokes from that high school match, largely because I was so awed by the course I was playing. Eighteen years would pass before I'd get another crack at Sleepy Hollow.

Scott, by contrast, had no idea what it's like to play on anything less than manicured fairways and pristine greens. On one level I was happy about that, but it also concerned me. My kid was thoroughly spoiled and largely oblivious to the practical realities of life. He had never worked to earn a penny; not even his allowance had come with strings attached. We'd tried forcing him and his brother to perform the standard tasks—set the table, clean their rooms, feed the dogs—but without much success, because we'd never made it an issue. Libby, being the most giving of mothers, had done everything possible for her kids and asked nothing in return. And I, being the classically detached dad, had let her set the tone. Neither of us had been tough enough.

Permissiveness had been our byword, and in one sense it had worked. We'd never sheltered our boys from movies or TV shows with violence, crude language, or sexual content, under the theory that to do so would foster a perverse fascination with the forbidden. Moreover, we'd never forced our social, political, or religious views on the kids. We'd always trusted our actions to set an example and trusted the kids to set their own standards.

While I'm no child psychologist, I do know that we've raised two reasonably well adjusted, well mannered, responsible sons. On the other hand, we've raised two kids who feel entitled to the best things in life, without much obligation to procure them.

Tim, as this book comes to press, is about to graduate from the top acting program in the country. He has become a fine and powerful dramatic actor and has won numerous roles in student productions, including a complex and emotionally charged lead role in Sam Shepard's *Fool for Love,* where he gave a performance worthy of James Dean (at least in the biased eye of this reviewer).

He is a true actor's actor, drawn only to the stage, as opposed to film or television. I applaud and admire his purity, but as he well knows, it also concerns me. I would rather see him aim for a broader range of things. Before starting college, he spent a summer auditioning and got callbacks for a couple of projects (including one of the bigger teen movies, *Road Trip*), but since becoming a serious student of acting, he has shunned anything that smacks of conmercialism.

A source of frustration for his mother and me, although not for Tim, is the success of one of his fellow students at Tisch, Ben Curtis. You won't recognize the name, but you will surely know the line he made famous: "Dude, you're gettin' a Dell!" At each of Tim's last two plays Ben was in the front row of the audience, applauding warmly. After the performances I can only assume that he hopped into a Maserati and drove to his weekend estate in the Hamptons.

Tim's aspiration has been to develop a repertory theater company, ideally a vehicle for off-off-Broadway productions of scripts by young playwrights. I love his passion, and I want him to follow his dream, but I fear it's a blueprint for starvation. Beginning next year, unless something breaks, Tim will cease to live in the style to which he has been accustomed. I know he'll survive. I just hope he'll be happy.

Fortunately, Tim has developed at least some sense of what it means to earn his way, having worked off and on since his junior year in high school as a busboy at one of our local restaurants. Fortunately also, his material needs are relatively modest. He has no particular taste for the finer things.

Scott does. Thanks in large part to the golf spoils I'd lavished on him, Scott long ago acquired a Robin Leach view of the world. He'd shown that he was a brighter-than-average kid, so I had confidence he'd find his way. Nonetheless, as I stared at him in that business-class seat to Tokyo, I decided he needed a reality check. Next summer he would become a caddie.

In the meantime we had three glorious rounds to play: at famed Hirono, a Charles Alison gem known as the Pine Valley of Japan, at the Kawana resort, a seaside course set on a cliff above the Japan Sea, and two rounds at the Taiheiyo Club, at the foot of snowcapped Mount Fuji.

Hirono and Kawana did not disappoint. The first may have been the most exclusive course I've visited anywhere, complete with an austere golf museum a few steps from the first tee where, unbelievably, a dust-covered leather bag of clubs, used by President Eisenhower, leaned against a wall, the clubs available for anyone to waggle. The wide fairways, expansive greens, mature pine trees, and superb conditioning were indeed similar to Pine Valley, maybe with a bit of Pinehurst thrown in. Kawana was picturesque and challenging— although no Pebble Beach—and its korai-grass greens (imagine Bermuda grass on steroids) were probably the slowest I'd ever seen on a prominent course, in the neighborhood of 6 on the Stimpmeter.

The best part of the trip had been saved for last, the stop at the Taiheiyo Masters. A week or so before our departure a fax had arrived at my office: Not only would I be playing in the pro-am, they had found a spot for Scott as well.

"Do you think we'll get paired with an American pro?" he asked as our bullet train took us from Kyoto to Fuji.

"We might. The Tour Championship was last week and the World Championships event at Valderrama isn't until next week, so a couple of guys might be over here. It's a pretty fat purse."

"I hope we get a big-name guy," said Scott. "I think I tend to play a little better when there are people watching."

"That makes one of us," said I.

One hundred and nineteen amateurs took part in the pro-am, and only two were Americans. As such, Scott and I were minor celebrities and major oddities, with Scott, the fair-haired, baby-faced kid, twice as odd as I. The most uncomfortable moment occurred when the two of us entered the expansive Taiheiyo clubhouse on the morning of the pro-am. When the twelve-foot-high double doors flung open, we suddenly faced a lobby full of Japanese tournament officials, clubhouse staff, and assorted hangers—nearly one hundred in all—and every one of them was staring straight at us. Not one of them spoke a word, not one of them moved a muscle, and not one of them took his eyes off us. We were the headlights and they were the deer.

Somehow we got through that gauntlet to breakfast, where we sat at one of the two non-Japanese tables, one table away from fellow celebroddities Sergio Garcia, Jose Maria Olazabal, Darren Clarke, Jean Van de Velde, and the three-time defending champion in this event, Lee Westwood. I didn't commune with them much except to note that Van de Velde, curiously, was the only one at the table who had not opted for French toast.

But I couldn't resist telling Calamity Jean how much I admired his performance that July at the British Open. For one thing, I may be the only person in the golf fraternity who agreed 100 percent with his shot selection on the final hole at

Carnoustie. For another, the way he'd handled the whole thing was beyond admirable. Van de Velde has a lot of class, and at Taiheiyo he turned out to be the least self-absorbed and friendliest of all the foreign stars.

At the range I noticed the first big difference between Japanese and American pro golf: the music. Go to a PGA Tour event and the practice tee is silent. At Taiheiyo we hit balls as a loudspeaker blared out a Japanese country-western band's version of "Stand by Your Man." I stood by Scott, who stood by Westwood, who stood by Olazabal. What a moment.

My pro partner turned out to be the only American Tour player in the tournament: Mark O'Meara, whom I'd known since the year he turned pro. We had a jolly day together along with the two other amateurs, one of whom was the course designer and the other a guy whose name I never got. All I knew was that he was a comic actor, billed as "the Joe Pesci of Japan."

Scott meanwhile became the instant darling of the Japanese caddies, who, as advertised, were women. At Taiheiyo they were decked out in white shoes, Black Watch plaid plus fours and vests, and enormous white baby bonnets that made them look like Scottish flying nuns. They did not actually carry the clubs and didn't even pull them in trolleys; they propelled them in electronically controlled vans that looked larger than most Japanese sedans and trundled along on remote-controlled paths, like rides at Walt Disney World. We players were free to hitch rides at any time, but I was afraid I might have to listen to a piped-in chorus of "It's a Small World."

The event was a shotgun start, and our team was the first of two groups assigned to the tenth tee. What sent us off was another sonic point of Asian differentiation: instead of a shotgun blast, a burst of fireworks—eye-popping, multicolored, slam-banging fireworks—set against the backdrop of Mount Fuji. All very understated.

My opening tee shot was a boomer, but with everyone's ears still ringing I felt I got far too little credit. I found the green with a wedge and then summarily three-putted to cost the team a net birdie. This set the pattern for my day.

The one strong point was my tee game. I outdrove O'Meara by an average of thirty yards all day long (okay, he played from the back tees—in fact, way back), but the point is, I drove the ball well. And a good thing that was, because an errant tee shot in Japan can produce one of the most embarrassing experiences in golf. I wasn't prepared for it the first time—a sound that's a cross between the screech of a lovesick alley cat and the blood-curdling shriek of someone who has just come face-to-face with Freddy Krueger: *"FAAAAAAAARRRRRRGHHHH!"*

It's the lady caddie, alerting those ahead to the incoming fire. Not "fore," but "far," which in truth means wide. The note is held for at least ten seconds, and is always bellowed at threshold-of-pain volume, so that anyone within earshot turns instantly to behold the offending party.

So thank goodness, I drove it straight. My irons were okay, which is all they ever are, but I putted with the touch of a sumo wrestler. One reason is that these were among the fastest greens I've ever putted—anywhere—and that includes Oakmont, Winged Foot, and Augusta National. The day we played they were nicely over 12 on the Stimpmeter, and by Sunday I'm told they were close to 14. In any case, with thirty-nine putts I posted a score somewhere in the mid-80s while letting down my team on countless occasions. We finished at five under par, tied for thirty-fourth out of forty teams.

Meanwhile, Scott, playing just in back of me, had himself a ball. After topping his opening tee shot, he played near-flawless golf and made the turn in 41, right about on his 12 handicap. Then on the back nine the little bugger poured in four pars-for-birdies. His pro was Asian Tour veteran Massy Kuramoto, who at one point yelled through the trees at me, "Junior play big good, every hole!" Together with his partners, *GOLF Magazine* Top 100 Teacher Laird Small and another unidentifiable actor (this one the alleged Japanese Al Pacino), he finished at minus 12, which was good enough for second place.

At the awards party I drowned myself in sake as the squirt smiled for flashing cameras and got praised in Japanese by Kuramoto. His prize was a beautiful loving cup, made by some fancy Tokyo jeweler. As he stepped down, Van de Velde, whose team finished near mine, told him, "Young Peper, you need to go back to school." It had to be one of the highlights of Scott's life.

But if that day was a triumph for Scott, the day that followed was even bigger. There is a second course at the Taiheiyo Club which, during tournament week, was open for play, and Scott and I were able to get a tee time for one last round before heading back to the States.

Neither of us played particularly well, but that kept the match interesting. We had not kept our hole-by-hole scores on a card, and neither of us had said a word about where he stood in relation to par, but we didn't need to. At this stage of the several-month quest, each of us watched the other's strokes like a hawk. I knew exactly where Scott stood in relation to me, and he knew the same.

On the days when I pulled several strokes ahead, the subject was never raised, but when the scores were close, one of us would inevitably say something about the status of our respective scores, just to be sure our independent calculations were in sync. Usually, it happened somewhere between the thirteenth and fifteenth holes.

This time I waited until the sixteenth green, where, after three-putting for a bogey to Scott's par, I said simply, "That puts us even."

"Yup" was all he said.

At 17, a par 3 of two hundred yards, all of it over water, Scott feathered his 5-wood onto the green, while I yanked a 4-iron into thick grass. When he two-putted and I failed to get up and down, he moved one ahead with one to go.

Feeling imperiled, I decided to bolster my chances with some trash talking.

"You may tie me, but you won't beat me. Not today, not in freaking Japan. That is absolutely unacceptable."

"I dunno, Dad. Remember the fortune I got in that cookie in the restaurant in Kyoto—it said I was about to do something remarkable."

"You had your 'remarkable' yesterday," I said. "Beating me would be something terrible."

"We'll see," he said, teeing up his ball. "I like my chances, the way you've been slopping it around the last few holes."

With that he pulled his drive into deep rough. Feeling triumphant at the success of my needling, I strode confidently to the tee, took a mighty swipe, and whipped my ball into even worse trouble on the other side of the fairway. It was a short par 4, but a pond guarded the front-right of the green, and both of us were forced to lay up to about eighty yards.

Scott, hitting first, played safely to the left side of the green, leaving a putt of over forty feet. That meant a bogey at best. Meanwhile, I had the pond between me and the stick, and the pin was up front. It wasn't an easy shot, but I knew that if I could get mine in there close, I'd salvage the 82–82 tie I needed.

Unfortunately, of all the shots in golf, the one that gives me the most aggravation is the eighty-yard wedge shot. With a sand wedge I invariably invoke my overswing-panic-deceleration move and either chunk it thirty yards or skull it 130. With a pitching wedge I'm incapable of throttling down. I'll make a smooth, abbreviated backswing, then have sudden doubts and unleash my trademark convulsive lunge. In these situations crisp impact is a fifty-fifty thing, and any shot that finishes on target is an accident.

What I needed for the shot facing me was a sudden, unexpected onset of finesse—and I didn't get it. Wedge struck turf a full three inches behind ball, and ball struck water a full three yards short of green. Final scores: Scott 81, Dad 84. The deed had been done.

For Scott it brought a sense of relief—the relief Phil Mickelson will surely feel when he finally gets his major. For me it brought a bit of melancholy, a bit of shame, and the certainty that the tide had turned. I suppose both of us felt an awkward pride as well. And yet neither of us felt total closure.

"Congratulations," I said about three-quarters-heartedly. "You did it."

"Well, it wasn't the greatest victory," he said in the same tone. "You sort of handed it to me."

"Hey, a win's a win, man," I said. "And you squeaked it in before 2000."

"Yeah, I guess it wasn't a moment too soon. It was just kind of weird doing it on the other side of the world."

"That's okay," I said. "As far as I'm concerned I'm not totally beaten yet. You've never outscored me head-to-head on American soil. We still have the Western Hemisphere to play for."

He would not wait long to make that official. Six weeks later, on another one of those spoiled golf-writer trips, we were in Hawaii. I'd booked the trip a year earlier, parlaying frequent flyer miles and PGA Tour press credentials to combine a visit to the Mercedes Championships at Kapalua with a family celebration of New Year 2000. I'd arranged for the four of us to greet the dawn of the new year at the top of the Mount Haleakala volcano, after which we would bicycle down the summit.

On the day before—literally the last day of 1999—I got a time for Scott and me at the Village Course at Kapalua. Playing the best golf I'd ever seen him play, he shot 74—two over par—to my 79. At last he had drilled me the way we wanted. When the fireworks went off that night, we both had something to celebrate. The year could not have ended more sweetly.

Along with that closure came closeness. Almost instantly, Scott seemed to give me a bit more respect, more deference. An unforced, unrequested filial piety seemed at work. The generosity of the victor was at work as well, along with a degree of pity, I suspect: the shared, silent recognition that the baton had been handed over, that the next millennium would belong, in so many ways, to him rather than me. Suddenly, in the same way that I'd always rooted for him to play well, to play better, Scott now seemed to be rooting for me.

With that in mind, and knowing I wanted him to get a bit of bag-toting experience under his belt before the summer, I offered him a job, as my caddie for the AT&T Pebble Beach Pro-Am. I'd been blessed with invitations to that greatest of all golf parties since 1992, the year I was able to coax a friend, neighbor, and fellow club member of mine to play in the tournament with me: Bill Murray.

Murray, by the estimation of most, has been the hit of the tournament ever since. If you happen to appreciate his annual Monterey antics, I will take credit for getting him there. If you find Bill's behavior inappropriate and disrespectful, well, you're wrong. The truth is that Bill Murray knows and respects golf's etiquette and traditions the way more people should. Furthermore, through not only his attendance but his appearances at various clinics and special functions during that week, he has single-handedly raised millions of dollars for the charities of the Pebble Beach Foundation, and that does not count the sizable donations he has made from his own pocket. Away from the limelight, Murray is one deeply introspective, highly principled, scarily intelligent, and ceaselessly generous man.

Besides, he knows what he's doing out there. He doesn't yank a woman out of the gallery until he sees in her eye that she's game. Two years after we played together, a well-known incident occurred in which he danced with an elderly lady in a greenside bunker of the eighteenth hole at Pebble Beach. PGA Tour Commissioner Deane Beman was viewing the tournament on television, and he reacted strongly, asking his henchmen to put a clamp on Murray. One of them, knowing I was close to Bill, called me during the tournament and asked me to intercede.

"The commissioner is concerned that when Bill reaches across the ropes and brings people onto the field of play, he'll give gallery members the feeling that they have the right to get involved. He's concerned about fans getting overzealous."

"Do you really think your officials can't control things?" I asked.

"You never know" was the reply. "Some of these people get pretty exuberant. The last thing we need is an incident like they have at those soccer games, where fans get trampled or something."

"Right," I said, not sure whether to believe what I was hearing. Never underestimate corporate paranoia.

The next day I bumped into Bill and his pro partner, Scott Simpson.

"Hey," said Bill, "we're headed over to the CBS tower to tell Jim Nantz and Ken Venturi we think Deane Beman is a Nazi. Wanna join us?"

"No, I believe I'll pass on that one," I said. "But the Tour people did call me last night. They wanted me to relay their concern."

"What's that?" said Bill.

"I guess what they're most concerned about is crowd control," I said.

Bill's reply was typical of his ability to deliver the perfect rejoinder with perfect timing.

"George," he said, "my *business* is crowd control."

In any case, by riding Murray's coattails, I'd wangled myself nine straight invites to the clambake. However, with the sale of the Pebble Beach Company to a consortium of investors led by Arnold Palmer, Clint Eastwood, Peter Ueberroth, and Dick Ferris, I sensed an imminent end to my good fortune. Numerous smaller investors (if you can call a $2-million stake small) had become involved in the purchase, and those people needed to be rewarded for their participation. The most logical way to do that was through invitations to the pro-am, thus reducing the chances for hangers-on like me. The 2000 tournament, I concluded, would likely be my last year— and thus the last opportunity to share the tournament with my son.

Besides, having Scott on the bag would save me about $750 in caddie fees for the week. The only thing I promised him for his lifting was a series of dinners at Italian restaurants and a pretournament round of golf at the most captivating golf course in creation, Cypress Point.

Since joining me for the entire week would mean five missed school days, Scott waited until Wednesday to fly out. I met him at the Monterey Airport and we drove directly to Cypress Point, where we were greeted by our host, and my dear friend of many years, Bob Sheppard.

I had been playing and practicing for three days. Scott had not touched a club in months, but he stepped to the first tee and laced a 250-yard drive down the middle. Each of us made five pars and four bogeys on the front to turn in 39.

Midway through the back nine, Bob, who had been battling an ailing hip, packed it in and left us to play alone. I was sorry to see him leave because he may just be the world's nicest man, but I must admit, there was something very special about being on the last few holes of Cypress Point, as the sun set over the Pacific, alone with my son.

We had produced another sprinkling of bogeys and pars until the surreally beautiful fifteenth, a par 3 of about 135 yards, where as sea lions barked from the rocks below, Scott struck a 9-iron that nearly went in the hole for an ace before stopping two feet away. At the famed and feared sixteenth—233 yards over the foaming surf—I hit my customary hurry-up push slice into the drink, but Scott managed to get it across, though into the ice plant, and took a bogey.

It was nearly six o'clock when we played the par-4 seventeenth, and as we walked along the cliffs that form the inner edge of that spectacular left-to-right dogleg, a lone sea lion, perched on a rock perhaps two hundred yards out to sea, extended his neck skyward and bayed loudly against the backdrop of a brilliant red sun. Suddenly, our golf shots seemed secondary. If golf is capable of providing a religious experience, this was surely it.

In the car on the way to our hotel Scott and I indulged in our customary counting up of the card. He had shot 78 to my 82.

"How many fairways did you hit, Dad?" he asked.

"Let's see . . . eleven," I said.

"I hit all fourteen," he announced.

"You're kidding. That's amazing. You know, not even the pros do that except once in a blue moon. Of course, you did snipe a couple of them pretty hard left. It's a good thing the ground was wet."

"Yeah. How many greens did you hit?"

"Hmm . . . eight."

"I hit nine. How many putts?"

"Thirty-one."

"Me, too," he said. There was silence in the car for a while.

"I guess our games are pretty close right now," said Scott.

"Yeah," said I, "I guess so.

As a caddie that week, Scott quickly adopted the support-ive lingo of all good caddies.

"We're goin' low today," he announced on the first tee Thursday, and when we didn't go low, he did his best to keep me encouraged. "You've got that shot . . . we can get it back . . . this is a perfect distance for you . . . nice and smooth, now . . . trust your line and knock it in . . . we're gonna make eagle here."

Alas, he had a heavy load to carry, and despite the help of an amiable, long-hitting, and deadly-putting partner in Robert Damron, I missed the cut for a Jack Lemmonesque ninth straight year. Granted, this tournament falls annually smack in the middle of my golf hibernation, but that's not an adequate excuse. They always give me a generous handicap—between seven and ten strokes—and I should be able to cobble some decent scores out of that. But I always choke. I had wanted to make the cut more than ever this year, to give Scott the chance to walk Pebble with the pros on Sunday.

"I'm sorry I played so poorly," I said as we made our way back to the hotel on Saturday. "You like the pressure more than I do."

He thought about that for a minute. "Yeah," he said, "but on my first tee shot in the pro-am in Japan—the only time I had big pressure—I did top it. I actually do like showing off for people, though. I think about them as I'm setting up, then I don't think about anything—I just hit it."

"Well, I'm glad we at least got in one round together this week," I said.

"I killed you at Cypress Point," he said, then, feeling guilty, added, "thanks to the advice you gave me to keep it slow and smooth." Then, sensing he'd softened too much, added, "I really had no choice coming off the plane cold."

"Remember when I hit it past you at 13? I clocked that drive, and so did you . . . Well, maybe it wasn't your very best, but it was mine."

It had been my very best, but I wasn't quite ready to admit it. "You're within ten yards of me now," I said, "and by the end of the season you'll be ten yards past me."

"You're still better at the short game, though. I need to learn a few shots, like that punched 7-iron you've always tried to teach me. You're right, I need to have that shot in my bag."

I'd never heard him admit that. The fact that he had showed the level of maturity he'd gained, but it also showed something else. It was the kind of remark he'd begun to let slip more frequently, a remark that I chose to interpret as Scott's way of telling me something we both knew but would never verbalize: "I love this game, Dad. Thanks for getting me into it."

"You know," I said, blinking back the mist in my eyes, "you're the best caddie I've ever had."

"That's because I know your game better than anyone."

Real
Competition

Other than golf, only one sport had ever captured Scott's fancy: lacrosse. His older brother had played it throughout high school and was one of the better players on the team, a midfielder with long, swift strides and a strong, sweeping forehand shot.

One day Tim brought home an extra stick so that he could practice his throwing and catching. At first I served as the other end of the battery, but when Scott appeared in the yard, just at the moment that I catapulted a ball within inches of our neighbor's Volvo, I happily relinquished my weapon.

By the following spring, when he was in seventh grade, Scott had become sufficiently adept at stick handling to earn a spot on the middle-school team. Despite his diminutive size (from the sidelines, Libby and I always spotted him immediately as the smallest kid on the field), he started every game at attack, where he scored a dozen or so goals for two years in a row. His finest hour came in the last home game of his eighth-grade season, when he duplicated Tim's varsity feat, scoring a hat trick—three goals—and earning the game ball.

When he jumped into the car for the ride home that evening, he was a happy boy and I was a proud papa. We talked a bit about the game for a mile or so, and then he star-tled me.

"I don't think I want to play varsity next year," he said.

"Why not?" I asked, my visions of four more seasons root-ing from the bleachers suddenly shattered.

"I think I want to play on the golf team instead," he said.

"Oh" said I, thrilled, but determined not to let him know it.

"You played on your high school team, right?"

"Yup. But I remember being in a quandary. I liked baseball a lot. Back then, baseball was cooler than golf—still is, I guess . . ."

"Not at my school. Our team stinks, and nobody goes to the games."

"Well, anyway, I knew I had an outside shot at making the varsity." (I had come a long way from my ignominious beanball tryout for Little League.)

"But you went out for golf, right?" said Scott.

"Yup—made the team as a freshman, too," I bragged.

"Do you think I can make it?"

"It depends on how strong your team is, but my guess is that you can. You're already a better player in eighth grade than I was in ninth, and I'd be surprised, given the size of your school, if the golf team is any stronger than the one I played on at Pearl River."

"What spot did you make?" he asked.

"Last man—number six. It came down to a three-way play-off: me, a sophomore, and a junior. I shot something like 44 for nine holes, and that was good enough," I said, recalling that golden evening on the ninth green at Blue Hill Golf Club, where it had all been settled.

"Mom thinks I should play lacrosse," he said.

"I know. So do I," I managed to choke out, a sense of duty to Libby preempting my true feelings. "It's good for you to play on a team, get the feeling of camaraderie, pulling together. There's not much of that in golf . . . but there's a little."

"There's also a lot of stuff in lacrosse that I don't like," he said.

"Like what?"

"Like running. One practice day last week we had to run three miles. Besides, I'm not that much of a team guy the way Tim is. That's one of the things I like about golf: Only you get the credit or the blame."

The onlyness.

"Well, I think that's Mom's point, that you need to get a little more of that team stuff," I said, trying gamely to plead a case for which I had zero zeal.

"Yeah, I know . . . Does the golf team have practices?"

"Mine did."

"What'd you do, go to a driving range?"

"No, we headed over to the local course at about four o'clock and played nine holes, two or three times a week until the season got going. Then we had matches about every other day."

"Yes! Now I definitely want to do golf and not lacrosse. There is never a moment during lacrosse practice when I want to be there."

A couple of weeks later, during a parent-teacher conference, I ran into the school athletic director, who also happened to be the golf coach.

"Hey, I hear your son wants to play on the golf team. That's great because we're looking for a fifth man. We've got a couple strong players, kids who shoot 40 or lower for nine holes, and we play four men in the matches, but we need some depth. My own son tried last summer—shot 88 one day—and got the bug, but I told him I need him on the baseball team."

"Thank you," I said. "That'll mean less competition for Scott."

I gave Scott the news as soon as I got home. "My guess is that if you can shoot 45, you'll make the team, and if you can shoot 38, you'll lead it," I said. "And by the way, the team plays on courses that are much easier than Sleepy Hollow."

"Cool" was the reply as I left him to dream his dreams.

That left only one impediment: Libby. We decided to double-team her, raising the golf-lacrosse issue at the dinner table.

"I talked to Tom Curry last night," I said, "and he said he thinks Scott could make the varsity golf team as a freshman. From what he told me I think he could make it easily."

"What about lacrosse?" she said.

"Mom, I hate the practices. Besides, I'm not that good at it, and I get banged up every game because I'm small."

"Okay," she said.

"Okay?" Scott and I said in incredulous unison.

"Yes," she said. "I think the team aspect would have been good for you, Scott, but I read an article the other day by a college admissions director, and he said that in terms of getting into the top schools it's more important to have an extracurricular record that demonstrates strong involvement and leadership in one or two activities than casual participation in several. I think you have a good chance to excel on the golf end, so you might as well go for it."

"Wow," I said, "that was way easier than we thought it would be."

"We?" she said.

"Well, uh, we've already had a chat about this."

"Why am I not surprised? Well, if I've given you guys such a wonderful surprise, I guess you both just owe me."

"Fine," Scott and I chimed, all three of us knowing the debt would never be paid.

As it turned out, spring tryouts for Scott's school team were a far cry from what I'd gone through. His team had no home course and thus nowhere to practice. Therefore, the kids couldn't prove themselves, at least not by posting scores. Instead, the dozen or so incumbent team members and hopefuls were relegated to a driving range where they hit balls off mats while the coach watched.

Only four kids played in the varsity matches, and as the coach had told me, there were four upperclassmen returning to the team.

"How do you compare with those guys?" I asked Scott after he'd been to a few ball-beating sessions.

"One of them might be better than I am, two of them are about the same, and the fourth guy is clearly worse. He can barely get the ball airborne, and his best drive is about two hundred yards."

"Is there anyone else trying out who looks any good?"

"No, they're all choppers," he said.

"So you'll surely make the team and probably play," I said.

"I really don't know, Dad," he said in his irritated "don't pressure me" voice. Underpromise and overdeliver has always been his mantra.

A week later the team of seven players was announced, and Scott made it. Simultaneously, the starting four for the opening match was announced, and Scott was not among them. The coach had gone with his four veterans. Scott was feeling frustrated, wondering if he would play at all.

193

At the time, I was at the Masters, so it was Libby who got the news when Scott came home from school, moping. By the time I called home that night she was in a fit—angry at the coach for not recognizing her son's talents, angry at the school for not having a home course on which the kids could prove themselves, and angry at me just on general principle.

Happily for all of us in the path of that wrath, in the opening match the number four kid shot a nifty 60 for nine holes. That put him firmly on the bench and Scott on the team.

Match number two would be played at one of the better courses in the area, White Beeches Country Club in Haworth, New Jersey. When the day rolled around, I was as excited as Scott. I wanted nothing more than to gallery the entire nine holes, and I would have happily taken half a vacation day to do so, but I knew that having me around would be less than cool in Scott's eyes. So I sneaked out of the office at four o'clock and drove the half hour or so out of Manhattan to the course, arriving nearly an hour before the kids came in.

Sitting on a bench near the clubhouse, I thought back on my own first high school match. I don't think I've ever been as nervous on a golf course as I was for that first interscholastic tee shot. This was back in the days before sports psychologists, and no one paid much attention to the mental challenges of the game, but I'd hit upon a method that worked for me when the pressure was on—Julius Boros mode. Boros, who had won two U.S. Opens despite a forty-two-inch waist, had a swing that was almost lackadaisically slow—a marked contrast to my own manic move. So whenever I felt pressure, I pretended I was old Jay, sweeping one lazily down the fairway. That mental image usually succeeded in reducing me from Mach speed to cyclonic, thus enhancing my chance of at least making contact with the ball.

Back then, as now, the best players on each team—the

number one and two guys—played in a foursome with their counterparts from the opposing team, and that group teed off first. Then came the third- and fourth-ranking guys, leaving the fifth and sixth placers to bring up the rear. This order of play was a good idea in that the better players could set the pace and set the standard. On the other hand, it was a questionable strategy in that the outcome would often rest on the shoulders of the hapless humps in the final group.

The front nine of my high school's home course had numerous parallel holes, which enabled the teammates to communicate with one another via hand signals, a simple thumbs-up or -down, followed by a number of fingers indicating the status of a match.

The last hole on our course was a par 4 that called for a blind tee shot over a hill. Players in the final group knew they were in a tight match when, as they came over the hill, they saw all of their teammates standing in back of the final green, watching intently. On days when the match had been locked up through the efforts of the guys in groups one and two, the green was empty and half the team was already in the bus.

Fortunately, my school had a strong team. We won the county championship each of the four years I was there, and our record was something like 48–3. It wasn't so much that we were great players as that every other school in the county was unbelievably weak. Still, in my freshman year I can remember a couple of gallery-at-nine moments.

At one of them I did something that shocked my teammates. I was a complete jackass to do it, but given my state of mind at the time, I couldn't resist.

My opponent was a huge football tackle from the town next to ours. He wasn't much of a golfer, but he acted as if he were, rarely speaking to me except to tell me what a world-conquering athlete he was. This had the effect of putting me off my game just enough to keep the match tight. I was two up on him with three holes to go, when I chipped my third shot on the par-4 seventh to within a foot of the hole. Bluto was off the green in three, forty feet away, needing a miracle to keep our match alive.

He didn't concede my one-footer, so I tapped it in. But foolishly, I did so without taking the flag stick out.

"You lose the hole," he said.

"You're kidding," I said, knowing even as I said it that he wasn't.

Now I was one up with two to go. We tied the next hole, but I was still steaming when we tramped over the hill at number 9 to see all eight guys and two coaches assembled at the back of the green. The hulk had blasted his tee shot into trees on the right, while I'd hit a decent drive down the middle. Five minutes later he was over the green in four, while I was on the front fringe in two. Directly between us, at the back of the green, was the pin.

Our match was essentially over. Big boy faced an impossible pitch down the slope of a fast green, and he needed to hole it for a bogey 5 while I had a straightforward uphill chip for birdie, needing only a tie to win the match. But I was away.

I'm not sure what possessed me, but I was still seeing red—in this case, my opponent's huge red golf bag with the name of his school team emblazoned on the side of it. He had set it down at the back of the green, a few feet from his ball and on a straight extension of the line from my ball to the hole. As I prepared to stroke my approach putt, I got an idea.

To the utter bewilderment of my teammates, I tossed my putter aside and pulled a 4-iron from my bag. Taking careful aim, I then hit a low, screaming chip shot across the green and smack into Bluto's bag.

"Gee, that one got away from me," I said to him mock-sheepishly, "and, by the way, you just lost the hole."

"Whaaaat?" he said, his eyes big as volleyballs.

"Rule 26-2," said I. "Should a competitor strike the caddie or equipment of an opposing player, it is deemed to be the opponent's fault. The penalty is loss of hole in match play. Nice match."

Because of jerks like me, that rule is no longer in the books. It was deleted in 1980. Scott, I hoped, would never have to stoop to such wickedness.

I'd been sitting on the bench for a half hour or so when in the distance I saw two groups of players walking in from the ninth green, which was in the middle of the course. First came the opponents, chatting happily. As they packed into their van, I heard them tell the driver that they'd won. Not the news I wanted to hear, not in Scott's debut.

Then came the good guys. Scott was in the center of the group, bag over his shoulder. I couldn't tell much from his body language. I tried to appear cool, only vaguely interested, but as he got within earshot, I couldn't resist.

"How'd you do?" I asked.

"Pretty good," he said, lowering his eyes.

"Really?"

"Yeah . . ."

It was the coach who gave me the words I wanted to hear.

"He was a tiger," he said. "Won his match, five holes to four, and played his guy tough all day. He's got lots of courage out there."

Scott had tied the team captain for the lowest score of the day, a 40. As we packed the clubs into the trunk, I don't know who was prouder, he or I. I wasn't even angry when he told me that he'd forgotten to bring his schoolbooks with him, meaning an extra twenty minutes of driving. It gave us the opportunity for a proper postmortem.

"I really did hit the ball well . . . the par was 37, so 40 was like 38 at Sleepy Hollow . . . I could have shot 38 or better . . . missed a two-footer on one hole and had a 360 lip-out on another . . . I was driving it great—had only one hundred yards for my second shots to three of the par 4s. It's a short course, but even so . . . At 8 my guy was on in two, ten feet. I was in the woods on a root and had to sort of chop down on the ball. I knocked it to ten feet and made it for the halve."

Scott's high school golf career was off and running. He would finish the year with six wins and one loss, and a scoring average of 40 for his matches. As the summer rolled around, he was feeling good about his game.

"I want to enter a couple of those local Metropolitan PGA events," he announced. "I checked the scores on the Internet, and I think I could do pretty well. They divide most of the fields into age groups, and now that I'm fifteen I'll have a bit of an edge in the thirteen-to-fifteen-year-old group. The winning scores are always in the mid-70s, and it looks like most of the courses are shorter and easier than Sleepy."

"Think you can win one?" I asked.

"Yeah, if I play well, I really think I can."

"Wow, that would be great. It would also be a help to you in getting into college. I know it's a long way off, and you've been doing well in school, but if you want to go to one of the top places, you'll need something to distinguish yourself."

"Yeah, yeah, I know, but I don't want to think about that stuff now. I just want to play some tournaments, okay?"

"Fair enough."

We were late in getting his name on the entry lists for tournaments but managed to make the deadline for six of them. A week before the first one, I got a call at the office from Libby.

"Scott's over at the club practicing," she said. "Can you pick him up after work?"

"I suppose so," I said with a sigh. On most days, that would have been a false sigh, since few things please me more than to pick him up after golf. But this had been one hellacious day at the office, one of those days when everything that could go wrong had gone wrong.

When I got into my car, I was in a foul mood, and that was before I encountered the worst traffic jam of the summer on the FDR Drive and before I was pulled over for speeding on the Sprain Brook Parkway. A trip that normally takes less than an hour had taken two hours, and seventy-five dollars.

With about five miles to go I called the pro shop from my cell phone and asked whether Scott was there.

"Yes, he's right here. He's been waiting for you," was the reply.

"Put him on," I said through gritted teeth.

"Hi, Dad. Where are you?"

"I'm in hell, and I don't want to drive all the way up to the pro shop, so just get your ass down to the front entrance to the club and meet me there."

"But—"

"No buts. I've been in this car too long already—just be at the damned gate in five minutes."

I barely waited for him to shut the door before peeling back into traffic, and since I was still absorbed in my aggravation, I said nothing for at least three miles. Then, finally, grudgingly, "How'd you play?"

"Pretty good," he said with an unusually heavy emphasis on the "good."

"What'd you shoot?"

"Seventy-two."

"Seventy-two?" I shouted, almost losing control of the car.

"You're kidding. That's incredible, that's wonderful! I want to know every shot."

"Well, at one point I was actually two under par. I shot par on the front, nearly aced the tenth, and then birdied the twelfth to go two under. Then I doubled 13. At 18 I needed an eagle to shoot 69—and I was trying—but I made a bogey."

"Wow, that's your lowest score ever."

"Yup, by three strokes, and it could've been better. What's the best you've ever had at Sleepy?" By this time Scott had beaten me several times on our home course and was looking for other ways to make his mark against me.

"Seventy—twice. And the second time I actually chipped in for birdie at 18 to do it."

"Have you ever shot under par anywhere?"

"Yup, twice. Two under par both times, once at Mauna Lani in Hawaii, and the other time was four years ago, in a tournament at Aspetuck Valley in Connecticut—a local qualifier for the MGA Met Net Championship—which Mr. Frank and I won by like five strokes. Until that day he had never broken 80 and I had never broken 70. He shot 78, and I shot 69. Man, we were really—"

"So you've never shot one under . . ."

"No," I laughed. "Never one under. Is that now your goal?"

"Yup, at least that, and winning a tournament."

"Well, go get 'em, partner," I said. "I think you're ready, and I can tell you one thing: You've certainly brightened my day."

His first junior tournament was at a course in Connecticut called Long Shore. Since Libby had dropped him off, I had pickup duty and that suited me fine, especially since his afternoon tee time meant I wouldn't have to cut out of work early.

As always, however, I purposely arrived in time to get in some covert gallerying. I caught up with Scott's group at the fifteenth, where they were waiting on the tee. He was stalking up and down the tee, practicing swinging occasionally. He seemed very focused. He was the first to play—that was good—but his drive was not, a yank into the woods, not far from the tree behind which I had skulked.

I scurried forward to my next outpost in time to see him punch his escape shot across the fairway and into a greenside bunker. From there he blasted to fifteen feet and missed the par putt. It didn't seem to upset him, however, and at the next hole he got it right back with a drive, a wedge, and a kick-in birdie. Seventeen was a replay of 15: pulled drive, second into the sand, blast out, and two putts for a bogey.

What struck me was his demeanor. This was not the same kid with whom I'd been playing. His steps were slow and measured, his head was always forward or down. He paced off every yardage, stalked every putt, took a careful practice swing before every shot, and no matter how and where the ball flew, his reaction was the same: impassive. He carried himself like a miniature tour pro.

At 18 he hit a perfect drive, dead center and well past those of the three kids with whom he was playing. But once again his approach found a bunker. By this time I could see no reason not to make myself visible to him, so I sidled up to the scorer's table, standing close enough to peer over the official's shoulders at the list of numbers posted. With all but two groups in, only a handful of the fifty or so kids had broken 80. The low score was a 73 followed by a couple of 75s, a 77, and a 78. I wondered if Scott would be joining that sub-80 group.

As Scott settled in for his bunker shot, he caught sight of me for the first time and gave me a discreet nod. His explosion stopped six feet from the hole, and the putt for par lipped out. When it did, for the first time he showed some frustration, wrenching his putter up and down in an ax-chop movement.

He had played the last four holes in two over par. My guess was that he'd shot somewhere in the low 80s.

What followed was an interminable moment of score checking and handshaking. Finally, he walked over to me.

"Well?"

"Seventy-four."

"Seventy-four!! That's terrific. Holy crow, you finished second! In fact, had you sunk that last putt, you would've won, or at least tied for first." I hugged him as I never had, shocked him a bit I think, because he stood stiff rather than hugging me back. But there were others around, and I suspect he figured I'd embarrassed the family enough. Inside, however, I know he felt just as joyous in that hug as I did.

"Yeah, I played well," he said as we walked to the car. "The par's 69, though. I made two double bogeys."

"Wow, then, how many birdies did you make?"

"Five—three on the back. I shot two over on the back and made only one par."

"Yeah, I saw the last four holes—three bogeys and a birdie."

"You did?"

"Yup, I was doing my skulk-in-the-trees thing."

The ride home was an hour and a half in horrendous traffic, but it went by in a flash as Scott prattled on about his round and I savored every syllable.

"I putted really well . . . double-bogeyed the first hole . . . hit a 5-wood to six feet on 12 and made birdie and then birdied 13 . . . I was one over with five to go . . . hit a phone cable on my drive at 10, can you believe that?"

These were golden moments for me—the times my son actually talked to me, talked with passion, sincerity, humility, and humor. Okay, it was just golf talk, but that didn't matter.

We were communicating in the best way we knew, using a language we both spoke fluently.

Of course, not all of his outings brought such glory and glibness. In fact, the next one left him in a terse frustration-aggression mood. It was a morning event, so I called him at home to get the report.

"So how'd you do?"

"Eighty. Worst course I've ever seen. Only 5,760 yards. What you like to call a trick track."

"Where'd you finish?"

"Dunno."

"What was the lowest score you saw?"

"I didn't see any scores, Dad, okay?" The hard-edged "Dad."

"Okay, I can see you're sensitive about this, so see ya."

Click.

By mid-August, however, Scott had played in his six events and had registered four top-five finishes: a second, a third, a fourth, and a fifth. Unfortunately, the victory he'd wanted so badly had eluded him.

On the other hand, he and his cohorts on Sleepy Hollow's interclub team had blitzed their way through the Westchester County interclub matches, beating the likes of Winged Foot, Scarsdale, Ardsley, and Knollwood en route to Sleepy Hollow's first such championship in thirty-two years. In the championship match against Scarsdale C.C. they won by a score of 26–1, the only lost point coming from Scott's match, despite his having shot a 73. Needless to say, his teammates gave him a full measure of good-natured razzing.

As a by-product of all this serious competition, Scott's handicap had plummeted. He'd begun the season as a 9, and I hadn't paid much attention to his progress until the weekend when, at the first tee, I checked my own handicap on the biweekly report that the USGA provides. Scanning the alphabetized list, I found my entry: Peper, George—Handicap Index 4.2; Course Handicap 4. And the entry beneath mine was: Peper, Scott—Handicap Index 4.2; Course Handicap 4.

We were dead smack even, down to a tenth of a stroke.

Indeed, Scott's game had become a near mirror of mine. He had developed into a relatively long and straight driver (although his swing remained far prettier than mine). His iron play was better than yours truly's—as is the iron play of nearly all 26 million golfers in America—and his short game had become almost as sharp as mine. (He was better on the flips and flops—the show-off shots—while I could still outdo him on the more pedestrian chips and bump shots.) On the greens I was a bit more reliable except under tournament pressure, when he routinely rose to the occasion while I choked.

We played in only one tournament together that summer, the Metropolitan Golf Association's annual Father-Son Championship, a one-day better-ball event that was held in Connecticut at the New Canaan Country Club. Had I putted as well as Scott did that day—in fact, had I putted even reasonably—we might have won. After a front side of even-par 36, thanks to a forty-footer and two fifteen-footers by Scott, we were in great position. (It was a tricky course, and 74 won the event.) But then I missed short putts at each of the first two holes on the back nine. That set the tone for two hours of shared ineptitude. Five over with three holes to go, we pulled out the stops at the sixteenth hole, a long, uphill 5, both of us hitting drivers off the deck for our second shots. We both nailed them, too, leaving less than thirty yards for an up-and-down birdie. Then we both skulled our wedges and made 6. We finished with a 78.

Still, it was a fun day in the country, highlighted by one moment I'll never forget. Scott and I were standing on the side of a green, waiting for one of our fellow competitors to pitch on, when I directed his attention to the tee of an adjoining hole.

There, sitting side by side on a bench, was an exceedingly corpulent father-son duo—each of them looked to be about five-foot-nine and 250 pounds. Each wore a baseball cap to keep the sun off his florid face, each waggled his driver with the club's shaft angled forty-five degrees toward the sky.

"Look at those two," I said. "It's amazing how similar they are. They even sit the same way, with their legs splayed out."

Scott laughed at the sight. "Of course, when you're built like that, you really don't have many options."

Then I looked at him and me. We were each standing on our left leg, the right leg crossed behind with the toe pointed down, while simultaneously leaning on our putters.

"You and I, on the other hand, have options," I said, pointing to our flamingo poses. "We just don't seem to be taking them."

"Wow," he said. "And I always stand like this, too. That's scary."

No, I thought, it's wonderful.

As Labor Day approached, Scott made an announcement, actually a veiled request.

"I don't want to play in the junior club championship this year," he said.

"Why not?" I asked, incredulous. His opponent, young Sanossian, had gone to college, leaving Scott as the odds-on favorite to take the title.

"Because I want to qualify for the real club championship instead," said Scott, "and the club rules say that if you play in the junior, you can't play in the real thing."

I had been aware of this rule and had always thought it was odd. The club rules allowed members to compete simultaneously in the senior championship and the club championship, so why not the junior? The truth is, I think many of the rules at my club, and at country clubs in general, are a little silly, a reflection of the paranoia of club boards and the fundamental lack of confidence they have in their members. Dress codes, restricted tee times, and other "club policies" generally arise because the members can't be trusted to control themselves. Rather than add offensive regulations, I say subtract offensive members.

But I didn't have a say in this matter, just a question for Scott.

"Do you think you're ready? I mean, you could waltz to the junior title and get a great trophy. You realize that because you're a kid, you can't compete in any of the lower flights. It's the championship flight or nothing."

"Yeah, I know that," he said.

"It's a flight of just eight guys, and since the defending champion is exempt from qualifying, there are only seven spots available. Usually, at least twenty guys go for it, including me."

"I know that, too," he said with a smile. "And usually, you don't make it."

"Thanks for reminding me. Well, the good news for you, my friend, is that this year I'm not going to attempt to qualify because Mom and I have to go to your cousin's wedding in Texas on the weekend of the first round of the championship. So I won't be able to beat your ass. But if you want to go for it, hey, why not? With all the tournament experience you've had this summer, you might just be ready, despite being fifteen years old."

"I'm ready," he said.

He was indeed. In the first of the two rounds he shot 79—not a sizzling score, but enough to place him among the top six scores in the traditionally weak field of aspirants. The next day he was paired with three of the longest hitters in the club, and I feared that he'd try to keep up with them. I didn't want to start giving him advice, but I couldn't resist leaving a note for him in the locker we shared: "You're paired with a trio of gorillas. Don't try to keep up with them, just play your own game—fairways and greens—and you'll beat all three of them."

It was trite advice but the best I could do. I wanted him to know I was there for him on his big day. I have no idea whether he read or heeded it. I was too chicken to ask and he was too proud to volunteer, but for whatever reasons, my prediction came through. Scott beat all three of the long-hitting adults with whom he was paired, and his second-round 78 put him in a tie for fourth among the qualifiers.

"He had a couple of chances to come unglued out there, and he never did," said one of his playing companions. "You should be very proud of not only his game but his head."

I was. I was very proud—and I was also very jealous. Scott had broken 80 twice in qualifying, something I'd never managed to do. On that same weekend, playing two rounds on the same course, but in the casual company of my buddies, I'd shot 76-73. Had I been qualifying, I would have tacked a quick five to ten strokes on each of those scores. Scott, I was delighted to see once more, didn't take the apple the way Dad did. I guessed it was time for me to start living my dreams vicariously through my son.

The other seven guys in the championship flight were an average of about thirty-five years old, more than twice Scott's age, and one of them was my good friend John Ervasti, one of the two best players in the club and a veteran of three U.S. Amateur Championships. He had not been on his game and he and Scott had tied at 157.

"Wow," I said to my son, "do you realize that now there are

only three degrees of separation between you and Tiger Woods?"

"Huh?"

"Well, you are now in a championship bracket with Mr. Ervasti. In 1995 Mr. Ervasti played in the U.S. Amateur at Newport and lost in the second round to Steve Scott. A year later Steve Scott made it to the final of the U.S. Amateur at Pumpkin Ridge before losing to Tiger Woods."

"Well, the amateur's a bit different than the Sleepy Hollow club championship, Dad."

"Hey, it's the people who count, and the way I see it, only three people stand between you and Tiger."

"Sure, Dad. You keep believing that."

"No, *you* keep believing that, and who knows what you might achieve?"

"Fine."

The following weekend, at virtually the same moment that Scott teed off for his opening-round match, Libby and I boarded a flight to Houston. The instant I got inside the terminal I phoned the club.

"They aren't in yet," said one of the assistant pros, "but word is that Scott was one down through 14. Call back in about a half hour."

This was torture. Why wasn't the first round of the Sleepy Hollow club championship televised by ESPN or the Golf Channel or someone? Didn't they know I was dying here?

We had an hour before our connecting flight to Austin. Twenty minutes later I called back.

"They're just coming up 18. Don't know whether the match is still going or they're just playing in. Call back in five."

Oh, the agony of the long-distance golf father. Three minutes later I got the news.

"Scotty holed a beauty on 18 to tie the match. They're about to head off number 1 in sudden death."

I was able to hang in for one hole—which they tied—and then Libby and I had to board the plane. It was not until an hour later, in the Austin terminal, that I learned Scott had lost on the second play-off hole.

"I was three down after nine but came back . . . We both shot like 76 . . . Yeah, I putted pretty well, especially the one at 18 . . . I really blew it in the play-off, though. Made double when a bogey would've probably kept it going."

"Hey, you have nothing to be ashamed of," I said. "Enjoy the fact that you got as far as you did—but don't have any wild parties while Mom and I are gone."

Scott had thought his season ended with that loss in the club championship, but at the last minute a space had opened up in the final Met PGA Junior event of the season. It was a big one, too. Whereas most of the junior tournaments are contested on comparatively undistinguished courses, this one was to be played at Stanwich Country Club. The site of the 2002 U.S. Mid-Amateur Championship, Stanwich is generally agreed to be the most difficult course in the New York metropolitan area, with a rating from the back tees of 76.0 and a USGA Slope rating of 144. Of course, the kids would not be playing it from the tips, but that didn't matter much because the difficulty of Stanwich is in its tightly bunkered and fiendishly contoured greens.

There was only one hitch. Scott was not quite in the field to play the event. In order to get in, he needed to show up on the morning of the tournament, and the earlier he appeared, the better his chances of playing. That meant arriving at the course well before the first tee time, which was at 7:30 A.M.

"Do you really want to do this?" Libby asked him the night before.

"Yeah, Mom," he said. "I'm hitting the ball well right now, and after this tournament I won't be able to play again until next spring."

"Okay," she said with a sigh that belied her endless pleasure in serving her sons.

The next morning she and Scott arose at 5:15. They arrived at Stanwich at 6:45, half an hour before any tournament officials appeared. At that point Libby returned home, leaving Scott to await word on whether he'd be worked into the starting times.

At eight o'clock she got a phone call from him. They'd found him a spot. In fact, they'd fitted him into the first group of the day, with three other fifteen-year-olds.

The three other kids—all of them low handicappers—returned scores of 88, 91, and 93. Those would be among the better rounds on that day, as in the field of fifty players only six broke 90.

Scott Peper shot a three-over-par 75 and won the tournament by eight strokes, beating not only everyone in his own age group but all the sixteen- and seventeen-year-olds as well. By his own admission it was the finest round of golf he'd ever played.

"I guess I saved the best for last," he said when he called me at the office that afternoon.

"I guess you did," said I. "I want to hear every single shot of that round, but it has to be the right time and place. This calls for a celebration. Tell Mom we're going out to dinner tonight." Beyond wanting to honor Scott, I figured his early-rising chauffeur deserved the night off.

"Sounds good. Can we do Italian?"

"Of course."

It wasn't one minute after ordering his mozzarella sticks and ravioli Bolognese that Scott got down to business.

"You remember the first hole is a short downhill dogleg left? I hit driver 9-iron to eight feet and nearly made it. Second hole I killed a drive, then hit a 4-iron . . ."

What ensued was a twenty-minute recap, interrupted with occasional questions and comments from me, of all seventy-five glorious, victorious strokes. As I watched him talk, I thought, this is like being at a Tiger Woods press conference. Only better.

I hope he never loses the urge to give me those shot-by-shot recounts of his rounds. No matter where our respective paths may take us and no matter how separated we may become geographically, I hope that now and then Scott will call me, whether from Pebble Beach or Podunk, and share the details of his latest round.

In his case alone I shall never tire of listening.

9

Mobility

With the end of summer both Scott and I once again put golf on a six-month back burner. Early that fall, however, we found ourselves in our old teacher-student roles again, but for a totally different reason: driving lessons. Scott's sixteenth birthday loomed on November 2, and he was determined to take his road test on that day.

New York is one of the more progressive—or lenient, as you choose to view it—states in terms of putting kids behind the wheel. I'm not sure whether this relates, as in some states, to the number of family-run farms in the rural areas—ergo, kids who need to operate tractors and other heavy machinery—or whether it simply reflects the generally liberal New York mind-set. Whatever the reason, Scott was a beneficiary, being a resident of New York but a student in New Jersey. Since Jersey kids aren't permitted to drive until age seventeen, and since Scott was one of the older kids in his grade, he slid into the driver's seat more than a year before most of his classmates.

The truth is, he had driven the car once before that, at the age of nine. One spring weekend I'd taken him and Tim on a fishing trip to the Catskill Mountains. We arrived at the campsite for dinner on Friday, and as a special activity that evening I'd planned to take them to Monticello Raceway, a venerable old trotter track that was just a few miles away. (Tim and I had done this a couple of years before, and we'd had a ball. I'd placed two-dollar bets for him and me on a half dozen or so races, and he'd actually won a few bucks.)

But this time, as we approached the raceway, something seemed strange. There was no traffic at all, and when we got there, we saw why. It was closed. We were a week too early for the racing season. So there we were, just the three of us, in an enormous barren parking lot at 7:00 P.M. with nothing to do. Then I got an inspiration.

"Gentlemen," I said, "you are about to do something much more exciting than watching horses race, and you are going to do it right here in this parking lot. Can you guess what it is?"

They both sat in mystified silence until Scott gave it his best shot.

"Play golf?"

"No, Scott," I said, "this will be even more fun than golf. Right here and now you are both going to drive the car."

Their eyes lit up instantly.

"Cool!" said twelve-year-old Tim.

"You're joking," said Scott.

"I'm not. We won't be going onto the road, but I'm going to let each of you take us for a spin within the confines of this parking lot." I put the car in Park and said, "Timothy, take the wheel."

As we walked behind the car to switch seats, I stopped and opened the trunk. From the backup set of golf clubs that had taken up permanent residence there, I withdrew a 4-wood.

"Dad," said Scott, "I thought you said we weren't going to play golf."

"We're not," said I. "Now get up there in the passenger's seat next to your brother. I'm gonna ride in the back."

"You are?" they said in unison, perplexed and, I suspect, a bit concerned.

"Yeah, and you'll see why in a moment." I positioned myself squarely in the center of the rear seat and poked the grip end of my 4-iron between the two front seats and down into the driver-side footwell, where I pressed the butt cap to the pad of the brake pedal. "This is how we're going to keep the car from going too fast."

Both boys listened intently as I explained the basics of operating the car. Then, as I clenched my fist tightly around the 4-wood clubhead, Tim slid the shift lever into Drive.

He moved forward slowly and tentatively but soon got a feel for the gas pedal and brake and within less than a minute was driving smoothly, navigating us deftly through a Dad-designated slalom of lampposts dotted across the lot. No jerky motions, no swerves, no sudden stops. In a pinch I think he could have driven us home.

After fifteen minutes or so his turn was up. We moved the driver's seat forward as far as it could go, and Scott got behind the wheel. Before I could say, "Remember to apply the gas slowly," the car bolted forward with such horrific speed that I swear we were briefly airborne. Instinctively, I plunged forward on my graphite-shafted hand brake and we screech-slammed to a stop that stripped six months of tread off my tires. Seat belts saved the boys, but I nearly impaled myself on my cleek.

"Okay, *that* was an adventure," I said, returning the shift lever to Park as my sons emerged from their brief terror in a burst of laughter. Suffice it to say that Scott required a bit more coaching than Tim. But he got it eventually.

Nearly seven years had passed when, on a Sunday afternoon in September 2000, Scott and I pulled into another empty parking lot, this time at a local office complex.

I didn't give him much in the way of coaching. He'd been observing his mother and me for months, and like most kids on the brink of driving, he already knew the mechanics of driving a car. Besides, I'd learned from my golf-teaching forays that in Scott's case less is more. I also realized that driver education, in contrast to golfer education, allows the teacher to bark commands at the same moment the pupil is performing. "Slow down *now* as you approach the corner" can be heeded far more easily than "Slow down *now* as you approach impact."

What struck me, however, was Scott's demeanor. In contrast to the cocky, know-it-all fakir of the fairway I'd come to know, Scott the student driver was delightfully deferential, inquisitive, and needful. A model pupil.

"Did I accelerate enough into that turn?" "Was that stop too sudden?" "Am I between the lines?" "Can we try the parallel parking again?" Ultimately, he wanted to pass the road test, but what he needed first was confirmation and approval from me.

Those few training sessions made me wistful for our first golf days together, just after he'd been bitten by the bug, when his only source of guidance, the first and last word on technique, was yours truly. Those days seemed like a long time ago. The sad truth—sad for me at least—was that Scott was growing up quickly in every way, and that with these first tentative forays behind the wheel he was testing his wings for an eventual flight from the nest.

On his birthday he did indeed pass his test and at the same moment took a big step out of childhood. Suddenly gone were the evenings when he'd emerge from his room, run down the hall, and flop onto the bed with us, clad only in his boxer shorts, his waist just flabby enough to show two dimples at the small of his back. Gone were the days on the golf course when, if we were being held up by players in front of us, he'd walk over to me and rest his head on my shoulder. (I was never quite sure whether that gesture meant "It's great being out here with you" or "My legs are tired." Either way, I loved it.)

One day that winter I arrived home from an extended business trip and was briefly shocked by the young fellow who greeted me at the back door. Scott's braces were gone, the shy metallic grin replaced by a big, perfect, white-toothed smile. He was in need of a haircut, and the color of his hair had seemed to darken a shade or two. It also seemed more dense than I'd remembered: incredibly thick and wavy—JFK Jr. hair. Maybe it was the hair, but he seemed at least an inch or so taller than before I'd left. When he stood up straight, he wasn't much shorter than I.

"You're five-foot-ten, maybe five-eleven," I said. "That's taller than Nicklaus or Palmer and just about the ideal height for golfers."

"I'm just glad I'm not a shrimp anymore," he said in a deep voice that suddenly sounded exactly like his older brother's. "Two years ago I was the shortest kid in my class. Now there are only two or three guys who are taller."

He'd added no weight—he still tipped the scales at barely 135 pounds—but the baby fat was gone, and although there was little muscle tone, I sensed that that was to come. There was so much to come.

The newly mobile Scott began to spend markedly more time out with his friends and less time home with his parents. The majority of his waking hours at home were spent in his bedroom behind closed doors, where in the manner of over-privileged American teenagers he engaged in relentless electronic multitasking: sending Instant Messages to his buddies on the computer while simultaneously listening to Dave Matthews, watching MTV, surfing the Net for sites pornographic and otherwise, burning CDs into his MP3 player, jabbering on the phone, and, occasionally, doing his homework.

As a result, he revealed little of his world to Libby and me. Even during dinner conversation he was less than forthcoming, despite frequent and dogged interrogation by his mother. Answers were typically monosyllabic. I could still get him talking about golf, but on most other subjects, notably his schoolwork and his social life, he remained as enigmatic as the Sphinx.

This absence of forthright communication was far more frustrating to Libby than to me, and it wasn't long before she resorted to guerrilla tactics of intelligence gathering. Her favorite gambit was to pause a bit more than briefly outside the closed door to Scott's room, hoping to hear something revelatory in his phone chatter. But she was not above rifling through his backpack and riffling through the papers on his desk—and I must admit, neither was I.

Invariably, however, this sleuthing turned up little or nothing: no blueprints for nuclear bombs, no hypodermic needles, not even a copy of *Playboy*. But one evening after an extended stand-by-the-door session, Libby broke a huge story.

"I think he has a girlfriend," she said.

"What? No way. What makes you say that?" I said.

"He's been on the phone for over half an hour with someone, and it's the tone of his voice—more giggly than usual, not the guy-to-guy voice. He's being much too nice—sweet—and we both know Scott doesn't do sweet."

"Well, he's sixteen years old," I said. "I guess it's about time."

Not long after that, Scott announced to Libby that he was having a friend over on Friday night.

"Oh, who?" she said.

"Amanda," said he.

Amanda, I must say, was an excellent choice. Tall, blond, and . . . well, let's just say Scott wasn't the only one in the family to have noticed her.

Their relationship lasted a few weeks. Since neither could drive at night, they'd hang out at our house or hers, presumably watching TV, playing video games, listening to music, and making out. One Saturday evening while Amanda was over, Scott's bedroom door closed, and neither Libby nor I made him open it.

"But you talk to him tomorrow," she said.

"About what?" I asked.

"You know what—sex!"

Gulp.

"Scott," I said the next morning as we drove to the golf course, "your mother and I are a little concerned about where you might be headed in your relationship with Amanda. I'm not going to ask you to tell me exactly where that is, because I don't want to know," I said, despite the fact that nothing was of greater interest to me. "Instead, I want to tell you something. Don't do anything stupid. We trust you—that's why we left you alone last night—but please, for your own sake, our sake, and Amanda's sake, don't do anything stupid."

My innate terror of confrontation prevented me from getting any more specific than that. For whatever reason, their dating ended about a week later, and soon after that Amanda was seen regularly with another lad in Scott's class. If Scott was crushed, he didn't let it show, and Libby and I soothed ourselves with the notion that it was Scott who ended things.

The only other aspect of his life where we were able to gather any hard data was his academic performance. We'd always known he was a bright kid. His scores on the various standardized tests had been good, and throughout grade school he'd gotten high marks and laudatory comments from his teachers. But Scott never talked much about his school-work unless we pumped him for specifics. He did his home-work but rarely seemed to kill himself. Oh, occasionally he'd stay up past midnight working on a paper or cramming for an exam, but even as he entered high school, he never seemed terribly taxed, despite a full schedule of Advanced Placement courses.

As his sophomore year came to a close and the idea of college began to loom, his mother and I started to take a more aggressive interest. This time it was I who hit investigative pay dirt.

Scott had been struggling with his putting, complaining about a lack of confidence over the short ones, and so I'd found a copy of Bob Rotella's *Putting Out of Your Mind*. I was dropping off the book on his bed when I noticed an official report of some kind from his school. It showed that Scott's grade point average of 4.3 placed him first in his class. His actual grades gave him something around a 3.8 (A minus), but the school policy was to increase by half a point any grade earned in an Advanced Placement course, and four of Scott's six courses were A.P.s.

"Why didn't you tell us you were number one in your class?" I asked him that night.

"I don't know," he said, eyes to the floor. "It's not really official. You know the school doesn't reveal actual class rank.

What that paper says is that grade point averages in my class range from a low of 2.6 to a high of 4.3. It doesn't say I'm number one. Besides, it's not really fair that they jump all those A.P. grades. And it's only for this year."

"Official or not, fair or not, one year or not, it's terrific news. I can't believe you wouldn't want to share it with Mom and me," I said.

"Whatever" was all he said.

Whatever. Well, whatever combination of Libby's and my genes converged to create his brainpower, it was the right one. That June we received the scores of the four A.P. exams he'd taken. (The A.P. exams are administered nationally, in part to help colleges and universities determine the strongest candidates for admission. They're graded on a curve from 1 to 5, with 5 being the best. A score of 4 or 5 will often exempt a student from college requirements in that area of study.) The results of the four exams Scott took in his sophomore year: calculus 5, European history 5, Latin 5, and physics 5.

Of course, those scores merely proved that he knew his subjects well. They said little about his native aptitude. For that we'd have to wait a few months, when he'd take the SATs.

In the meantime Scott had more important tests on his mind: golf tests. It had been only a mediocre year for him on the high school team. The graduation of two seniors meant that he'd moved up to second position on the roster, and his scores—averaging 39 for the nine-hole matches—showed that he should have been playing number one. But Scott had no problem playing at the second spot.

"Eric's a senior and he's played on the team for four years," he said. "He's not much worse than I am—in fact, he hits the ball better, he just can't putt. Besides, this way I get easier opponents. Usually, in our league for some reason, the second man on the team is a lot worse than the number one player."

Indeed, Scott had won all but two of his fourteen matches and earned a spot on the all-county team. But these were small-pond achievements and he knew it.

"Do you think I could get into an AJGA event?" he asked me one day. He was referring to the American Junior Golf Association, the PGA Tour of competitive golf for kids. They run a couple dozen high-quality tournaments each year, showcasing the nation's best high school players. Many of those kids go on to earn scholarships and become college standouts, with several becoming tour pros. Tiger Woods, Phil Mickelson, and David Duval all showed their mettle as top AJGA players.

"You'd have to qualify," I said, "and that's not easy. But I know the executive director. Let me give him a call."

Through the good graces of the AJGA's Stephen Hamblin, Scott got a sort of sponsor's exemption into the Sand Barrens Invitational in southern New Jersey, about three hours from our home.

He practiced hard for the two weeks before and got his game into as good shape as I'd ever seen it. As a pretournament training treat I gave him a surprise.

"On Sunday, when we head down to the tournament, I've arranged for us to play a practice round at a special place," I said. "Pine Valley."

"Cool," he said. "Isn't that like the hardest course in the world?"

"I don't know about hardest," I said, "but it is ranked by *GOLF Magazine* as the number one course in the world."

"Awesome," he said.

Awesome it was, a beautiful summer day that brought Scott, me, and *GOLF Magazine* Managing Editor Peter Morrice together with Pine Valley member and old friend Jim Finegan. Finegan, a retired Philadelphia advertising executive and frequent contributor to *GOLF*'s pages, is arguably the most knowledgeable person in the world on the golf courses of the British Isles, not to mention one of the game's most graceful writers. He has written three marvelous guidebooks to those courses, although calling them guidebooks is like calling *Moby-Dick* a primer on whale fishing.

Finegan is also a former senior champion at Pine Valley, despite a distinct lack of physical might. He's five feet seven inches tall max, can't weigh more than 130 pounds, and has the self-described "wrists of a sixth-grade girl." Jim hits his drive "precisely 187 yards and not an inch longer," but he hits it 187 yards dead straight every time. In the course of eighteen holes he rarely strikes more than three or four shots with less than 100 percent purity. On one occasion he and I played with Callaway's chief club designer, Dick Helmstetter. After watching him for a few holes, Dick said, "Would you be willing to come to California and live the rest of your life in our test facility? Now that Paul Runyan is gone, you may be the only man on earth who swings the club at just sixty miles per hour yet stripes it perfectly every time."

In our round that day Finegan, at age seventy-two, covered Pine Valley in eighty-one immaculate shots. Rarely have I witnessed a more impressive display of ball striking.

Scott also put on a show. I'd prepared him with tales of terror of Pine Valley, a course I'd played a dozen or so times but rarely with much success. "It doesn't play as tough as it looks," I warned him, "but then, no course plays as tough as Pine Valley looks." The first six holes routinely eat my lunch, and after that I kind of lose the fire. The best score I've managed there is 81—and it felt like a 65.

But Scott had developed a better game, and a far stronger mind, than his father's. After an effortless driver/9-iron par at the first, he birdied number 2, maybe the hardest hole on the course, and got through the dastardly first third of the course in even par. After that a couple of bad drives and a few over-aggressive tactical decisions caught up with him, and he finished with a 78.

"Young man," said Finegan after the round, "you have all the shots. What you need now is a game."

On our way out Scott asked me what our venerable friend had meant by that. "I think he's saying that you need to start putting it all together, get some consistency, and start deploying all those shots at the right moments—start managing the course better, using your head as well as your swing. Basically, you need to start getting more out of your talent. Look at Finegan—he gets the absolute maximum out of his."

"Yeah, he does. But he's almost like a freak. Getting a game, as he calls it, is not easy," said Scott.

"Tell me about it," I said. "No one said playing golf is easy, and from my experience, playing great golf is damned near impossible."

Scott was to get a stronger dose of reality later that week. About seventy of the eighty-four kids who assembled for that AJGA event, in Finegan's words, had games. On the practice tee, except for their Bermuda shorts, they looked like pros—not just in their swings but in their mannerisms, the way they handled themselves. And the shots that came off their clubfaces were not just powerful, they had character: spin, trajectory, and shape.

The day before the tournament proper they held a "junior-am," in which I played. My team's junior turned out to be one of the nation's top girl players, Elizabeth Janangelo from West Hartford, Connecticut. Such a prime prospect was she that she'd already been accepted at Duke University, despite not yet having started her senior year in high school. And boy, could she play.

Although not a particularly big girl, she drove the ball as

far as I did, and much straighter. On most holes she had wedges to the green, and most of those wedges she stuck close. The next day she opened the tournament with a 66 and went on to win, her fourth AJGA title.

The majority of the competitors were from points south. Scott was paired with two kids from North Carolina and Alabama, both of them schooled veterans who managed their swings, their games, and themselves methodically, determinedly, and confidently.

I was somehow able to stifle my curiosity until the twelfth green, where I arrived just in time to see Scott make a bogey.

"How's it going?" I asked nervously.

"Well, I was okay—one over through seven," he said, "and then I made back-to-back triples."

He would suffer a similar fate on the inward nine en route to his most inglorious moment as a golfer: an 87 in a national event.

I consoled him as best I could, not really knowing what to say. ("Want a beer?" was probably my best line.) "Well, one thing I can tell you is that you did your best. I know that, because I saw your focus and routine, intact right down to the last approach shot. You didn't give up, and I'm proud of you for that. And by the way, you didn't have the highest score in the field. One kid in the group in front of yours was even par through six and then took a 13 at number 7. That destroyed him and he shot 96.

"Besides, you have four 5s on your A.P. exams. I bet there's not another kid in the field who can claim that. And that's a lot more important than your golf score."

At that point Scott rolled his eyes, and I realized I was *over*consoling. The truth is, he wasn't as crushed as I thought. Mostly he was thunderstruck.

"I just never thought I could do that," he said with a rueful chuckle. Then he drifted into his usual postmortem. "You know, I parred eleven of the eighteen holes. I just went fifteen over on the other seven. I didn't have any doubles—just four triples. With pars on those four holes, it's a 75. It's actually pretty funny."

He'd be needing that perspective on the second day when things got better but only a bit. With an 82 he missed the cut and finished among the bottom half dozen or so players in the field. It was a very humbling experience. If Scott hadn't realized it before, he knew now that he just didn't have the stuff to become a nationally prominent player, and likely never would.

What he could possibly become is a prominent local player and without question, a top club golfer, and for the remainder of that summer, that became the focus of his thoughts. The Sleepy Hollow club championship loomed. Last year he had qualified. This year he was determined to go further than that, maybe even win.

On rounds of 77-72 Scott earned the fourth of seven spots, just as he had a year earlier. On the morning of the first-round matches I went to the club to check his progress. His opponent was a friend of mine, a corporate lawyer three times Scott's age.

"Scott hit sort of a skanky drive off 1," said one of the assistant pros, "and I didn't see their match again until 11, where he was way left of the green, down near the creek. If I had to guess, I'd say he was behind."

I sat down in a chair on the patio just behind the eighteenth green and waited and watched. At length I saw his match on the distant seventeenth green. He'd missed the green and made no better than bogey. When he teed off second at 18, I figured the match was probably over, and they were just playing the hole in rather than walking in—either that or he was on the ropes.

Both Scott and his opponent reached the green of the uphill 405-yard par 4, each with a lengthy putt. When they got close enough, I gave Scott the "So what's up?" signal. He responded with an index finger followed by a thumb pointed toward the sky—he was one up!

His opponent putted first and, from sixty feet, nearly holed it for a birdie before tapping in. Now, from about fifty feet below the hole, Scott needed to two-putt for the win. He took four practice strokes (wasn't that too many?) and then rapped the ball firmly up the slope. It stopped two feet below the hole—a gimme most days, but not in this situation. I would have missed it comprehensively—probably left it short—but Scott stepped up and slam-dunked it into the back of the hole. He'd made it to the final four!

Scott's opponent in the semifinals turned out to be the defending champion, another forty something who had been good enough in his heyday to win not only the Sleepy Hollow title but the Winged Foot club championship as well. Scott played well, but it wasn't enough, and he lost 3 and 2.

"Well," I said as we headed home, "last year you made it to the quarterfinals, this year the semis. Next year maybe you'll go all the way." There was no reply, but I know he was thinking the same thing.

A couple of weeks later I ran into one of the other competitors from the championship flight.

"I played with your son in round two of the qualifying," he said. "Man, is he impressive."

"Really?" I said. "Thanks for saying that. I guess he's become a pretty good ball striker."

"Well, it wasn't so much the ball striking that impressed me," he said, "it was his control, his focus, his unflappable manner out there. He has talent, but frankly, there are other kids in the club who are more talented. What Scott has is an ability to hold himself together, to post a score, whether his game is on or not. There were a couple of moments during the round when he got himself into some big trouble, could've blown to a triple bogey or worse, but he gutted out a double and then came back with pars and birdies. How old is he, sixteen, and he's one of the more polished competitors in the club."

I had only one regret about that club championship. The field had lacked one player that Scott wanted badly to go up against: me.

For two or three years we'd been talking, teasing, and fantasizing about facing each other in the club championship. In the mid-1990s I'd qualified a couple of times, back when he was too young. Then when he'd made it a year ago, I'd been unable to enter because of a conflict with my niece's wedding.

Finally, it had seemed, in 2001 we'd have a chance to take each other on. Scott's game was clearly ready, and even mine was starting to click. That July, I'd shot a 71 that included a 33 on the front side. I was set to give the kid a run for his money.

Then in early August I began feeling a recurrent pain in my left hip. It didn't seem like much at first, just a quick stab every now and then, mostly when I tied my shoes or got in and out of the car, and so I didn't give it much thought. But within a couple of weeks it began to return with greater frequency and then expanded into a generalized ache whenever I was on my feet for more than a few minutes.

Months earlier Scott and I had sent in an entry for the Nike Father-Son Championship, a terrific tournament that annually attracts more than six hundred teams from around the country to Myrtle Beach, South Carolina, for a three-day golf and funfest. Now, just a few days before that event, I began to wonder whether I'd be able to play three rounds of golf.

I wasn't—at least not capably. Even in a cart I struggled,

limping back and forth to my ball and making odd spin-out swings to avoid stressing the leg. As Scott played mid-70s golf, including one nine-hole stretch with four birdies, I dragged Team Peper to a finish near the cellar of our flight.

Just after Labor Day I went to an orthopedist and got the news. I had an aggressive form of osteoarthritis, and not just in my left hip but in both of them. It came as no surprise. My mother had had the same condition, as had my grandmother—it limped in the family.

"Medication will ease the pain," said the doctor, handing me a prescription for Celebrex, "but sooner or later you'll have to have surgery."

"What kind of surgery?" I asked.

"Arthroplasty—a total hip replacement," he said. "Ultimately, on the right hip as well."

That was a shock. After all, just a year earlier, I'd celebrated turning fifty with three golf buddies of the same age by playing fifty holes of golf in one day, and I'd walked all fifty holes. Now I couldn't walk five holes without being reduced to a Quasimodo-like shuffle.

It didn't seem fair. At my age I didn't deserve crippling arthritis, didn't deserve to be facing major surgery. The choice I now faced was not a pleasant one. If I didn't go for the operation, my quality of life would be sharply diminished, and my golf days were over; if I did go for it, who knows what the result might be?

I wallowed in self-pity for a day or two before I realized there were many things I didn't deserve from the first half century of my life—all of them positive, and beginning with my family.

Just as on Labor Day weekend Scott had made me proud with his performance in the club championship, his brother on the following weekend had made me equally proud with his most impressive work to date as an actor, in an off-Broadway production of Sam Shepard's *Buried Child*. Tim's role had included a passionate and powerful soliloquy in the last act that had brought tears to his parents' eyes. Yes, when it came to the two most important things in life, both Libby and I had been extremely lucky, and we were about to appreciate our blessings as never before.

On the Tuesday morning following Tim's performance I was at my desk in New York City, going through my usual routine. There's a TV in my office and the first thing I do each day is tune it to the Golf Channel for the 7:00 A.M. rebroadcast of the previous night's *Golf Central* news show. Then I flip to the *Today* show and half listen to Katie and Matt as I dig into the day's tasks.

There was nothing remarkable about that Tuesday morning until Katie Couric broke into the patter with the world-altering words "We've just had a report that a plane has struck one of the towers of the World Trade Center." America's most harrowing day had begun.

My first thought was of Tim at NYU, living off campus in an apartment just a few blocks from the Trade Center area. A call to his cell phone got only his recorded message. Next I phoned Libby at home. No answer there either, which was unusual for nine in the morning. Nearly two hours passed before I heard from her.

"Where the hell have you been?" I said angrily before she could say more than hello. "I've been trying you and trying Tim all morning. I still haven't heard from him. Do you even realize what's going on?"

"Yes," she said in a strangely quiet and polite voice. "Tim is fine. I've talked to him. George, I'm at Fran's."

"Fran's—what the hell are you doing there?" I said, still irked.

"Stacey."

"What about Stacey?" I said, referring to the daughter of two of our oldest and dearest friends, Fran and Semo Sennas.

"George," Libby said, her voice beginning to crack, "Stacey works at the World Trade Center."

"Oh my God," I said. "I'll be there as fast as I can."

The remainder of that day is a blur. With all the major bridges and tunnels out of Manhattan blocked, the drive home, with two stranded colleagues hitching a ride, was a circuitous five hours. On the kitchen phone was a voice message from Tim—he wanted to be home, too, but he was having trouble getting out of Manhattan. He'd just missed catching literally the last vehicle across the George Washington Bridge, a flatbed pickup onto which two dozen desperate people had jumped.

At about five o'clock Tim called to say he was taking the Hoboken Ferry. An hour later Scott and I picked him up near Edgewater, New Jersey. He was clearly shaken.

"I was at St. Vincent's Hospital most of the afternoon," he said.

"Why?" I asked.

"It's around the corner from my apartment, and that's where they said the survivors would be taken, so I went over hoping to get some news on Stacey. I posed as her brother. But they had no record of her. It was all so weird. All of these stretchers and ambulances were lined up on Seventh Avenue, all these E.R. people were there, ready to go to work, but nobody was brought to the hospital. Nobody."

Stacey Sennas McGowan was a remarkable, radiant woman of thirty-eight, with a devoted husband and two darling little girls, aged five and three. I'd known her all her life, watched her grow from a tomboy into a vivacious dark-eyed young beauty whose megawatt smile reflected her one-in-a-million warmth and generosity of spirit. She had been president of her class at Nyack High School as well as an outstanding lacrosse player, good enough to play for Boston College, where her friends nicknamed her Crush for the exuberant hugs with which she greeted everyone. "Hers was a hug that would render every other hug you receive for the rest of your life a complete insult to hugging," said her best friend, Pat Corry, in delivering her eulogy. But Stacey was also a bright and gifted businesswoman who had risen to the position of managing director at the investment firm of Sandler O'Neill. She'd had much to live for, much to give, and so much life ahead of her.

It was nearly seven o'clock that evening when the boys and I reached the Sennas home, and by that time a dozen or so others had gathered to offer what help and hope they could. It was then that I learned that the situation was even worse.

Welles Crowther, the twenty-three-year-old son of another couple we'd been close to for years, was also among the missing. Like Stacey, he'd been an outstanding lacrosse player, first at Nyack and then at Boston College. In fact, one summer he'd coached at a local lacrosse camp that Tim had attended. And thanks in part to Welles's tutelage, Tim had been named the top offensive player of the camp.

Welles had the outgoing charm of his father, Jeff, and although he'd only been in the business world for a few months, he'd already begun to distinguish himself. Like Stacey, however, he'd been employed at Sandler O'Neill, on the 104th floor of Tower Two.

Libby would spend most of the next ten days with Fran Sennas, while making frequent visits to Alison Crowther, as hope gave way to resignation. No words can begin to describe their loss, or the loss of so many others as a result of that brutal day.

I'm not sure to what degree September 11 changed the lives of people throughout the nation, but I know that in the New York area things are still not back to normal and may never be. The grief and anger have ebbed to a great degree, but the sense of uncertainty and vulnerability is still there. These days, every so often when I drive across the George Washington Bridge, a little voice in me says, "Let's get quickly to the other side, just in case one of those trucks alongside you is not what it appears to be." For months I heard that voice every morning and evening. Soon, I hope, it will be gone.

People, they say, are leading their lives differently: hugging their children more often, spending more time with the family. I guess that's true of us Pepers. I know we're all a bit closer than we were a couple of years ago, but I think that's also a function of our boys growing up and maturing. As for me, shallow and self-serving as this may sound, one of the biggest effects of September 11 was that it made me want to play more golf—with Scott in particular.

Golf is a blessed refuge. Moreover, just as it confounds and humbles us, it teaches. It teaches the simple lesson that on some days bad things happen, things that are beyond our control. All we can do is summon the courage and understanding to accept them, maintain our faith, and believe that if we persevere and do the best we can, the bad will be replaced by good. After September 11 I needed golf more than ever.

Thus, even as I popped first Celebrex and then Vioxx, even as I tried six weeks of acupuncture to cure my aching hips, I knew I'd be going under the knife—and soon. I was determined not to miss the 2002 golf season.

Internet research gave me the good news that a hip replacement is no big deal: It's 99.4 percent nonfatal, and nearly all patients experience a huge improvement in mobility. So I decided not only to get the surgery done as soon as possible but to go for a "double," both hips on the same day. Only 3 percent of hip replacements are bilaterals, and relatively few doctors attempt them, but I knew I was young enough and healthy enough to withstand the longer operation, and I had neither the patience nor the bravery to go through it twice. Besides, the out-of-office time—six weeks—was the same for a simultaneous two-hipper as for a single, so why not get it all over with at once? I wanted to get back to normal life—and normal golf—as soon as possible.

My Internet research also told me that I wanted cement-less ceramic-on-ceramic hips. Ceramics are all the rage these days, as they last far longer than the metal, plastic, and other faux bones that have traditionally been used for ball-and-socket jobs: forty years or more as opposed to ten to fifteen. But the Federal Drug Administration had not approved them for the United States, despite the fact that they'd been used success-fully for decades in Europe. The FDA had, however, allowed ten hospitals across the country to conduct a clinical trial of the ceramics.

One of those was the Ranawat Orthopedic Clinic at Lenox Hill Hospital in New York City, so it was there that I decided to get my bodywork done. Their head guy, Dr. Chitranjan Ranawat, is one of this country's top orthopedic surgeons and has rerigged everyone from Joe Namath to the prime minister of India. But when I visited the office, on December 26, I learned three things that didn't please me: (1) The Ranawat Clinic was no longer participating in the ceramic trial; (2) they weren't sufficiently impressed with the deterioration of my right hip to grant me a double ("Hip surgeries are not like M&M's," the surgeon told me. "You don't just hand them out."); and (3) they had recently done a hip replacement on sports-writer/commentator Dick Schaap, who five days before my visit had died from postoperative complications of his surgery.

(In fairness to the hospital, I should point out that Schaap had had a number of health issues—he was a big smoker, for one—and he'd died of acute respiratory distress syndrome, which occurs in a small number of surgical cases.)

Nonetheless, my pair of sore hips were suddenly connected to a pair of cold feet. That afternoon, in search of some expert guidance, I placed a phone call to another member of the *GOLF Magazine* editorial masthead, and the only person I knew who had recently gone through a hip replacement: Jack Nicklaus. Like just about everyone else on the day after Christmas, Jack was at home with a light schedule, and in me he had someone who genuinely wanted to hear every last detail of his surgery. We chatted for nearly forty-five minutes.

As you might expect, the meticulous Mr. Nicklaus had researched his options thoroughly. In listening to him I remembered a line that had circulated among the wags in the golf press: "You know why Jack waited so long to get his hip replaced? He wanted to be sure he couldn't do it himself."

Actually, Jack had waited because his personal trainer, Pete Egoscue, devised an exercise regimen that bought him some time. "I was bone-on-bone for five years before I even considered surgery," he told me, referring to the loss of cartilage cushioning the ball and socket that causes the hip pain. The first thing Nicklaus did was try to talk me into the same program. But I had about as much interest in exercise as in organic chemistry, so we quickly got on the topic of surgery.

It turns out Jack's second choice as a surgeon was my own Dr. Ranawat, but he'd backed off because "the ceramics Ranawat used were from France, and they proved to have some problems with reliability." That explained why Lenox Hill had dropped out of the clinical trial.

Instead, Nicklaus had opted for Dr. Benjamin Bierbaum, a Boston surgeon (and golfer—he lives on the fifteenth hole of the Country Club and is a member there as well as at the Kittansett Club, two of *GOLF Magazine*'s top one hundred courses). Bierbaum imports his prostheses from Germany, and they've proved to be more tough and dependable than the French ones (which comes as no surprise to this reporter).

Jack kindly offered to place a call, and his word was magic. By the end of that day I had not only a January 3 appointment to see Dr. Bierbaum but a tentative January 14 date for surgery. Typically, Bierbaum's docket is so booked with sufferers from all over the world that the wait is three to four months, but just that day a patient had canceled for January 14—or at least that's what I was told—and I'd been jumped to the top of the waiting list.

The good news: Dr. Bierbaum was happy to include me in the ceramic program. The bad news: he was not happy to do both hips on the same day. Although my X rays and MRIs showed nearly equal deterioration on both sides, the range of motion of the right hip was still pretty good. However, my persistent, shameless begging brought him around.

The worst part was the anticipation. Happily, with only eleven days to think about it, I didn't get too panicked, and I somehow managed to sleep well the night before. It was the five hours or so at the New England Baptist Hospital, between checking in and "checking out" through anesthesia that were a bit trying. But they have a terrific staff, and one big earth mother of a nurse took me under her wing and helped keep me calm. Another nurse told me Jack had been a lot jumpier than I was when he went through it, and that helped, too. (Jack called me the day after the surgery, and when I asked him about this, he denied it.) They stuck about six needles and tubes into various parts of my body, including an IV they said would deliver the anesthesia. That's the last thing I remember until I woke up in post-op.

The tubes were still in me, I was hoarse from the breathing tube that had been in my throat during the operation, which had lasted nearly five hours, both of my legs were supported by slings, an ice bag lay outside each of my thighs, and my calves were wrapped in balloon stockings that inflated and pumped my legs once per minute to promote blood flow. But boy, did it feel good to wake up alive and mended!

My eyes opened to the sweetest of all sights: Libby at my bedside. I gave her a kiss, then said, "One word . . . Macallan," referring to the single-malt Scotch that was the one thing I needed at that moment to make my relief complete. Of course, alcohol wouldn't be touching my lips for a couple of weeks, and I wouldn't get even water—just ice chips—for a few hours, but on the right side of my bed was a blessed little button that allowed me to self-inject with morphine every ten minutes.

Thanks in large part to the morphine, there was minimal pain. They ask you to rate your pain several times a day on a scale of 0 to 10, with 10 being excruciating, and the worst I ever felt was 3 or 4 (compared to a constant 6 to 9 in my left leg and 2 to 3 in my right leg prior to surgery).

Dr. Bierbaum dropped by that evening, assured me that all had gone well, and said that the deterioration he'd found in my right hip during the operation confirmed that my pleas for a bilateral had been justified. That made me feel almost as good as the morphine.

I actually walked—okay, took a couple of wobbly steps with the aid of two nurses and a walker—the next morning. Three days later I was on crutches in a rehab unit, and five days after that I was home, doing a battery of twenty-eight stretching and strengthening exercises three times a day, ten repetitions of each exercise on each hip—1,680 reps a day.

Libby, not surprisingly, turned out to be the best nurse

since Florence Nightingale, and thanks to my computer, the looming deadline for this book, and NBC's wall-to-wall broadcast of the 2002 Winter Olympics, the recuperation period went by quickly.

What did surprise me was the level of Scott's concern. Time after time, when I attempted a maneuver that was beyond the limits of my prescribed rehab, he was quick to admonish me—even more quick and more stern than Libby.

"Dad, don't try that!" he shouted at me, and it was a welcome kind of scolding. It told me that maybe Scott, too, wanted us to play a few more rounds together.

By the end of February I was back in the office, walking with the aid of a 6-iron, and by the end of March I was ready to get back on the golf course.

The timing was perfect—spring break—and we'd been able to cadge my cousin's Palm Beach condo for five days. I don't think I've ever looked forward to an opening day more than I did that one.

The course was Palm Beach Polo Club, a demanding Pete Dye design where water seems to come into play on every hole. But the venue was unimportant. I was out in the Florida sunshine on two strong legs and starting the golf season side by side with my son.

We had the first starting time of the day, and we opened the practice tee at dawn. It was a beautiful morning, as brimming with hope as I was. After some perfunctory stretching (I've never been much for organized exercise) I hit a few tentative chip and pitch shots and, feeling no pain or awkwardness, moved into the full wedges and irons.

It was great to feel the strike of club on ball again. Within a short time I was swinging with confidence—and without pain except minor muscle aches. Miraculously, many of the shots flew straight and with reasonable distance. The only difficulty came on the driver, which I seemed to hit with nothing but a low hook. That, I reasoned, was to be expected. Better height and flight would return as the strength and coordination in my legs were restored.

Best of all, I was able to slop it around the course in eighty-eight strokes! Not in about thirty-five years had I been so pleased simply to break 90. In truth, it wasn't much worse than a lot of my season-opening rounds, especially considering the difficulty of the course. A couple of friends I knew who had had hip replacements claimed they'd played the best golf of their lives after the surgery. Maybe I would, too. At the end of that day I think I was every bit as excited about my new mobility as Scott was on the day he'd passed his road test.

On this day, however, he wasn't too pleased with his golf. After visiting half a dozen water hazards, he'd shot about the same score I had. Not the start he'd wanted. But his day was about to brighten considerably.

A month or so earlier, Scott had taken the Scholastic Aptitude Tests. The SATs are standardized tests, administered nationwide on a handful of dates each year. They're regarded as a sort of I.Q. test for high school students and are used by most of the top colleges and universities in the country as a prime way of evaluating academic potential. One test measures verbal ability, the other math, and each is scored on a scale of 200 to 800. Generally, a combined score of 1,100 or higher is respectable, anything over 1,300 is considered strong, and anything over 1,500 indicates a superb mind. All things being equal, a score of at least 1,450 is needed these days to give a kid a reasonable chance of gaining admission to the very top schools. We'd crossed our fingers that Scott would break that magic 1,450 barrier. A year earlier he'd done well on the PSAT ("P" for Preliminary) that is used to predict performance on the big test. As with his golf he seemed to rise to the occasion when the pressure was on. He was particularly strong in math, and a year earlier his performance on a nationwide test had qualified him to take a college course at Columbia University, a course so beyond my grasp that even the title frightened me: Fractals and Chaos. Clearly, Scott's genetic ability in math had skipped a generation.

Normally, SAT scores are not reported until about two months after the test date, but Libby had learned from a friend that, for a nominal fee and the price of a phone call, results could be obtained after only five weeks. She even knew the earliest date she could call for the recorded recitation of scores—and the earliest time.

That time was two o'clock on our first day of spring vacation. When Scott and I returned from golf, there was no greeting, no "How did you guys play?" or "How did your hips hold up, honey?" from Libby, just "I've been trying the SAT number for an hour and the recording keeps saying, 'Call back at four o'clock.'"

And so at four o'clock Scott called.

His mother and I, along with Libby's mother, who was vacationing with us, sat breathless as Scott punched button after button on the phone in response to the computer-voiced gauntlet of requests: name, Social Security number, test date, credit card number and expiration date. The process took only two minutes, but they were two very long and tense minutes for all of us.

At length a smile lit up his face.

"What is it?" Libby screamed. "What did you get?"

But Scott just held up a palm as if to say, "Wait a minute."

Then he smiled again and slowly hung up the phone, as a sort of stunned expression began to take over his face.

"Well?" we all said in unison

"Uh . . . I got 800 on the math . . . and 800 on the verbal."

My "You're kidding!" was drowned out by Libby's "Whoooeeeee!!" and Grandma's "Good gracious!" and suddenly we were all in one big jumping family hug.

Twin 800s—1,600! Nobody scores 1,600. I knew my kid was bright, but this was spooky bright. Not only was Scott more intelligent than either Libby or I, he was more intelligent than anyone in our respective families or, for that matter, anyone we knew! He'd just done the mental equivalent of qualifying for the U.S. Open.

That day was only the beginning. Later that spring he took three SAT II tests, similarly required exams but in specific subject areas, in Scott's case math level II, physics, and writing. His scores on those, respectively, were 800, 800, and 760. Then at the end of the school year he took six more Advanced Placement tests and scored another set of perfect 5s, earning the distinction of National A.P. Scholar, one of only two kids in New Jersey and fewer than two hundred nationwide.

All right, enough number-dropping. The best news is that, at least as I saw it, Scott was suddenly in the driver's seat when it came to college applications. It was no longer a question of which school he'd be fortunate enough to get into but which school would be fortunate enough to get him. Barring a cataclysm of some kind in the first three months of his senior year, he would be able to go to the college of his choice.

But which would that be? Our mailbox had begun to swell with unsolicited brochures and catalogs from colleges and universities throughout the land. (Apparently, either the SAT people or the A.P. folks or both do a nice business selling their mailing lists.) Most of the places were not on Scott's radar screen, and he never opened any of the mail, but occasionally, a brochure caught at least his mother's eye.

"You should take a hard look at this one," she said, sliding him a packet of information from Stanford University. "I did a semester there, and hated it, but you might like it."

"Is it warm?" Scott asked.

"A lot warmer than the East Coast is in winter," said Libby. "You can play golf there all year round."

"Yeah," I added, "but he couldn't make the team."

"Why not?" she said, and I could see Scott had the same question.

"Look at who has come out of there recently. Tiger Woods, Notah Begay, Casey Martin—and they were all on the same team. At Scott's age those guys were all shooting in the 60s."

"No, they weren't, Dad," said Scott. "Tiger was, but not the other guys."

"Don't bet on it. They were at least five strokes per round better than you are now." I'm not sure why I was being so brutal. Guilt took over. "But I've spent some time with all three of those guys," I said. "They're bright, but they're not nearly as bright as you."

"He could play on an Ivy League team, like Harvard or Princeton, couldn't he?" asked Libby.

"Yeah, especially Harvard," I said, "where they got a lot of guys from the Northeast who have short seasons. I suspect that if you can shoot 75 regularly, you could play for most Ivy teams."

"Where couldn't I play?" asked Scott.

"Maybe not at Princeton," I said. "They're the perennial Ivy League champs. And certainly not at any of the big southern schools—Duke, for instance."

"The golf part might be important," he said.

"Why's that?" said I.

"Well, I think that no matter where I go I'm gonna get a good education, so right now the main thing to me is to find a place where I'm gonna have the best time: the best social life, the most fun playing golf, the stuff that goes on outside the classrooms."

"You know something," I said. "I can't fault your reasoning one bit."

In keeping with that philosophy, Scott had decided that he wanted to pick one school and apply for early admission in December. ("I want to be able to relax and enjoy myself senior year at school.") And so, over the next few months he and I would pay visits to the places on his list.

Two of them were eliminated quickly: Georgetown ("Too many priests skulking around") and Yale ("The golf course was not as great as you said—it was in terrible condition—and the town was kind of creepy"). Long ago I'd spent some time at Yale, working toward a Ph.D. in comparative literature, back when I fancied the notion of being called Dr. Peper. I loved the bucolic, quirky C. B. Macdonald golf course and still do, but I must admit that the town of New Haven, although never a garden spot, has recently fallen on hard times.

Duke was deemed acceptable, albeit with a campus so spread out it required a bus shuttle between its two halves, and the golf course there was a beauty, recently renovated by Rees Jones. But in the end Scott was shooting higher on the scale of academic clout.

That meant one of three schools: Harvard, Princeton, or Stanford. In late summer we visited Stanford, and I did everything possible to sell him on it. On a crisp, cloudless, blue-sky morning we toured San Francisco from Nob Hill to the Golden Gate, gorged ourselves on Dungeness crab at Fisherman's Wharf, and then headed south to the Palo Alto campus. We took a quick golf cart tour of the back nine of the Stanford course, arguably the finest collegiate layout in the country and once ranked eighty-eighth on *GOLF Magazine*'s top one hundred courses in the world. After that, Scott had a one-on-one chat with the Nobel Prize–winning head of the Stanford physics department, after which he and I joined the one-hour walking tour of the attractive campus.

"Well, are you starting to sort things out any?" I asked hopefully.

"Yeah, I don't think I want to apply here," he said.

"Why not?" I said.

"It's so spread out—it looks as if you need a bicycle to go anywhere. And the campus newspaper said that only 40 percent of the incoming class is Caucasian. I think it might be less easy for me to fit in quickly and easily here than it would somewhere else."

Scott, I knew, had zero prejudices, but college is a bold new world, and I could understand his take. "Yeah, that might be true," I said, "and it's also true that most of the kids here are from California and very few are from our part of the country." (A cynical friend of mine had concluded that the only kids from the East who go to Stanford are those who are running away from something.)

And so it came down to Harvard and Princeton, the two schools that, by rating and reputation, are the best in the country.

"I like the idea of being right in Boston," Scott said, "but Harvard seems to be kind of cutthroat competitive, and I get the impression that everyone there is really impressed with themselves. Plus, if you want to take advanced courses in math or physics, you have to go to MIT."

"Well, that's a factor," I said, "and who knows what the transit system will be like there over the next four years. They're still screwing around with the Big Dig."

"What's that?" he asked.

"A complex bus and subway system they've been putting in. It's way overbudget and way overdue, and the city has been one big construction site for years. However, there is one major plus to Harvard."

"What?"

"The home course for the golf team is the Country Club" (site of the 1988 U.S. Open and 1999 Ryder Cup Matches).

"Yeah, but didn't you tell me it's nowhere near the campus?"

"That's right . . . whereas the Princeton course is out the back door of one of the freshman dorms."

"Yeah," he said, "and I think the chance is good that I'll be playing for fun rather than on the team."

"Who knows," I said. "Your handicap is 3 and you have a year to get it lower. I think you'd have a good shot."

"Maybe, but I don't want to make golf the center of my life in college. I used to think I would. I used to think I'd want a job in golf, like you have, but not anymore."

"Believe me, you don't want a job in golf. There aren't too many good ones. I got lucky. Besides, as a predecessor of mine, Herb Graffis, once said, 'We work in the toy department.' You have the stuff to do better than that. You can do something more serious, more important—and probably more lucrative, too."

"Is it true what Mr. O'Brien told me, that you can be a complete idiot and make $250,000 a year on Wall Street?"

"I don't know. In any case, that's not what I meant by something more serious and important."

"Hmm . . . Well, at this point I kind of like advertising. Whenever I watch a TV commercial, I find myself wondering how it came together, who came up with the ideas, who figured what market to shoot at. It's kind of creative and practical at the same time. Right now I'm thinking about advertising, maybe the financial world, or maybe law."

"Well, you have plenty of time to get it sorted out," I said.

"Yeah, I guess so . . . but I think I've decided where I want to apply. I'm gonna go for early decision at Princeton."

Those words were magic to me. As much as I'd tried not to make it a part of his decision, as much as I'd tried to offer all the options and sell him on each of their strengths, I'd wanted very much for Scott to opt for Princeton.

It wouldn't be easy for him, even with those fancy numbers he'd posted. Only 12 percent of applicants are admitted, and each year hundreds of kids with 1,600 total SATs are rejected by Princeton. But Scott had one other advantage, an advantage he and I had spent months trying to minimize but couldn't ignore. He was the son of an alumnus: I graduated from Princeton in 1972.

10

Valediction

Slow it down, man," said Scott.

The two of us were alone, side by side at a driving range near our home, and I'd been hitting my usual rich variety of iron shots: fats, thins, slices, and pulls, along with the occasional shank. As always, the culprit was the blinding speed of my downswing.

Why is it, I wondered, that the tempo of my golf swing is so irreversibly dreadful when, with respect to every other aspect of life, my timing has been perfect?

By virtue of my birth year, 1950, I was able to catch a gravy train that has run smoothly for half a century. In fact, any middle-class American born during the first half of the 1950s may count himself or herself as a member of the largest lucky sperm club ever: the boomingest of the baby boomers. From day one we've had just about the best of everything life can offer.

Think about it. We came of age in the prime of the Beatles—any earlier and we'd have had to suffer through Elvis, any later and it would have been Michael Jackson. Our sports heroes were real heroes—Mickey Mantle, Johnny Unitas, Bill Bradley, Gordie Howe—not millionaires with rap sheets.

Color television arrived just in time for our Saturday mornings, and the birth control pill arrived just in time for our Saturday nights. Among the first to sample McDonald's and Burger King, we were also the lead market for lite beer and liposuction.

Unless we were incredibly unlucky, we escaped polio (we were too young), and unless we were equally unlucky (or foolish), we escaped AIDS (we were too old). In between, we had more fun than any generation before or since. Our high school and college years brought Woodstock, miniskirts, free love, and recreational pharmaceuticals. Protesting was in, and since there were so many of us, everyone had to listen, even Congress, which lowered the voting age to eighteen just so we could pull the lever.

Granted, we came of age during the assassinations of the Kennedy brothers and Martin Luther King Jr., we stared straight in the face of Kent State, Cambodia, and Watergate, and it was our numbers that came up in the first National Draft Lottery. But just our luck, the Vietnam cease-fire was declared before most of us could go to war.

Best of all for the golfers among us, as the twentieth century neared a close and the seeds of decrepitude began to germinate in our games, along came 45-inch titanium-shafted 400cc metal woods, 60-degree wedges, and golf balls that soared and bounced like flubber. And as fans we've had a double bonanza. We were there for the entire glorious career of Jack Nicklaus, and now we have a front-row seat for the phenomenon that is Tiger Woods.

I was mulling all this that afternoon at the driving range as I sat on a bench and watched Scott hit sky-high 230-yard 2-irons. Scott and I have reached the stage where we have vastly different practice regimens. Ideally, I need to hit between one and two dozen balls, especially if I'm warming up before a round. Fewer than a dozen and I'm too stiff, more than two dozen and I start to get what the economists call diminishing returns. Scott, by contrast, can hit no balls or two hundred balls and head to the first tee with equal comfort and confidence.

In any case, as I mused on the fortuitous timing of life, it occurred to me that the age separation between Scott and me, thirty-four years, was almost exactly the same as the gap between Tiger and Jack, with each of us Pepers about a decade younger than his generational icon. And just as Tiger had seized control of the worldwide game, with Jack fading quietly into the background, an undeniable shift had occurred in Scott's and my world.

In that summer of his seventeenth year he had shown that, while he was still a kid, adulthood was on the way. For the first time he'd gotten a real job, as an intern at the Metropolitan Golf Association, where he worked in the communications department, relaying scores of local tournaments to the news media. The long summer days he'd always filled with golf were now spent in an office or on the road to and from the tournament sites. On the busiest days he logged up to twelve hours, and over the course of the summer he earned nearly $4,000, while learning some valuable life lessons: what it's like to work with a team of people, depend on them, and have them depend on you.

He hadn't grown up totally, and for an extremely bright kid he continued to do some remarkably stupid things, as he reminded us in the form of two incidents, the first of them a speeding ticket for doing eighty-seven miles per hour in a sixty-mile zone—his *third* speeding ticket since getting his license. That required me to hire an attorney to plea-bargain. The result was, instead of losing his license, his driving privileges were suspended for thirty days and he was fined $180. Scott paid the fine from his MGA earnings. He also paid half of the $700 attorney fee; sucker that I am, I paid the other half.

His other bonehead move came when he threw a party while Libby and I were away for the weekend. Under interrogation later, Scott admitted that two dozen kids had attended, only about half of whom he knew. They did minor damage to our kitchen and generally made a mess of the place. Scott did a characteristically poor job of cleaning up the evidence, and Libby found beer bottles in the bushes for weeks afterward. But the worst thing was that one of the kids had gone into Tim's room and stolen his laptop computer. Scott, to his credit, took full and immediate responsibility and said he'd buy Tim a replacement. I once again caved and paid half of the $1,300 bill.

Yes, Scott still had one foot planted firmly in his childhood. At the same time, he had matured in myriad ways—physically, mentally, emotionally, psychologically. I'd like to think that at least a part of that growth derived from his involvement with the game of golf.

I don't know that he learned about honesty or humility or responsibility or resilience or perseverance from playing golf, but I'm convinced that golf at least helped him see those qualities. The game surely taught him, just as it has taught me and continues to teach me each time I play.

Indeed, in many ways the two of us had taken an eleven-year course together, an extended coeducation through golf. In getting to know him I'd reached a better understanding of myself. In the act of teaching him—or at least trying to teach him—I'd learned things about how to behave, both on the golf course and off. My guess is that most parents learn something about patience, deference, and self-sacrifice simply in the course of raising their kids. For me it didn't come that quickly or easily. Fathering alone hadn't done the trick. I'd needed golf to make me catch on.

Now, with his primary education near an end, Scott was about to leave us. I was happy about the young man we—Libby, George, and golf—had raised, but like all parents who face this moment, those feelings of pride and joy were tinged with some sadness and apprehension, along with a bit of fear—not so much for Scott as for me.

By next year he would be out of the house for good, on his way down a new and exciting path, with the world to conquer. At the same time, I was nearing the end of my working life. Retirement was looming, and with it a host of uncertainties, accompanied by the impending ravages of age. My double hip job had turned out to be a piece of cake, but it had nonetheless prompted contemplations of mortality.

Of course, this was all part of the natural succession of things, the passage of time. The only element of my future I couldn't accept was the golf part. The simple truth was that I was about to lose the best golf buddy I'd ever had. Losing *to* Scott—in Japan, Hawaii, and so many times and places since—had been the easy part. Losing *him* will be painful beyond imagination.

On that morning it had hit home. I was in my den, paying some bills, when Scott walked in.

"I'm going over to hit some balls," he said. "Wanna come with me?"

The words had struck like a knife. It was precisely the same invitation I'd first extended to him when he was six years old. Now, more than a decade later, he was extending it back to me.

Maybe the reality was that we weren't coming to an end—we were just coming full circle. And what a glorious circle it had been. From those first days when I'd quietly coaxed him, silently begged for him to be bitten by golf. Through the times I'd rooted hard, then rooted softly. To the matches I'd tried not to win and then the matches I'd tried not to lose. To the current matches in which I simply try to stay close and give him a game.

Now, as I continued to sit and watch him practice, he had moved to his driver, pounding out three-hundred-yard tee shots that seemed never to come down. After one of them I let out a "Wow!," the same kind I'd heard so many times from him, so many years ago. In a way we'd returned to those golden times, when each of us rooted hard and unconditionally for the other to play his best.

But now the learning period is over, the competition stage has passed. In a short time something will be lost by both of us. On the other hand, what Scott and I have left is the best and purest part: a shared love, appreciation, and admiration for the game of golf, which, through its mystical power and confounding charm, will always let us show our love, appreciation, and admiration of each other.

I had hoped to give this book a fairy-tale ending, with an account of how Scott and I at last met in our club championship. Well, that didn't happen. My postsurgery game didn't come back quite as quickly as I'd hoped, and so I never even entered the qualifying rounds. As for Scott, he both entered and made it, a 73 in the second round taking him for a third straight year to the fourth-seeded position.

I thought he might actually go all the way, and his play on the first hole of his opening match said he would—a solid drive followed by an approach that stopped four inches from the cup. But his opponent matched that opening birdie and then went on to shoot the round of his life—a 66 that handed Scott a 6-and-5 defeat.

Maybe that's as it should have been. Maybe the best is yet to come—for both of us. Our last serious outing in the summer of 2002 offered hope. Six months to the day after my surgery, on a perfect Sunday morning, I walked our hilly course without a hint of pain and turned in a very solid 75. At my side Scott shot a near-immaculate 71, only a double bogey at 18 keeping him from his first round ever in the 60s.

Those numbers we threw at each other said, "Hey, it ain't over yet." Maybe, just maybe, next year Scott and I will meet in that club championship. Whatever may happen, whatever the next year and the years after that may bring, I hope we have many, many battles ahead of us.

Epilogue

My most vivid memory of golf with my father is less than flattering. Having been introduced to the game for only a year or so, I had not yet finely tuned my ability to control the golf club. My swing was all over the place. Sometimes I took it back with my whole body, like a wobbly upside-down pendulum. Sometimes I took it back without breaking my joints and came back down on the ball with a firm flap. As with any golfer who had not yet reached nine years of age, I had myriad swats (not swings), each of which could appear at any moment.

My eclectic assortment of golf swats produced just as varied results. Some of those results worked for me, others were just funny to watch—as was the case with my most vivid memory. My dad and I were on the course in a rare outing that included my brother, Tim, before he realized he didn't actually like golf. We were all enjoying the male camaraderie and father-son bonding of the day, when I hit the most implausible of shots. It didn't go in the hole; it didn't go near the hole; in fact, it really didn't go anywhere at all. It ended up basically in the same place it started. It was how it got there that was amazing.

I stepped up to the ball in the heavy rough after a mighty drive of perhaps fifty yards. The fairway lay ahead, calling me to stripe one down the center and roll it up onto the green some three hundred yards away. (Although I was small, I had a big imagination.) I took out my 3-wood, intent on giving the ball a major thrash. I ripped the club down with all my puny strength and struck the ball as hard as I had ever struck it. Yet, in the chaos of my swaying swat, I nearly missed the ball completely.

I finished with a beautiful pose as if I'd busted it down the fairway (the truth is I thought I had). But as I scanned the horizon, I saw no ball. Instead, I *felt* it, as it shot up from the ground and pelted me in the butt! Apparently I'd managed to nick the very tip of the ball and send it into the ground with so much overspin that it spun there for a few seconds before shooting straight up at me. We all burst into hysterical laughter, for ten minutes straight, and for the ten minutes following each retelling of the story.

As I think back on that story I can see myself posing as I always did after a good shot. I can see myself getting spanked by my own ball and jumping into the air. I can even see my dad, my brother, and myself lying on the ground laughing. But I don't remember any of it.

The story has been told so many times over and over again that it has become a fact to me. It's become as real to me as yesterday. But the sad truth is I don't really remember it. In fact, I don't remember most of the stories in this book. I don't

remember my first time on the range. I don't remember finishing my first round on the "big" course and immediately asking
my dad if we can go chip and putt. I don't remember standing
in front of my dad as he sunk the most pressure-filled putt of
his life to win our first Parent Child Championship. I learned a
lot reading this book.

I used to think that the greatest part of sharing this amazing game with my father was the memories that we'd always
have. It's true we do have a lot. We have those crazy stories
and those tight matches. But that's not the most amazing
thing we share. My dad and I will forever have a bond. We will
always be drawn back together by the calling of the golf
course. No matter where he or I end up we will never be far-
ther apart than the nearest golf course.

The relationship we have can't be summed up in a single
memory or anecdote. The truth is that the memories we share
are a distant second to the tie that will never be broken. Even
though I can't remember the first time he and I walked to the
tee together, that moment marked the beginning of something
special between the two of us, something that will never fade
away, even if his or my memory of it does.

Scott Peper
December 1, 2002

Postscript

In November 2002, shortly after completing the manuscript of this book, George Peper retired after twenty-five years as the editor in chief of *GOLF Magazine*. This fall, he and Libby will move to Scotland, to the residence they bought twenty years ago, alongside the eighteenth fairway of the Old Course at St. Andrews. Their plan is to spend two years renovating it and then sell it in the summer of 2005, when the British Open returns to St. Andrews. Meanwhile, George will continue his career as a freelance writer while attempting to establish a record of perfect attendance on the Old Course.

In December, Scott Peper was admitted early decision to Princeton, where he will try to do something his old man couldn't do thirty-five years ago: make the varsity golf team.

In the meantime the matches between father and son continue.